How
High/Scope
Grew

~

How
High/Scope
Grew

~

A Memoir

David P. Weikart

HIGH/SCOPE®
P R E S S

Ypsilanti, Michigan

Published by

HIGH/SCOPE® PRESS
A division of the High/Scope Educational Research Foundation
600 North River Street
Ypsilanti, Michigan 48198-2898
(734)485-2000, FAX (734)485-0704
Web site: *www.highscope.org*
E-mail: *press@highscope.org*

Editors: Lynn Taylor, Nancy Brickman
Cover design, text design: Judy Seling, Seling Design

Library of Congress Cataloging-in-Publication Data
Weikart, David P.
How High/Scope grew : a memoir / David P. Weikart.
    p. cm.
Includes bibliographical references.
  ISBN 1-57379-206-3 (soft cover : alk. paper)
  1. Weikart, David P. 2. Educators--United States--Biography. 3.
High/Scope Educational Research Foundation--History. I. Title.
  LB885.W43A3 2004
  370'.92—dc22

                            2004000932

Printed in the United States of America
10 9 8 7 6 5 4 3 2 1

～

To my parents, Catherine and Hubert Weikart,
who laid the foundation for my intellectual curiosity
and interest in both the natural world and service to others

To my wife, Phyllis Saxton Weikart, who joined me
in imagining what we might accomplish and
encouraged me to stay with the vision

To my children, Cynthia Weikart Embry,
Catherine Weikart Yeckel, Jennifer Weikart Danko,
and Gretchen Weikart, and their families,
who represent the future and the hopes
toward which I struggled

～

Contents

∼

How
High/Scope
Grew

~

Introduction

"How did it happen? Starting with nothing, how did you manage to develop an institution and an educational approach that has had such wide-ranging influence?"

"How did a small nonprofit manage to keep a research study going for 40 years?"

"How did the High/Scope Educational Research Foundation survive for decades, when economic and social factors forced similar institutions to close their doors?"

Because High/Scope is unique, I am often asked questions like these. This book is my answer. It is not a scholarly account of our curriculum or research, which are rigorously documented elsewhere. Instead, it is a very personal memoir of decisions and their consequences, of painful failures and surprising successes, of ideas that were dead-ends and others that bloomed beyond our wildest dreams.

I wrote this book for students in education who want to know how a major educational approach was developed. I wrote it for researchers who dream of making their "grand designs" a reality and for practicing educators who wonder if it is worth it to struggle against tradition and bureaucracy to make a difference in the lives of children. I wrote it for Foundation staff who want to know about the "early days" of High/Scope. I wrote it for my children and grandchildren, who wonder why "Pa" was always so busy, and for my wife, Phyllis, who enabled it all to happen because she was willing to undertake the personal sacrifices and financial risks necessary to develop High/Scope. Finally, I wrote it for all the children and families who have benefited or will benefit from these decades of work.

Over the last 40 years (1962–2001) I have had the opportunity to build an institution and create an educational approach to serve children and their families. While the course of this development was certainly not a straight line, the work has had a strong element of consistency. In hindsight, the effort almost appears to be well planned, but a closer look at actual events reveals an extended sequence of choice points—ideas were generated; actions were taken; well-laid plans were rebuffed; work was influenced by others; fortuitous support arrived from grantors; data were gathered and conclusions drawn. All of these happenings, along with a willingness of staff and others to cooperate, contributed to the evolution of the High/Scope Foundation. In this book, I describe many of these events in chronological order, by topic. In each area, I relate the history from my personal perspective. Where I thought them relevant, some pictures and illustrations are included. There are also some real stories from behind the scenes that have never appeared in the formal reports. Lists of references describing the actual outcomes of the work discussed can be found in the appendices for relevant chapters, since I only provide brief summaries. Because these lists of resources are not exhaustive, readers may also want to consult current High/Scope catalogs and the web page (*www.highscope.org*) for more recent references and outcomes.

The first chapter details the history of my lifelong involvement in outdoor activities and camping. This longstanding commitment and resulting experiences led to the establishment of

"It is a very personal memoir of decisions and their consequences, of painful failures and surprising successes, of ideas that were dead-ends and others that bloomed beyond our wildest dreams."

High/Scope Camp and to the High/Scope adolescent program. Combined with my family background, the camping experiences formed my basic approach to education, which led me to initiate High/Scope's research studies and underpinned the development of the High/Scope Curriculum.

The succeeding chapters look at essential areas of the Foundation's ongoing work. Chapter 2 describes the High/Scope Perry Preschool Study and also includes information on the development of the High/Scope Curriculum. The interesting issue of differential curriculum effects is presented in Chapter 3. Our multiyear efforts to solve the riddle of how to deliver effective parent-infant education are discussed in Chapter 4. Chapter 5 presents our work at the elementary-school level. Following this, Chapter 6 takes a look at the history of our successful international development work.

The funding and administrative issues and choices that have allowed the Foundation to conduct its work are the topic of the next few chapters. Fundraising is the core of project operation, and as I've discovered, it is not a science. Nevertheless, Chapter 7 offers some general fundraising principles drawn from my experience with foundations and government agencies. Chapter 8 describes the financial development of the institution. A long list of High/Scope's grants and contracts over the years is presented in the appendices and begins on p. 301. While the list is neither wholly accurate nor all inclusive, a quick examination provides a sense of the range of institutions and amounts involved. (The list is not complete because records are kept for the auditor and not for the historian.) Chapter 9 traces the gradual evolution of High/Scope Press as a service to educators. While print materials were always available from the Foundation, it was not until the late 1970s that the need for an organized effort was recognized with the formation of High/Scope Press. The evolving role and membership of the High/Scope Board of Directors is presented in Chapter 10. Moving from advisory to policymaking and strategic planning over the years, the board has played a central role in the success of the Foundation.

~

The final two chapters represent my effort to summarize two issues. In Chapter 11, I present some ideas on why I, as an individual, was privileged to create High/Scope, both the curriculum approach and the institution. In talking with others over the years, I've recognized that many factors must converge for endeavors such as these to be successful. And while I really do not know exactly how and why we succeeded, this chapter offers some guesses. The final chapter looks at what I believe can be learned from High/Scope's past work and how this knowledge can be used in planning for the future. Certainly no one has yet solved the problem of how to provide appropriate education for children and the necessary support to their families. However, it is my hope that High/Scope's body of validated work can provide some direction and insights that will be used by others in this regard. I am aware that moving from an idea and a theory of education into validated practice on a national scale involves more that one career lifetime. I can only hope that the foundation of knowledge already built will enable High/Scope as an institution to continue its efforts to improve the life chances of children and families through effective educational practices.

1

The Beginning: High/Scope Camp

The outdoors has always played an important part in my life, probably because it was central to my family's interaction with the world. On their honeymoon, my parents, Catherine and Hubert Weikart, went hiking for several weeks in the Green Mountains of Vermont. They were active members of the Youngstown (Ohio) Nature Club with a special interest in bird watching. Through their work as community social workers directing settlement houses in Youngstown, they supervised a fresh air camp, Christ Mission, in the countryside. Deep in the woods on the property next door to the camp was a small, rustic one-room cabin that we used for occasional outdoor weekend visits, usually tied to settlement house staff meetings. Cooking meals over wood-fueled campfires and creating huge pots of "bean-hole beans" in 24-hour, buried fire pits provided the centerpieces for many social gatherings. My dad's specialty was a large raisin and apple pie baked in a buried Dutch oven. As a family, we took advantage of hikes through Mill Creek Park, an extensive and beautifully situated wild city park organized for miles around a series of lakes and a broad stream that meandered down to the Mahoning River. Many of my earliest memories and family stories are of picnics and gatherings in the park for nature walks, birthday parties (I found my new replacement teddy bear behind an ancient oak at age 3), and social gatherings for service club breakfasts.

~

Because of this family exposure to the outdoors, I responded enthusiastically to my parents' suggestion that I spend the summer of 1946 working at a residential camp. While doing general maintenance and dishes by hand for 120 girls at the YWCA camp on Lake Erie may not seem like much of an opportunity, it impressed me at age 14. I learned to swim and to enjoy camp singing. I also learned a little about women.

Hubert and Catherine Weikart instilled a love of the outdoors in their children.

In the spring of 1947, when I was 15, my father died at age 45 after a short illness. That summer my older sister, Emily, 17, and I stayed home with our two younger brothers, Hubert and James, 12 and 8, to help our mother reorganize our family. We lived near Idora Park, a local amusement park that had a large swimming pool. The Red Cross offered senior lifesaving courses, and my mother encouraged Emily and me to take the program. I was only 15 and not really old enough (the required age was 16); however, since my birthday was in August and I was big for my age, they permitted me to enroll. This experience built on what I had learned the previous year and gave me a useful skill. It also laid the groundwork for me to take a Red Cross water safety instructor course two years later.

Early Camping Experience

In the summer of 1948, the director of the Youngstown YWCA provided me with an introduction and recommendation to Sydney and Lillian Ussher, newly hired directors for Camp Riverdale for boys on Long Lake in the New York Adirondacks. My summer job put to good use my earlier dishwashing experience. I was a member of a three-man dishwashing crew covering three meals a day, seven days a week, for 180 campers. We did all the work by hand. After dish chores, I usually helped out on the camp waterfront, learning canoeing and, using my senior life-saving status, assisting with swimming instruction. This extra volunteer duty was recognized, to my amazement, with the suggestion by the Usshers that I leave my dishwashing chores behind and accompany a small group of campers on a five-day canoe trip through the rivers and lakes of the area, ending at one of the Saranac lakes. This trip was a watershed event in my development; it exposed me to an entirely new way to experience the outdoors. It was clear that such a trip restructured relationships among staff and campers, and that my new skills in woodcraft and knowledge of nature had real applications. The trip gave me a strong appetite for more outdoor camping and canoeing.

The author's high school graduation photo, 1949

In the summer of 1949, at age 17, I followed the Usshers to Sebago Lake, Maine, when they purchased Camp Wawenock to launch their own camping community. My responsibilities for the summer were mainly maintenance chores. However, my level of skill for the job may be partly revealed by the problem I had with the camp ice cream maker. Wawenock had a crew of local men who sawed large blocks of ice out of Sebago Lake each winter to fill the camp's ice house. Horses pulled the blocks, skidded onto wagons, across the ice and up the hill to the ice house. Once filled, the edges of the ice blocks were packed and the tops were covered with deep layers of sawdust to insulate the ice until the summer. Each Sunday morning of the camp session, I was responsible (with the help of eager friends on the staff) for making five gallons of ice cream for the day's dinner dessert. This involved several steps: bringing the ice cream container, filled with liquid mixture by the cook, to the machine; inserting the stirring paddle; tightly securing the cover; and packing the space around the container with salt and ice retrieved from the ice house. After some 40 to 45 minutes, we would begin periodic tasting of the concoction to check for consistency and flavor. My problem was that there was always a hard, frozen half-inch ring left on the inside wall of the container. The last time I made the ice cream, I made the embarrassing discovery that I had been inserting the stirring paddle backwards. Rather than float behind, the blade was supposed to precede the paddle around the edge, thus scraping it clean. Well, at least for the last time, it was made properly, though I don't think it changed the taste at all, at least not much!

Camps With a Recreational Focus

In the summer of 1950, after my first year at Oberlin College, Oberlin, Ohio, I began to work for Weldon ("Chief") Hester at Camp Lawrence Cory, a large YMCA boys' camp operated by the Rochester (New York) YMCA on Keuka Lake in the Finger Lakes region. I worked there as a general counselor, trip and outpost (camping) director, and finally as program director in

Oberlin College graduation, 1953

successive summers through 1953, and again in 1956 and 1957 after my discharge from the U.S. Marine Corps. To improve my skills, each summer before camp I attended special counselor training programs in various skill areas: aquatics, handling small craft (including canoeing), and outdoor camping. The training, usually offered in either Maine or North Carolina, included a two-week outdoor camping program provided by the Maine Guide Association. That program placed a heavy emphasis on outdoor cooking. An indifferent indoor cook, I discovered reflector-oven baking, a craft that opened a window for expert skill development while providing a pastime I continue to enjoy. The participation in these extra programs gave me many new skills and reaffirmed my commitment to camping. Indeed, my interest was so strong that I decided that whatever career I was to pursue would have to leave my summers free so I could continue to work in residential camps. Thus, my career interests began to focus on teaching or school counseling, my avocational recreational interests determining my professional vocation!

The author, on a camping trip, engaging in one of his favorite pastimes—reflector oven baking (2000)

The daily program at Camp Cory, reflecting traditions that grew out of the fresh-air camps of the 1930s, emphasized healthy outdoor activities, competition on the athletic fields and in the water, and a firm commitment to God and country. When I first started at the camp, I noticed that a group of old-line staff seemed to have organized the program as a vacation for themselves. The camp variety show was produced by the staff *for* the staff, with the campers serving as their unwitting captive audience. Friday night boxing sessions were times for staff to enable children with grudges to duke it out (safety gear was carefully used), but little care was taken to match the youngsters for size and weight. Instead, the intensity of their grudges ruled who would fight whom. Staff believed sports should have a hard, competitive edge to develop the boys' assertiveness and desire to win, because "guys had to be tough." Craft shop was the place where the boys could assemble pre-designed kits, all purchased from the camp store.

"I decided that whatever career I was to pursue would have to leave my summers free so I could continue to work in residential camps."

During my second and third years at Camp Cory, I worked as director of outpost camping, and thus I was away from the main camp most of the time, avoiding the issues faced by the rest of the staff. While leading groups out of camp, I had the time to help them learn outdoor skills, especially baking. Indeed, one day the YMCA camping committee visited the outpost program I was operating on an abandoned farm some miles from camp. The 12 boys and I served them baked chicken with hot biscuits for the main course and finished up the meal with cherry pie. They left endorsing the outpost program and requesting reservations for next year! However, I wanted the whole camp program to improve, and I began to recruit program staff from Oberlin who were skilled in waterfront activities, music, and crafts, as well as general camp counseling. I felt that I could be of assistance to the director, and that fresh ideas from new staff would help.

When I was appointed program director in 1953, about 25 percent of the staff came from Oberlin, and I was able to move the program toward a more child-centered approach. This meant camper participation in the variety shows, a boxing night that dropped boxing in favor of a wide range of physical skills where all could participate, and singing that focused on traditional folk music instead of shouted nonsense songs. In addi-

"I was able to move the program toward a more child-centered approach."

tion, once during each two-week session a large event such as a Paul Bunyan Day or a United Nations Festival would be initiated, with everyone contributing their knowledge and skills. The program still provided the boys with plenty of fresh air and exercise, the flag was raised each day, grace was said at each meal, and sports and waterfront activities were still the center of the camp experience. However, general counselors spent more time with their cabin groups, and during program periods all campers had the opportunity to successfully participate since there was less emphasis on "the winner." Upon return from the military in 1955, I worked at Camp Cory for two more years as program director and, at the request of Chief Hester, continued my program development efforts.

I assumed one special responsibility at the end of my second summer (1951). Chief asked me to lead a canoe trip of 10 boys into Algonquin Park in northern Ontario. He went along to guide us through the lake system that first year. Each year after the first, I took the trip along with another staff member and spent 10 days on the water. In 1952 while at the Maine Guide

~

camp, I learned of an unusually fine wilderness trip northeast of North Bay, Ontario, in Quebec, starting at Kippawa Lake. With many portages, the route went northeast through a series of small lakes to the head waters of the Kippawa River. Following the river with its many rapids, the route went south to the magnificent 60-foot Kippawa Falls and then west by another series of lakes to the staging area. The whole trip encompassed a rough triangle. These challenging canoe trips became the highlight of each summer for me, with the smell of pine and spruce on every breeze, the loons calling as they patrolled offshore, the brilliant displays of northern lights, fine cooking with the reflector-baking ovens, the great blue fields of wild blueberries for pies and breakfasts, the exhilaration of shooting rapids, the deep sleep experienced after a physically exhausting day, and the fascinating development of easy friendships among the group as the trip progressed. While difficult to organize and lead (after

"These challenging canoe trips became the highlight of each summer for me."

The author returns to Kippawa Falls in Quebec (2000).

all, 14- to 16-year-old adolescents are just beginning to develop work skills and a sense of group responsibility), these ventures reaffirmed for me my own sense of mission and the value of youth participation in these adventures.

Camps With an Arts Focus

At the end of summer in 1957, I married Phyllis J. Saxton in a beautiful New England Congregational Church in Shelton, Connecticut. With our return in the fall to the University of Michigan in Ann Arbor to continue our graduate studies and to start our new family, we knew we had to find a way to serve together as staff in summer camp programs. When I met Phyllis in the fall of 1956, she was finishing her second year of a master's program in physical and health education. As part of that program, during the summer she taught a water safety instructor course for the University of Michigan and was director of all camp waterfront activities at Interlochen Music Camp in northern Michigan. We returned

The author and his wife, Phyllis, 1957.

to Interlochen as a team in 1958, and Phyllis staffed her usual course and waterfront position, while I directed the junior boys division. It was not a happy experience. While Phyllis's work went as planned, I found my work to be very difficult. The junior boys were at Interlochen, obviously, to continue their musical development. This meant that as director I was to see that they practiced as scheduled, got to their "real" staff on time for lessons and rehearsals, and only engaged in safe physical exercise. "Safe" meant no activities that might strain or break fingers, as the recovery time would prevent their participation in the musical activities. Essentially, the counseling staff were to "hold" the junior boys for care and feeding while they were not engaged in their "real" program. This required us to keep them physically limited by focusing only on swimming, rowing, and hiking while avoiding volleyball, baseball, basketball, tetherball, etc. For obvious reasons, this approach gained us no thanks from the late-elementary-age boys. By the end of the summer, both Phyllis and I realized that we had lost our interest in this kind of camping. The standard approaches to organized camping as represented by Camp Cory and the specialized approaches as represented by Interlochen were not what either of us wanted. We were ready to begin a new venture.

Camps With a Social and Intellectual Focus

In August 1958, I received an invitation from Don Randall, an Oberlin friend whom I had recruited several years earlier for the Camp Cory staff, to visit him at an unusual camp he thought I would like to learn about. Perhaps, he wrote, it offered a view of programming that more reflected the direction in which I seemed to be headed. Don was serving as a nature studies counselor at Camp Rising Sun in Rhinebeck, New York, a camp for talented adolescent boys, all of whom attended on a full scholarship provided by the founder, George "Freddie" Jonas. When I went to visit, I was astounded. The program was organized around the idea that the boys should be self-governing as much as possible; that intellectual pursuits in science, math, drama, writing, among others, should be the activity focus; and that music was an important part of the camp experience for everyone. Sports activities were an after-supper recreational event; competition was not a requirement. It was expected that intrinsic motivation and rewards would drive program activities. Staff and campers worked together on construction projects, special events, plays, musical activities, and general group discussions. The program's primary goal was that boys, having received an opportunity to flourish in such an environment, would as adults pass on the values they had learned by helping others.

"The standard approaches to organized camping were not what either of us wanted."

15

The camper group was primarily composed of a rich mix of youth from New York City with the careful addition of boys from other countries and from around the United States. Unlike Camp Cory, which focused on entertainment and fun, and Interlochen, which prized skill development in the arts, Rising Sun valued thinking and problem solving within a socially responsible environment. This approach was closer to the way I was thinking as I worked in the public schools and attempted to improve education for children. I had just been appointed director of special services for the Ypsilanti Public Schools in Ypsilanti, Michigan, and as a school psychologist was beginning to see the necessity of reforming schools to better meet the needs of children and families.

When I talked with Phyllis on my return from Rising Sun, it seemed as if a new world of opportunity had opened up for both of us, one neither of us had known about previously. Here was another way to be of service to youth, to enjoy and use the opportunity of residential camping to develop important knowledge and skills in both campers and staff. This approach fit comfortably with my personal experiences and educational goals. Even more important for my long-range career, it enabled me to begin to give voice to the type of educational curriculum I would develop and promote throughout my professional life.

"This approach enabled me to begin to give voice to the type of educational curriculum I would develop and promote throughout my professional life."

In the summer of 1959, Phyllis and I joined the staff of Camp Rising Sun. I accepted the position of trip director, with responsibility for organizing and leading out-of-camp hiking and canoeing trips. Phyllis was five months pregnant with our first child, but still managed to introduce folk dance as an activity to 56 reluctant but game adolescent boys. They were won over when they experienced a very successful evening of folk dance with the girls from a neighboring camp. They were impressed by the lack of awkwardness when they compared the evening with what they usually experienced in high school at dances. These early and very successful movement and music experiences

Phyllis Weikart and daughter Cindy Embry lead a folk dance session during one of Phyllis's summer training programs.

encouraged Phyllis to develop a program of movement and folk dance education that is nationally recognized today as one of the most effective, developmentally based teaching approaches to movement and folk dance.

We returned to Rising Sun in the summers of 1960, 1961, and 1962. I worked as camp director and Phyllis continued offering movement and folk dancing, now to a much more receptive audience. Our second child was born in the spring of 1961, and with two young children, much of Phyllis's time was devoted to family responsibilities. During these years as camp director, I worked to nudge the program into a more active and less personally critical format for campers. For example, after each week's publication of the camp newspaper, the *Sun Dial*, a camper and staff group critique was held to point out the writing problems in the various articles. It was hardly a way either to improve writing skills or to encourage contributions to the next issue. Some of my changes created friction with the camp's founder and philanthropist. Indeed, with hindsight, the problem I encountered is obvious. George Jonas, who established the camp in the 1930s and created its successful format, was in his seventies and wished to maintain the program as he knew it. I, all of 30 years of age, wished to see the program evolve to respond to what I felt was a more supportive and engaging format for all the participants: one with more active involvement and less time sitting and talking about action; with fewer boys who saw themselves as less valued because they weren't selected for this or that activity or honor; and with reduced emphasis on a few major events, such as camp-produced shows or special trips that selected only a small number of the boys for participation and recognition. However, youthful enthusiasm is not enough to change established ways, and I was not invited back to direct the program for the summer of 1963. The camp governing board had it right: I had the experience and the youth to have confidence in going my own way, and I was not prepared to set aside that independence to carry out the traditional rules of operating Rising Sun. As long as Jonas would be supervising, they needed someone who could work within the camp's traditional framework. I was not that person.

Initiation of High/Scope Camp

In the fall of 1962, several important events occurred to influence my professional approach to residential camping. Weldon (Chief) Hester, my mentor from Camp Cory, contacted me in late October and asked if I would consider directing a completely new camp that the Rochester YMCA was constructing deep in the Adirondack wilderness. It was located on an isolated lake with access to various waterways and mountain hiking trails. I would be given a free hand to develop the program as I saw fit, under the supervision of the Y's camping committee, of course. To me, it was the opportunity of a lifetime! I accepted the invitation to visit the facility in November and talk further. I liked working for Chief, an earthy man of action and firm opinions on which you could anchor your own beliefs and attitudes. However, five days before I was to go, I called him and said I didn't believe I should do it and that I was afraid to even look at the site, as I knew the temptation to accept would be overpowering. I couldn't go because I was ready to do something on my own. I have always regretted that decision because I can't help wondering what adventures and challenges that job might have provided in my development. Yet, I have never regretted that decision because of the great satisfaction I have had in the development of High/Scope, its curriculum, and research.

The second formative event was the acceptance by the Washtenaw County Intermediate School Board and the Ypsilanti School Board of my proposal to look for a residential camping site to provide programs to children with special needs as part of my growing special education department. The only requirement they set was that the camp be nearby, preferably located within Washtenaw County. This idea was approved in October, almost in conjunction with the Hester call. I contacted a countywide real estate firm and asked for assistance in finding a site. I and several members of an ad hoc camping committee began looking at possible sites, but the process was a dismal failure. The properties we visited were rundown and usually very inappropriate for the use we intended. In early December, after a two-month search, the two boards called off the search and suggested we move on to other issues, at least for a year. I was disappointed, because I had turned down the New York camp opportunity in part to pursue this school-based effort, and it now seemed unlikely that we would gain the support needed to resume this effort.

"Rising Sun valued thinking and problem solving within a socially responsible environment and was closer to the way I was thinking as I worked in the public schools and attempted to improve education for children."

Then the third event occurred. Our realtor arrived in the second week of December with pictures of a facility that he had just discovered, two tattered-looking old houses in the country offered by the Catholic Archdiocese of Detroit. They had been using the property since 1942 as a summer camp for boys who were in their care as wards of the court. They no longer planned

∽

The red brick house in Clinton, Michigan, as it was when pur-chased in 1962 (top left) and as it is today (top right) and the rear view of the stucco house as it is today (lower left).

to use it either as a boys' home or as a summer camp and wanted to dispose of it as excess property. Had I not had the experience at Camp Rising Sun, which used two old farm houses for various functions (Camp Cory had a more traditional camp facility), I would not have been interested in the property. As it was, I said that the authorization period for the schools was over and I didn't think there was much more I could do. Knowing the potential of the facility, or perhaps seeing his commission a-glimmering, the realtor insisted that I at least visit the location. Since it was only 25 miles away, I agreed to meet him there several days later in the midafternoon.

Arriving as scheduled on a very cold mid-December day with the snow 10 inches deep on the ground and still falling, I did not believe the site could show its best qualities. Nevertheless, as we began looking at the buildings I quickly knew I had come home. If I ever wanted to do a residential camping program in southeastern Michigan, this was the facility. The underground electric, water, and septic systems had been upgraded to commercial standards by the Archdiocese with a foundation grant in anticipation of converting the facility into a boys' home. The wellhouse was buried in the ground and had concrete walls and ceiling with a 6-inch-deep driven well and 1500-gallon pressure tank. Unusually high-quality building techniques had been used when the buildings were constructed in 1925. In the north building, poured concrete had been used for the lower floor and the ceiling, and there were fieldstone fireplaces in the living room and recreation room. The building had so many twists and turns I got lost going from the main floor to the upper floor. The south building was a mirror of the north, but with a small dining hall attached. Like the other buildings, the main floor of the three-story barn was of poured concrete. The barn had horse stalls and grain storage bins. With all of its space, it had great potential as a recreation and arts building. There was also a small natural swimming area—an enlarged area in the stream that flowed in the valley between the two homes. Surrounding the houses, the 100-acre site included fields that could be used for recreation areas. While the buildings and furnishings were in mild disrepair, they were sound and functional. It was clear that this was the facility and location that would work for me, and as I returned home to discuss it with Phyllis, I was very excited. The only problem, as she pointed out a few minutes into the discussion, was that we had neither public nor private resources to buy such a facility, no matter how creatively I might think we could operate a residential program there.

"It was clear that this was the facility and location that would work for me."

At this point, two friends and their wives stepped in, John and Jane Salcau and Raymond ("Pete") and Ida Kingston. Both John and Pete were principals of elementary schools in Ypsilanti and were members of my small school-reform group, which was working on what would later be called the High/Scope Perry Preschool Project. Their decision to join Phyllis and me in purchasing and operating the facility made it possible to move forward. Among us, we had enough money to jointly obtain a land contract from the Archdiocese. John had outstanding administrative skills, and he and his wife helped to organize the operation, including setting up an accounting system. Pete and Ida were masters at home maintenance and seemed to know everyone who might be of help in starting up a repair program, so they took on the responsibilities of building maintenance and renovation. Phyllis and I knew camping, and operating the program became our responsibility. Since we were starting from scratch and with a very limited budget, such friends were indispensable. Had it not been for their efforts, in all likelihood High/Scope would not exist today. The Kingstons stayed involved for the first year and helped us solve the most pressing repair and facility issues. (I didn't know, for example, that septic fields had to be cleared of all trees and other growth, leaving only the grass. I thought the young maples would add a splash of color in the fall.) One weekend, John and I arrived early to remove some old Bradley metal showers from the boy's shower room. Pete was coming later to plumb in the new ones. John and I worked diligently for two hours and made no progress; we couldn't get inside the covers to loosen the galvanized pipes. Pete arrived; took one look, at our amateur efforts, and laughed; he had the six shower assemblies out in 10 minutes. The Kingstons participated for one year working on restoring the facility to a basic operational level. The Salcaus stayed with us for three years; they assisted with the recruitment of campers, set up the financial operation systems, and helped solve the issue of how a new program gains credibility with parents. (Being a well-respected elementary school principal carries a lot of weight, while being the new school psychologist in town carries very little.) After this initial assistance from our friends, Phyllis and I were able to assume full operation of the program in 1966.

How High/Scope Got Its Name

In early January of 1963, we three couples decided on the name "High/Scope." This decision occurred at the end of a long evening of heady and serious discussion of purpose and goals, laced with the silliness that only plunging over your head into a venture can produce. We decided that we had to create a name for the program, and none of us wanted to use an Indian name (as was so typical of many camps), nor did we even want a name with "camp" in it. We were seeking the participation of gifted and talented adolescents, a group who might not identify with that tradition. We considered sensible names: Bridgewater, our location's township name, and Saulk Trail, the name of the old Indian and trapper route from Detroit to Chicago. Playful names were also put forward such as Rusty Bottom (our stream through camp was named Iron Creek). Finally, exhausted and realizing it was almost midnight, John stood up, raised his now empty glass, and said, "Let's name it *High Scope*—'high' to signify our aspiration level and 'scope' to signify the breadth of vision we hope to reach." Later that month, an unemployed Austrian graphic artist with time on his hands was engaged to design our initial logo and added the slash in the name (as he put it, "To join the two little words into one big whole"). Thus, the camp was named High/Scope, and, when the Foundation was formed in 1970, the name was used to create the corporate name, *High/Scope Educational Research Foundation.*

This stump of wood, designed by High/Scope camper Donal Moore, remains at the entrance to the camp facility. Moore is now a member of the High/Scope Board of Directors.

High/Scope Camp: The Early Years of the Adolescent Program

Starting a new program in a new facility, at least one new to us, was a major challenge. Purchasing a facility on a land contract was one thing; organizing the financial resources to pay staff, buy necessary program supplies, serve three meals a day, and

repair structural damage was quite another. To attack these challenges, we made a number of key decisions. We knew we wanted to serve adolescents, so we set the age range of participants
at 12 to 17 years. We knew the camp would be coeducational;
none of us wanted a single-sex camp. (Phyllis and I already had
three daughters and a fourth was to be born in 1964. The Salcaus and Kingstons had both daughters and sons.) We felt the
program we were designing would best serve talented and gifted
youth who had an area of serious interest or had the potential to
develop such an area. As the camp developed, this criterion was
applied very loosely, because we discovered that youth with a
variety of interests and aptitudes thrived in our environment. We
also decided from the outset to enroll a culturally and racially diverse group. So, in addition to those who could afford to enroll,
we sought out families with youngsters who could benefit from
the experience but who could not afford to pay all or even part
of the tuition (we provided tuition waivers). These waivers went
primarily to minority youth; this represented a major commitment, as we supported these youth directly from our own very
limited incomes (there were no third-party scholarship funds).
As part of our diversity goal, we also wanted the camp to have
an international aspect, to increase the opportunity for greater
understanding of other political systems, languages, and cultural
points of view.

To achieve this end, we worked with foreign schools and
organizations to gain enrollments, again granting tuition waivers.
Our first student from overseas, Ignacio Ponce de Leon of
Colombia, arrived the first summer of 1963. Ponce de Leon was
attending the United Nations International School in New York
and was recommended by their teaching staff. The second foreign student arrived the next year. That student, Janet Clark,
came from England. Clark was the first of a long line of students
from Seaford, which is located along the southern coast of the
United Kingdom. A friend, Leonard Sealey, a British educator
working at the Educational Development Center in Mas-
sachusetts as part of their open education model in National

Follow Through, took an interest in our camp program and its philosophy. With his help, we arranged for Seaford youth to attend the program. This pattern of assistance from someone who knew of our work and was connected to a school in another country helped us to reach agreements with schools in Germany, Norway, Austria, Hungary, Australia, Colombia, Peru, Chile, and Brazil that lasted for varying lengths of time. In the 1960s, camp participants from the local area would collect the harvest of an apple orchard at High/Scope to earn some funds to help defray the international transportation costs that the tuition waiver did not cover. As the orchard aged and as camp enrollment became less local and more national, its maintenance and harvesting became too difficult and this out-of-season activity was ended.

"We knew we wanted to serve adolescents, so we set the age range of participants at 12 to 17 years."

Another major decision was a very practical one. We decided that the food served at the program should be good enough to create enthusiasm among both staff and campers. All of us had attended institutional programs where the food was an object of ridicule—we didn't want to deal with that issue in our program. To implement this decision meant hiring cooks who could bake breads and rolls, brownies, cookies, and cakes and who would use fresh ingredients when making the kinds of foods teenagers liked to eat. This was an expensive decision because it is always cheaper to hire only one cook who opens cans and heats frozen, portion-controlled meals rather than two who make everything from scratch. But the years have proven it to be a good decision, for meal times at camp were and continue to be a lengthy time of not only enjoying good food but also talking, singing, and sharing what members of different groups are accomplishing.

Finally, we wanted to provide a program that would involve youth in thinking about issues that would actively engage them, provide opportunities for them to be creative while trying new skills and entertaining new ideas, and enable them to successfully meet both intellectual and social challenges in a psychologically safe environment. To this end, Phyllis and I developed a daily routine based for the most part on our experiences at Camp Rising Sun. We implemented certain program elements that were not acceptable there, such as a specific daily routine, large-group events where all could participate in various ways, and more focus on active involvement in problem solving where students could actually apply ideas rather than just talk about them.

The Program: A Basic Framework

Though the actual structure of the program has evolved over the years, the basic approach has endured. As mentioned, many program elements came from our four years of experience at Camp Rising Sun, but this base was extended and enriched by ideas drawn from our other camping experiences and our educational philosophy. Special emphasis was given to linking abstract concepts to the actual camp experience of the participants. For example, although we had the typical discussions of brotherhood and social responsibility so beloved by teenagers, we also encouraged discussions that framed these issues in practical terms: Should I do room cleanup for my bunkmates when they have other obligations? In the same vein, speculations about political issues were fine, but we also asked youths to discuss how we could run the camp community meetings so that everyone would feel comfortable expressing their views. Likewise, besides listening to campers debate global warming issues, staff were encouraged to find, describe, and use natural rocks, grasses, and woods in artistic displays or in construction. Throughout the program, campers were encouraged to engage in knowledge-based activities, and thus produced some very practical results.

"Special emphasis was given to linking abstract concepts to the actual camp experience of the participants."

With such an orientation, our camp program moves at a very different pace from that in school classrooms. The most significant results of this focus on applying knowledge in active, concrete ways are that participants became very involved in the

~

program, move in very different directions from the same starting point, reach greatly different endpoints, and feel valued and enthusiastic because they are able to manage their own learning. Following are brief discussions of the common program elements we identified as supporting such youth development: room groups, instructions, and work projects, among others.

Room Groups

Over the years the program has always placed an emphasis on *room groups* of four to six individuals (including the counselor) to serve as a particular unit of friendship and support. These same-sex groups are preestablished to be as diverse as the overall enrollment will permit. If we have four girls from the same city, for example, they will most likely be placed in four separate groups; if several boys speak German as a native language, they will be placed in different room groups. These room

"The room group and counselor are the 'home base' for each camper."

groups live together and are encouraged to share their experiences in the program both informally and in structured activities. The group might read or tell a story together; gather ideas for a skit or other presentation; learn new songs; talk about their homes, cultures, and countries; or deal with specific problems any of them might encounter during the experience. Talking at night after lights are out is encouraged. (The room group's role includes making time for the silliness of the adolescent. At one moment the group members may be sharing their deepest personal aspirations or fears, at the next moment they may be convulsed in laughter about some description of a common bodily function more expected from 8-year-olds.) The room group and counselor are the "home base" for each camper. The groups do morning work crews together (washing dishes, cleaning baths, sweeping various program areas); this is followed by a period of time in which each group can do any program activity they wish to plan and undertake as a group. Occasionally, the members of a room group do not work well together. After all, these are adolescents trying to integrate new, often extraordinary ideas into their world view, so sometimes shifts in group assignments must be made. Typically, however, members of a group experience an outstanding opportunity for personal, social, and intellectual growth.

Instructions

One of the two major program time blocks is *instruction,* a self-selected small-group experience based primarily on the arts or sciences. An instruction may consist of a single-topic session for one morning (lasting an hour and 45 minutes) or an extensive series of up to 10 sessions (15–16 hours) focusing on a more complex topic. The central purpose of this program unit is to enable campers to learn interesting things in their own style, gaining confidence that they can be effective learners and active participants. While topics are usually developed by staff, the primary goal is not to teach content, although that is important, but to involve the adolescent in self-directed learning in which the leader offers support without criticism. Instruction topics are introduced through short descriptive write-ups prepared by the session leaders (usually staff but occasionally campers). These "blurbs" are posted and campers make a first- or second-choice request from among the 10 or 12 on display, most receiving their first choice.

Some typical topics for shorter sessions include taking, developing, and printing photographs; using a specialized shop tool; assessing plant adaptation to the environment by digging up various plant root systems; examining water quality in the stream and ponds; making charcoal drawings of the buildings; planning an evening program for the whole group on estimation of the number of pebbles in the driveway or the height of selected trees.

The longer sessions provide time for an in-depth look at a complex topic. For example, a group might plan, prepare, and stage a play such as *Waiting for Godot;* dramatize a selection from a favorite children's book; paint a large mural to hang on an outside wall; use the tools in the shop to build a wooden race car; or create stained glass "windows" to hang in the large dining room picture windows. While these carefully designed instructions vary every year to reflect the specific talents and interests of campers and staff, they are all organized to permit youths to plan the experience and actively resolve problems and meet intellectual challenges without staff directing the solution. Opportunities are provided for camper presentations of the work process, findings, or product to the entire group after mealtimes or during evening programs. This engagement in problem solving, discussion, and review of what has been experienced are what make the instructional periods so important. The process is also a fundamental principle of the High/Scope approach to education.

Work Projects

Work projects are another major program element. Designed to allow youths to produce tangible products as a result of their thinking and labors, these activities allow them to make and follow plans, use tools, negotiate various responsibilities, and learn new physical work skills.

When campers return to visit High/Scope years after attendance, they always look for the project they worked on. They ask, Is it still there? Is it still of use to subsequent generations of campers? They do this because of the investment they made in these efforts and because such products are usually the only concrete things they leave at camp. The projects have ranged from making glazed tiles to decorate a fieldstone fireplace mantle, building two massive 4- by 12-foot cherry barn doors, making picnic tables for outdoor meeting spaces, creating an observatory at the top of the barn silo, constructing a treehouse hung high in the basswood trees, digging a drain system for the volleyball court, cutting nature trails in the woods, designing a power-generating water wheel at the falls (it finally powered a flashlight bulb), assembling assorted bridges across Iron Creek, and building stairways and wooden decks.

Of all the activities done at camp, work projects demand the most of the youngsters. Many have never worked with tools. It is almost painful to have to help campers and even staff learn such simple skills as how to use a shovel to move earth or a ham-

"What if young people's daily experiences in school could draw upon such self-determination and commitment, rather than be the outcome of adult decisions and goals? Wouldn't education for all youth be more effective?"

mer to drive nails, and to sympathize with campers who get dirty when working (though one young girl from Peru, dressed as always in the best of informal fashion, enthusiastically managed the pouring of an entire concrete dam barrier with only a single smudge and absolutely no hesitation or complaint). Yet within the context of developing a self-image, succeeding in mastering these basics provides a simple but powerful experience that seems to stay with a person for life. It appears that doing for one's self and accomplishing something that is outside of personal expectations is a vital element in a teen's personal growth. An example will illustrate: As a personal spare-time undertaking, one 16-year-old Austrian camper spent much of his time first designing and then building a dollhouse for his sister—not a single-room, American-style house, but a multiroom, European-style mansion. When he finished, the structure was clearly a dollhouse, but no self-respecting doll would have ever paid the contractor, since the builder's vision far outstripped his actual abilities! Yet this teen displayed radiant joy at mastering some basic tool skills and producing his sister's dollhouse. He knew that the structure was very rough, but it was his, made by his own hands, fueled by his determination—not a project directed by an adult to meet a vague curriculum objective or to demonstrate "intellectual discipline." Many youth have so little chance to develop their own ideas to their own satisfaction that, given the chance, they are thrilled with the opportunity and realize that their skills will improve over time. What if young people's daily experiences in school could draw upon such self-determination and commitment, rather than be the outcome of adult decisions and goals? Wouldn't education for all youth be more effective?

Other aspects of work projects present challenges and opportunities to staff. As with the dollhouse project, the typical adolescent's ability to envision what might be done often exceeds his or her capacity to implement that vision. Thus, staff have to make certain that the project under consideration can be accomplished successfully—failed work projects are unusually discouraging. There is also a tendency, perhaps learned in schools, to extend and expand the time spent in discussion of work, time that could be better spent actually working on the project. Engaging quickly in physical work is one of the purposes of project time, since delays may doom a potentially successful project. There are also many small issues staff must resolve. Getting sweaty at a work task and not a sports activity is a new concept for many youth. Most work on projects takes place outdoors in the sun or rain, with poison ivy to be considered and the wrath of the Michigan mosquito to be endured. For campers coming from an indoor city life, the "wilds" of the countryside are new and even frightening, especially for those not certain initially that they want the camp experience. Yet, even in the face of such realistic problems, work projects are persistently rated by both campers and staff as one of the most successful aspects of the camp program.

Summer Whisper

Hum in my ear

again. Your song

is a high summer whisper

followed by an itch.

—Poem by an unidentified
summer camper

Other Program Elements

There are many other elements that combine to make up the total program experience. *Evening programs* are offered daily. These include skits and tableaus, active games on the playing fields or in a five-acre maze we have developed, problem-solving science experiences like creating a small, self-propelled vehicle, creating and acting out tall tales, building kites or bridges out of balsa wood, or solving social problems through small-group debate on choices their group as a whole must make. Several activities recur every year because of their longstanding value to the group experience. One is *folk dancing.* From the start of camp, developing a group repertoire of dances has been important to developing a sense of community. Taught by Phyllis and our daughter Cindy Embry, the group learns to execute simple steps and maintain a steady beat. After a special series of workshops totaling 12 hours, they are able to enjoy intermediate dance—many have developed an enthusiasm for more. When asked what they liked best about camp, the answer is often "folk dance." I believe this response is shorthand for both the dance experience and the strong sense of community and camaraderie that the dance activity produces.

Another one of the essential program elements is *council.* Down the path by the garden, across the small creek, along the wooded hillside, up the winding trail, and into the clearing at the top is the "council ring"—old logs circling around a simple fire pit. Once a week, campers and staff gather beside the barn and walk 10 minutes in silence to participate in council. The session opens with a song, perhaps a reading, a short thematic skit, or something relevant to introduce a general idea for the night's consideration. Not a discussion, not a performance, not an inspirational lecture, council is a time for individuals to consider issues that affect both the self and the group. The announced topic may, in the end, not be considered for long, because individuals can speak as they wish. As in a Quaker meeting, there is no demand for continuity, "answering" an earlier comment is seldom necessary, and there is usually an interval between contributions. Council serves as an opportunity for the group to integrate the experiences of the week and provides time for them to think about what is coming next. While the council topic at times relates to the campers' home and school experiences and the relationships there, more typically it focuses on some aspect of camp. In the first councils, for example, teens may discuss the problems and difficulties inherent in being away from home, while later in the four-week session the discussion often relates to making the most of their camp opportunities and their relationships with a group of 50 new friends. The camp environment is so different from high school, where personal status is often dependent upon clique membership or association with a boyfriend or girlfriend, and where social standing is easily earned or lost. At camp, the cohesiveness of the large group opens the camper's imagination to new possibilities and often is seen as an opportunity for a new beginning.

After council, *room-group discussions* can take a serious turn as council issues are related to personal experiences. Sometimes, as an adult, I have difficulty understanding the personal revelations these talented teenagers describe, but I have grown to accept the wisdom of a group process in which the well-spoken leaders and the softer, shier group members seem to meet on an equal footing. In these discussions, the entire group of campers and staff (who seldom speak at council) seem to acquire a better understanding of themselves and the program opportunities.

> *"At camp, the cohesiveness of the large group opens the camper's imagination to new possibilities and often is seen as an opportunity for a new beginning."*

Lots of other things happen during the program. On *visitors' Sunday,* families of current participants visit and those from earlier years drop by. *Dining hall singing* is important as it provides another opportunity for group participation. *Sunday evening cookouts* in the valley at the campfire circle provide opportunities for formation of casual friendship groups. *Field trips,* originally to art museums, zoos, wild-life areas, and parks, are now to college campuses and community service groups. *All-day canoe trips* are offered on the Irish Hills chain of lakes.

Special work projects, also occur from time to time—for example, restoring the swimming pond beach by spreading sand, or weeding the garden when it gets ahead of the work crew. (One summer, such a rescue was under way in the camp garden. After about 15 minutes of sweat, deer flies, and mosquitoes, a camper from Peru stood up and announced that he wasn't going to do this anymore: "In my country the peasants do this!" The outburst sparked an interesting discussion, both for him and some Americans who had no understanding of the issues of social class and culture involved.)

Finally, *sports* such as volleyball, soccer, softball, frisbee, and special low-competition games play an important role at the end of each afternoon before swim time. Aspects of competitive organization, such as teams and scorekeeping, are kept to a minimum; cooperative play is encouraged; and all are asked to select something they would like to play so teams are mixed in gender and skill level. (This organizational approach has also raised cultural issues. A circle of puzzled Americans learned a lesson about cultural differences when a vigorous Norwegian girl pointed out after a soccer game that she was as good as most of the

An early session of High/Scope Camp: The author's mother, Catherine Weikart, is second row left; the author is in the fourth row, standing in front of the young man with dark glasses, and Phyllis Weikart is to his right (wearing a white shirt).

boys. In response, a fine male athlete from Chile informed her that girls should be, well, at home with the babies. While the ensuing spirited discussion did not change many minds, the role of women from different national and religious perspectives got a thorough airing.)

I recommend *Learning Comes to Life* (available from High/Scope Press), a book written by Ellen Ilfeld, for a full description of the program from her perspective as a former camper and staff member who participated during the 1960s and early 1970s. Ilfeld provides illustrations and comments from staff and campers.

High/Scope Camp Sponsorship

Original Sponsors

Sponsorship of the High/Scope Camp program has changed since it was founded in 1963. As noted earlier, three couples established the program and ran it the first year. After the Kingstons dropped out at the start of the second year, the two remaining couples continued to operate the program. When the Salcaus left after the third year (1965), Phyllis and I took full responsibility for the organization. This obligation included directing the program, recruiting campers, selecting staff, operating the food service, maintaining the facility, developing the site, financial accounting, purchasing equipment and supplies, making mortgage payments, and insuring that the funds were available to accomplish all this. Without the full participation and cooperation of Phyllis and the help of my late mother, Catherine Weikart (who helped both in the program and in taking care of our four daughters when they were young), the camp could not have operated. Running a summer program while maintaining full-time jobs to insure income the rest of the year has certain consequences. Imagine, no summer vacations! Little time off was possible during the winter, either, because of the need to maintain the facility and supervise off-season rental groups on the weekends. These groups provided essential income supplements to support the summer program. But also imagine the delightful environment the program gave us as a wonderful place to raise our children with deep, rich experiences in a safe outdoor location! It was an environment of our own making for our own children as well as others. It was demanding, but it was what we wanted to do, the way we wished to make our contribution to improve the life prospects of youth.

Camp operated in the 1960s as an eight-week program. Youth could choose to come for two, four, six, or eight weeks. We found the longer term campers came primarily for six weeks, and those electing two-week sessions preferred the last two weeks. There was a clear ebb and flow to the summer. The first two weeks were exciting, as everything was fresh and challenging. Staff and campers alike were fully open to the experience. Once in a while, some problem would emerge. Smoking was always an issue, and we always followed the same rule: Choose to abstain and you are welcome to stay, continue smoking and you are choosing to go home. Drugs, including alcohol, were under the same rule for both campers and staff.

Sometimes other problems intruded. Two Korean 18-year-olds thought they were here on a holiday tour and couldn't understand why there was a program with requirements. A 17-year-old camper from Austria didn't come to the first program meeting after lunch on the first day. His room counselor remained with the group and I searched for the camper. He was in his room sobbing. Such behavior in a boy his age, one selected from many by his school principal, deeply concerned me. The problem turned out to be that he missed his girlfriend, with whom he had been living. Parents and principal thought that High/Scope in America would be a good experience as well as giving him some time away. After two days of tears, he boarded a plane back to Vienna. What a waste of resources for all of us! A hearing-impaired 16-year-old boy from Ohio was obviously frustrated with the program, in spite of heroic efforts by his room group and staff. Then, one morning, he was missing.

In hindsight, we realized he had made careful plans to leave camp —collecting food, a cook tin, matches, knife, and a map. After a day of great concern, consultation with parents and police, and road searches, he arrived at his home determined not to return to camp. Several years later he wrote from a fish-packing plant in Alaska, asking about job possibilities. He felt he had learned so much at camp before he left! Over the many years, such events were the exception not the rule. Teenagers are in an extraordinarily important period of development, the final organizational stage before adulthood. It is a time of trial and sometimes, often more than we would wish, error. In safe, thoughtful environments like High/Scope's, key developmental issues can be successfully negotiated or at least approached. All youth could use such an opportunity.

In 1970, when the High/Scope Educational Research Foundation was established, we maintained the camp period at eight weeks. However, by 1975, we reduced it to seven weeks, and in 1978, to six weeks. The six-week period seemed to be the one which most appealed to families, and it provided more scheduling options for after-camp rental groups, whose use of the facility helped to offset fixed costs.

> *"Teenagers are in an extraordinarily important period of development, the final organizational stage before adulthood. It is a time of trial and sometimes, often more than we would wish, error. In safe, thoughtful environments like High/Scope's, key developmental issues can be successfully negotiated or at least approached. All youth could use such an opportunity."*

When the time was reduced to seven weeks in 1975, Phyllis began her summer program to train music, physical education, and classroom teachers in movement and folk dance, since space became available at the end of the camp season.

We were not sorry to give up the rental of the facility to high school marching bands or football teams, the usual after-season August rental groups. Not only were they very hard on the facility but the management of such groups by their leaders was usually so authoritarian that it was difficult to see youth treated in such a way.

⌒

It wasn't all humorless, however. One summer, the assistant director from a marching band using camp came rushing up to the dining hall office where Phyllis was working. In desperation, he rapidly conveyed that some girls had food poisoning and were prone on the field. "Only girls, no boys?" Phyllis asked. "Yes!" he cried, "Call ambulances!" Phyllis was a trained camp health director and had a master's degree in health education; better yet, she had four daughters and 25 years experience running summer camp programs. She assured him that she would come immediately to appraise the situation. Upon arrival, she saw that it was as he had said. Twelve girls were spread about the field, prostrate, with clusters of surviving girls and most of the still healthy boys around each. The mental image that came to mind as Phyllis surveyed the field was of downed queen bees with the remnants of their hives fluttering around. She asked the assistant director to move all the upright band members back to formation, to practice at the far end of the field. Under protest, he obeyed. This left the 12 "queens" unattended. Phyllis waited a few minutes. Then she approached each one and asked how she felt. Lying on the damp grass of the field and nervous without their attendants, they each suddenly felt much better, thank you. "Ready to rejoin the group?" All but one experienced a miraculous cure on the spot and rushed to join the band. The last one took a little longer, returning to her room alone before a sudden and complete recovery. "Saint" Phyllis, 12 miracles to her credit, returned to the office thinking about how complex boy-girl relationships are for teenagers. The food was untainted, and the band performed well for the parent performance later in the week.

High/Scope Foundation Sponsorship

In 1979, George Johnson, director of federal programs for the COOR Intermediate School District in four northern Michigan counties (Crawford, Oscoda, Ogemaw, Roscommon) contacted staff member Charles Wallgren at the High/Scope Foundation with an interesting request. He wanted to identify CETA-qualified (Cooperative Education Training Act) disadvantaged youth who were good achievers in his local school districts. His goal was to provide them with a solid educational experience that would encourage them to develop their abilities and build their commitment to learning. He had heard of the High/Scope camp program and wanted to see what we could do. For a trial run, he sent four youth to that summer's camp to gain their perspective. Encouraged by their reports, he then worked with me to develop a month-long program that started in mid-May, with the students missing some of the regular school year.

This event was the catalyst for another decision: It seemed like a good idea for the High/Scope Foundation Board of Directors to take over all of the youth programs at camp. Phyllis and I felt we needed to begin to develop a formal adolescent department at the Foundation. They agreed. Thus in 1980, the new program for the COOR schools was operated by the Foundation using the High/Scope camp facilities. I hired experienced staff to operate this new program in the same manner as they had the traditional High/Scope summer camp. I continued to direct the original summer program, now under the auspices of the Foundation, and Phyllis continued to expand her teacher-training work. In 1989, George Johnson, of COOR, and Arthur Jefferson, superintendent of Detroit Public Schools, discussed the possibility of the Detroit district providing half of the enrollment for the May program. Their goal was to have rural white youth from northern Michigan and inner-city black youth from Detroit experience the program together, a unique way to help different members of our state population learn about one another within a program with a strong educational focus. The selection criteria were that the youths must be disadvantaged as defined by being financially eligible for the free lunch program and show evidence that they could be good academic achievers. This new program was named "Institute for IDEAS" (the acronym stands for Initiative, Diversity, Expectations, Achievement, Service) by David Bruno and the staff of High/Scope's adolescent department in recognition that we were

⁓

in effect an extension of the schools. In salute to that status, *campers* became *students* and the *camp* became the *Institute*. This shift took on special status in the fall of 1995 when the United States Department of Education's Program Effectiveness Panel certified the Institute for IDEAS as a research-validated program for inclusion in the National Diffusion Network. I believe we are the only nonschool-based program to achieve such stature.

"This new program was named 'Institute for IDEAS' (the acronym stands for Initiative, Diversity, Expectations, Achievement, Service)."

In the summer of 1995, the original summer program was reduced to two weeks for its last summer of operation. And with this event I closed out my career in residential camping (1945–1995). Those 48 years (I missed 1947 because of my dad's death, and 1954– 1955 while I was in the United States Marine Corps) were of enormous importance in my personal and professional development. An important sense of accomplishment for me comes from personal observations that the youth I served changed in important and beneficial ways. Their letters would come to me long after their camp session, and they would refer again and again to the life-altering aspect of their experience. One young man, now married with children, wrote that when he came to camp he was "on the wrong side of the educational curve." Now, he reported, he had a job involving major responsibility with the Walt Disney Company, and he thanked me for sparking a change in his attitude and for making him see how best to use his talents. Another sense of accomplishment comes from the experience of using my own interests and skills in woodcraft and the outdoors for the benefit of others. While the hiking and canoeing trips I led were demanding, they were also unusually fulfilling. Sharing knowledge of cooking on an open fire, helping others identify birds, and encouraging youth to recognize trees by both bark and leaf enabled me to work in areas of personal interest. I believe that individuals can and should use their own interests and skills to enable others to mature as effective adults. Camp provided me with that kind of opportunity.

At a professional level, operating the camp program kept me in direct and personal contact with both youth and their college-age leaders. As the High/Scope Curriculum evolved at the preschool level, we were able to use some of our ideas from the teen program operation for the preschool program. My commitment to give teachers a major voice in the development of the High/Scope approach pushed me to listen to the program participants as I shaped my views on education. When I look at the strength of the High/Scope approach, I feel it comes from this strong base in reality.

I am still not cut off from camping. I still participate by providing assistance as needed to the High/Scope Adolescent Department as they operate the Institute. And I must admit that such programs should be run by younger staff who are in touch with the youth of today. But the core of the program developed since 1963 remains as a sturdy base to support both the youth and staff who participate today.

As things end, others begin. In August of 1994, a second four-week adolescent program began, designed to run from mid-August through the first part of September. The May–June program continued to serve northern Michigan and Detroit youth; the August–September program began serving students from the international schools who had participated in the former summer program, private enrollments, and students from schools and social service agencies that the Adolescent Department was working with as part of their agency staff development program. Phyllis continued to use the facility in the weeks between mid-June and mid-August for teacher training sessions in movement and music.

The primary purpose of the program remains the same as it has since its founding in 1963. Through the Institute for IDEAS, youth who show intellectual and leadership promise are given the opportunity to develop a broader understanding of the educational process and to increase their participation and service in their regular school and agency programs.

Adolescent Department

In recent years the Adolescent Department has expanded beyond organizing and delivering the summer programs. John Weiss, a department director (1995–2002), developed a concept of serving both school- and community-based organizations. As the staff worked with these groups, Weiss realized that the most vexing problem the agencies faced was training their youth volunteers to be leaders. From this observation, he developed a program to train both adults and youth in program planning and service delivery based on the High/Scope program model. He gradually altered the Institute for IDEAS enrollment to give priority to student leaders from the groups we served. Thus, the focus of the department enlarged to include year-round work with agencies at their locations.

"The most vexing problem the agencies faced was training their youth volunteers to be leaders."

In one example of this work, the High/Scope program enabled an entire community to improve youth programs. Rick Hugey, program officer of the Gilmore Foundation in Kalamazoo, Michigan, learned about our service to youth, and he visited the IDEAS program in August 1998. Impressed by the program's emphasis on youth leadership, he and Weiss developed a broad plan targeted at the youth-serving agencies in Kalamazoo. Through Hugey's efforts, Gilmore provided us with a small pilot grant to undertake some initial discussion with agencies in the area. An enthusiastic response by community agencies to a High/Scope Adult/Youth Training Institute conducted under this grant led the United Way to develop the Kalamazoo Youth Development Network. The goal of the participating funding agencies was a three-year training and support program targeting a majority of youth-serving programs in the area. The project trained 75 adults and 75 youth leaders. Early success in the application of the training and favorable reports by youth who participated in the summer IDEAS program led to a five-year extension of this work.

Participants in a recent (2003) High/Scope IDEAS Institute at the High/Scope Retreat and Meeting Center (formerly known as "High/Scope Camp").

A second example of the Adolescent Department's work with outside agencies is its work with an alternative school. Weiss met with Scott Thompkins, director of Lakewood Educational Alternative Program in Lakewood, Michigan, during the IDEAS program in August 1996. Thompkins's enthusiastic goal was to model a school-based program on the High/Scope IDEAS Institute. His staff became involved after a staff training program that fall. In both 1997 and 1998, the school received federal money from the Goals 2000 program to integrate ongoing training and site support. Thompkins developed a project approach to learning using the State of Michigan educational benchmarks as a curriculum guide. Using High/Scope methodology, he then engaged his high school youth in planning their own learning projects guided by the educational benchmarks.

The outcomes of this intensive development of the High/Scope methods in an alternative high school are encouraging. Their student scores on state standardized tests have significantly increased, surpassing Michigan state averages in math, writing, science, and reading. With renewed Goals 2000 funding, the effort continues. High/Scope's Adolescent Department works with the school throughout the year and their youth leaders participate in both the school training and in the High/Scope Institute for IDEAS.

With this experience of community leadership training, the adolescent department is working with a wide range of agencies and schools to improve the quality and effectiveness of services to youth.

2

High/Scope's Preschool Research and Curriculum Development

The initiation of the High/Scope Perry Preschool Study was the result of a confluence of wide-ranging social forces and personal factors. The civil rights movement and accompanying social upheaval were enabling major societal change, and after four years at Oberlin College, a two-year tour of duty with the U.S. Marine Corps in Korea and Japan, and three years of graduate studies at the University of Michigan in Ann Arbor, I was eager to enter the workforce and make my own contribution to society. However, in the fall of 1958 when I began my professional career as school psychologist and director of special services for the Ypsilanti, Michigan, public school system, I wasn't thinking in terms of clearly defined goals and long-term studies. I was eager for professional challenges, but ignorant, really, of where those challenges would eventually take me. I don't believe any researcher wakes up one morning and says, "Today I'll begin that 40-year study I've been thinking about!" Instead, such efforts usually emerge from a gradual accretion of ideas considered and embraced, one experience at a time—at least that's the way it was for me. When the idea of an early education project began to form in 1959, it was the result of my

∼

desire to meet a local need identified through my professional experience in the schools. Yet, in retrospect, I can see that other factors were at work as well, and that none of the long-term studies initiated over the years could have happened without three key elements:

- A genuine set of debatable questions that demanded answers so that public policy, both educational and financial, could be established.

- A group of staff who cared about the questions and who were willing to work creatively, diligently, and objectively to find answers.

- A commitment to develop strong research designs, so that the outcome data would effectively support recommendations for action.

A longitudinal study can develop without an initial "grand design." Long-term studies may evolve as logical questions lead from a first step, to a second, and then beyond. But these early research steps must be organized well enough to support the longitudinal structure that eventually is built on their foundation.

Throughout my professional career, I have been interested in changing the practice of education to enable children and youth, especially disadvantaged children and youth, to attain greater personal, social, and economic success. Thus, my work has been characterized by curriculum innovation applied through intervention projects. The Perry research and the other studies I undertook asked a broad question: What would happen if a child's experiences were influenced by an educational intervention that enabled both the child and the family to become effectively involved in an educational program?

"Such efforts usually emerge from a gradual accretion of ideas considered and embraced, one experience at a time—at least that's the way it was for me."

The major underlying assumption was that the environment plays a major role in child development. This type of question required employment of the classical experimental group/control group research design, whenever possible.

Of course, the types of interventions I conducted were the products of the social and political times; the theories that guided this work represented the thinking of the period. For example, while I was enrolled as a graduate student at the University of Michigan in the education and psychology program, I was exposed primarily to current American researchers. Such well-established European theorists as Piaget were not part of the curriculum readings of the 1950s. Also, as with any longitudinal study spanning these particular 40 years, the work that began at the dawn of the computer age has been expedited over the decades by the evolution of that technology.

"The major underlying assumption was that the environment plays a major role in child development."

Significant Influences on the High/Scope Preschool Study and Curriculum Approach

The 1960s' focus on social change had a significant influence on the development of the High/Scope Perry Preschool Study. Throughout the struggle for civil rights, African-Americans and many whites demanded an end to the racial injustice evident in both northern and southern communities. In Ypsilanti, for example, all African-American children attended one elementary school since they lived in a single, restricted neighborhood. This strict school segregation broke down in the higher grades because the community had only two middle schools and one high school. There were black teachers at the black-dominated elementary school, but few at the other levels. These staffing and housing practices were the result of conventions applied by social consensus rather than law. As the civil rights movement gained force, an impetus developed for changing these traditional practices. A new consensus was formed, based on social justice.

In my role as school psychologist and director of special services with the Ypsilanti school system, I was new on the scene. I was the first to hold my position under new state fund-

〜

ing. To gain focus, I felt that one of my first tasks was to understand the impact of instruction within the system. In my report on systemwide achievement testing at a school principals' meeting during my first year on the job (1958), I presented charts of achievement test outcomes documenting what I saw as a serious problem. My intent was to begin an extended dialogue among the school leaders concerning potential solutions. Over the previous 10 years of standardized achievement testing (1948–1957), no class in the predominantly African-American school ever exceeded the 10th percentile on national norms for any tested subject; yet in the elementary school across town, which primarily served the children of white, middle-class university professionals, no class ever scored less than the 90th percentile. The principals' reaction was electric; several went to the window to have a smoke (it was the 1950s and smoking at meetings was accepted), several left the room without comment, one pushed back from the table, tightly crossing his arms and legs. Of the 12 principals, only a small group of three—Eugene Beatty, Raymond "Pete" Kingston, and John Salcau—were reform oriented and really focused on the topic. (Kingston and Salcau also joined me to establish High/Scope Camp five years later.) The very limited discussion ended with the announcement that everything possible was already being done; the test scores just represented the way children were. What could you expect? Their ability was what they were born with. With reform of the elementary school curriculum clearly out of the question, or at least out of my reach during the first year of my first professional job, my attention turned to alternatives.

> *"With reform of the elementary school curriculum clearly out of the question, or at least out of my reach during the first year of my first professional job, my attention turned to alternatives."*

After a period of discussion with special services staff and the three reform-minded principals, the idea of intervention at the preschool level emerged. Such a step had much to commend it. First of all, these years were the age-level *before* state-required school attendance began; thus, a program serving this group was no threat because it required no changes in the schools as a whole. Second, around 1956 the state had passed laws allowing counties to levy a special tax to add to state funds for special education services. Then in 1957, Washtenaw County voters passed a .5-mil levy to support such program expansion. In a new extension of state regulations, these funds could be used for 3- and 4-year-old children in local school districts. Thus, the resources to operate early education programs were available. Third, one of the principals in our small group of reformers was Eugene Beatty of Perry Elementary School, which the majority of African-American children attend-ed. Thus, we had a building principal who was happy to support such an intervention and will-ing to permit his attendance area and school to be used. Finally, I had a staff deeply committed to social change and the goals of the civil rights movement, giving me the neces-sary internal departmental support to undertake the project.

"We had a building principal who was happy to support such an intervention and willing to permit his attendance area and school to be used."

From a theoretical view, I was on more difficult ground. In a review of the literature, I found little support for such a novel undertaking in a public school with disadvantaged chil-dren, or indeed, with anyone. My program idea preceded by several years J. McVicker Hunt's extraordinary 1961 book, *In-telligence and Experience,* which laid the intellectual groundwork for questioning the idea of measured intelligence as a genetic trait. This meant I was working in a context where most people felt that IQ was God-given and, unfortunately, low-IQ minority children were just born that way. Yet, I was bothered when I discovered that I could assign a youngster an IQ with fair accu-racy simply by knowing the address of the family. (A girl on Harriet Street would usually obtain an IQ score of 82 to 86; a boy, 78 to 82.) Further, the studies in the 1930s conducted by Beth Lucy Wellman, Harold Skeels, Marie Skodak, and others on institutionally versus noninstitutionally reared low-IQ chil-dren at the Iowa Child Welfare Station offered some support for the belief that intervention could be effective. When there

49

was major environmental manipulation (such as placement out-side the institution with a family versus such limiting circum-stances as placement of a child in a state facility for the retard-ed), this could have a profound effect, dramatically raising a child's IQ score.

Finally, as a zoology minor in my graduate program at the University of Michigan, I was impressed by the 1960 studies on maze performance of cage-reared versus playground-reared rats by Stanford University researchers David Krech, Michael Rosenzweig, and Edward Bennett. These studies strongly suggested that problems caused by limited environ-ments could be ameliorated by stimulus-rich opportunities that more approximated the real-world rat environment. (Caution is needed in using information from studies on rats. Most such stud-ies focus on rats' spatial ability; humans are far more complex.) For me, the idea of enriched opportunities for poor children from limited backgrounds seemed justified by the findings from these sets of studies. Excited by these ideas, I was disappointed to dis-cover that most of the available early childhood research focused on higher-income children and wasn't relevant to the population we were trying to serve. However, in the social ferment of the times, the slender research evidence at hand seemed enough of a base to proceed.

"Most of the available early childhood research focused on higher-income children and wasn't rele-vant to the population we were trying to serve."

Developing the High/Scope Perry Preschool Study

With need driving decision, the High/Scope Perry Preschool Study thus began as a response to my frustration with the pace of needed changes in a small, local school system. The national political and social events of the time demanded change, and newspapers reported angry protests, massive marches, prayer meetings, and candlelight vigils throughout the country. Action was in the air. At 29, I was young, idealistic, and impatient to make things happen. Because of my age and inexperience, I just assumed that change would occur because it was necessary. Several events converged at this point to shape the program.

First, with the backing of the three principals and the promise of a place to hold the program, the school board gave permission to begin, providing I could locate the funds to cover direct expenses. With the recent changes in state regulations and with the new county special education millage, I knew I could finance the program.

Second, while establishing preschool classes was neither encouraged nor discouraged in the state legislation, state special education officials became alarmed that I was actually going to operate a classroom-based program (with home visits each week). When state officials had drafted the regulations to permit local authorities to spend county and state special education funds on 3- and 4-year-olds, they had envisioned a parent advisory service providing referrals to counseling and medical agencies. They saw these programs as primarily reaching physically or emotionally impaired preschool children. Serving socially and economically disadvantaged children who only superficially fit the criteria for mental impairment was not their idea of effective use of the resources. After extensive review of our plans and evidence from the scraps of research I provided, they nevertheless approved our application for preschool classroom funds. In an effort to contain what they saw as a risky venture, they required that I employ only teachers who were state-certified in three areas: preschool education, elementary education, and special education. Apparently, they felt I would be able to operate a sound program if I met these standards. (Or perhaps they assumed I could never find such teachers in a period of severe teacher shortage and they could thus avoid the entire issue!)

"With need driving decision, the High/Scope Perry Preschool Study thus began as a response to my frustration with the pace of needed changes in a small, local school system."

❧

51

Third, a series of meetings occurred with university professors in child development and special education that I had recruited as advisors on the proposed project. After reviewing our plans, the basic advice from several of these experts was *not* to operate the program. Because the children we planned to enroll would not have a mental age of 6 on the Stanford-Binet IQ test, the advisors believed such youngsters would not be mature enough to benefit from a school-based program. They felt that 3- and 4-year-olds, especially from disadvantaged backgrounds, would be unable to handle any program that I might plan to offer, and that in fact the program might actually harm the children.

All three events were important in influencing program development, but none was as important as the last. With such startling advice from seasoned professionals, it seemed unethical to just disregard their opinion and continue with our plans. However, after several weeks of discussion with the special services staff and the three principals, we decided that the advisors had asked (but not answered) a legitimate question, Does participation by disadvantaged children in an early education program improve their intellectual and academic abilities? Or, simply put, Does preschool work? With this challenging question to be answered, the High/Scope Perry Preschool Study was conceived as a tightly designed research project.

The High/Scope Perry Preschool Study Begins

The study officially began in October 1962. From 1962 until the spring of 1967, it was an actual service project with both program and no-program groups (randomly assigned children were placed in one group or the other primarily by chance). The children assigned to the program group attended preschool three hours a day, five days a week, during the regular school year and had a 90-minute home visit by the same teacher each week. The children of the no-program group remained in the community, at home with their parents, without any of the services the program group received. Since it began, the project also has operated as a longitudinal study. From ages 3–10, both groups' progress was assessed each year. Assessment occurred again at ages 14–15, 19, and 27. In 1999, interviews at ages 39–41 were initiated.

The study's power to answer the basic research question presented earlier rests on four pillars. Of these, the first and foremost is the random assignment of sample, as difficult as that was to accomplish. Such assignment meant that once identified as a poor child with a limited level of assessed intelligence, each child had an equal chance to be in either group. There was only one significant difference between the groups when the project started—maternal employment. (The maternal employment difference disappeared in the age-15 study.) If systematic, consistent differences appeared either shortly after the end of the project or later during the follow-up phase, such differences could thus be interpreted as the result of the preschool experience.

"The High/Scope Perry Preschool Study is robust enough to support its extensive longitudinal structure and its astonishing conclusions."

The second pillar of the study design is the fact that once assigned, no family in either group failed to participate. To reach this goal, we sometimes needed the school principal and members of several neighborhood service clubs to talk with the families; I was determined that the study would not be flawed by involving only those who wished to participate. Once screened for the study criteria and randomly assigned to either the program or no-program group, all families assigned to either group agreed to be involved for the duration of the two-year program.

The third pillar is that no one entered the study because they requested the service (and after a few years of operation there were always requests) or because staff or service agencies felt a particular child had a special need to enroll. Maintaining this principle was often difficult because teachers doing the initial screening in the community occasionally identified families in great need. However, this policy was essential to avoid the problems in data interpretation that would have occurred if those desiring the service were assigned to the program group while those who had little interest were assigned to the no-program group or were not considered at all in sample assignment.

The final pillar is the fact that throughout the study there has been little loss of sample. By age 27, only 5 percent of all the data were missing. High retention of participants and complete data are an absolute necessity for a long-term, small-sample study such as this one. With this attention to the integrity of the sample, its random assignment, and the location of all participants for follow-up, the High/Scope Perry Preschool Study is robust enough to support its extensive longitudinal structure and its astonishing conclusions.

When the study first began, it was not conceived as an extensive longitudinal study. The research questions were limited to early education effects on intellectual development and the resulting benefits for elementary school performance. However, as director of special services, I found it was natural to compile the data from the groups each year. I also found that it was natural to establish a sequential-wave design for the small groups entering the program each year. That's what schools do: enroll children annually. I had the staff and the opportunity. As parents, staff, and community reported great satisfaction with the service, there was strong support from the building principal to continue.

While almost all service projects achieve participant satisfaction, the most important aspects for us were the research findings. Before kindergarten, the major end-of-project outcome was an extraordinary increase in children's assessed performance on the Stanford-Binet IQ test. We were exhilarated by the results and vindicated in our faith that we could provide an effective intervention in the lives of poor children at risk of school failure. The average gain of 15 IQ points moved most of these disadvantaged children out of the mildly retarded IQ range and into the normal range. These results justified our course of action, we felt. We saw our efforts as part of the social and civil change going on around us; we were contributing to the improvement

of the nation. Poor children could now come to the uncompro-
mising elementary schools better able to engage in traditional
education. We couldn't change the schools, but we could help
children be better prepared.

A worrisome problem emerged, however,
as we continued our yearly follow-up assessment. *"We couldn't change*
In the early elementary grades the program *the schools, but we*
group's measured level of achievement was not *could help children*
significantly different from that of the no-program *be better prepared."*
group. This elementary school finding put a damper on our enthusiasm. However, by third grade things appeared to change again.
While the measured IQ of the program group drifted down to the
level of the no-program group, the program group significantly
out-performed the no-program group in achievement test scores
and teacher ratings of better classroom behavior. This pattern has
remained steady throughout the study. Critics pointed to the
washout of IQ gains; reformers pointed to the achievement gains.
I declared a victory and started three new intervention projects in
1967–1968. These projects—the High/Scope Preschool Curriculum Comparison Study, the High/Scope Curriculum Model in the
national Follow Through Project, and the Ypsilanti-Carnegie Infant
Education Project—will be discussed in later chapters.

Employing the Research Staff

Because the High/Scope Perry Preschool Study included a
strong research component, acquiring competent research staff
was essential to the work. On the whole, locating research staff
was less of a problem than finding teachers. I was still a graduate
student at the University of Michigan and had contact with fel-
low students whom I could hire for short-term assignments. In
my school district position, I had a social worker and a regular
staff of school diagnosticians who were eager to take part in the
work. Their assignments were pieced together both to meet
state standards for program reimbursement and to assure the
quality needed to operate the study.

Over the years, the study has had four waves of research staff. The first wave (1960–1964) worked with me to establish the project, gain initial funding, and create the theory base for the curriculum. The second wave (1965–1968) was instrumental in establishing the complicated follow-up procedures, especially those designed to maintain the integrity of the data and the objectivity of independent data collectors and coders so that they had no knowledge of the group to which particular subjects were assigned. These researchers also assisted in the design of the parallel longitudinal studies, especially the Preschool Curriculum Comparison Study. The third wave (1969–1973) joined me to implement these new longitudinal studies. Most of these three waves of staff were graduate students at the University of Michigan, and they tended to move on as they completed their degrees. In 1974, we hired a fourth and more permanent wave of recent Ph.D. graduates. This group has been responsible for the ongoing high-quality data collection and coding. They have also participated in producing an extensive monograph collection documenting each phase of these studies. In particular, Larry Schweinhart gradually has assumed major responsibility for the High/Scope Perry Preschool Study and other research as chair of the Foundation's Research Department. (In 2003, he become president of the Foundation.)

In retrospect, I have been fortunate to have had more than 100 talented and dedicated research staff at all levels engaged in the study. Indeed, one of the staff accepted a congressional fellowship in Washington after five years at High/Scope. One evening midway through his fellowship year, a congressional committee staffer asked him, "Now, tell me, how does Weikart cook the data to come up with such consistently positive results?" My staff member just happened to be the one in charge of data collection, supervising both the interviewers and the recorders of official state and county records. His response was personal astonishment followed by anger and the comment, "With so many people involved in the study over so many years, if there were such a problem, you wouldn't have to ask me. You would already know!"

~

Obtaining the Financing

Obtaining money for any project is always difficult when you
have to depend upon the kindness of strangers; obtaining money
for an innovative study for an extended period of time is even
more difficult. The initial funding of the High/Scope Perry
Preschool Study came from four sources. The funds that paid
for daily project services to children and families came from the
State of Michigan. These funds were supplemented by the
Washtenaw County Intermediate School District and by the Ypsilanti Public Schools, which provided administrative services and
classroom space. The fourth source, which supported the direct
research costs, was a Cooperative Education Research Grant from the U.S. Office of Education
(then part of the U. S. Department of Health,
Education, and Welfare). This four-year grant of
$120,000, a princely sum in those days, started in
January 1964, 18 months after the launch of the
project. The grant was obtained with the cooperation and support of the Michigan Department of
Education, which had to submit the application

*"In retrospect, I
have been fortunate
to have had more
than 100 talented
and dedicated
research staff at
all levels engaged
in the study."*

and receive the funds. The department, represented by Dr. John
Porter (later to become Michigan's chief state school officer and
then president of Eastern Michigan University), was most helpful both in reviewing drafts of the proposal and in forwarding it
to Washington with recommendations. Years later, I talked with
Robert Thorndike, one of the five-person review committee,
who said that it was their first grant to a public school (most
went to universities). They believed that for a public school staff
to undertake such research at the preschool level was a little
risky and odd, but innovative and full of promise. I thanked him
for his confidence.

The end of the project in 1967 was also the end of the research grant. From then until 1970, the study relied on regularly
hired special services staff and small-scale Washtenaw County
Intermediate School District assistance for data collection and

coding. In 1970, I wrote Tom James, president of the newly established Spencer Foundation, for assistance with the follow-up work. After receiving our proposal, he suggested I visit him at his office at the John Hancock Building in Chicago. I, of course, agreed. During the meeting we discussed the weather, conditions of living and working in such a tall, modern structure (the way the coffee swayed in a cup on the upper floors), and the future direction of education in America, but only superficially discussed the study. I was disappointed with this failed opportunity to obtain funding for a study to which I had committed a decade of my life. Thus, it came as a great and welcome surprise to receive notification a month later of a three-year grant for $300,000. James endorsed our work and enabled the High/Scope Perry Preschool Study to continue. I was so inexperienced that I didn't recognize the meeting for what it was—a relaxed session during which James could assess the individual behind the project. (It was only my third grant.) Later funding for the Perry Study came from the Ford Foundation, U.S. Office of Special Education, and Carnegie Corporation of New York, among others.

In my efforts to obtain funds for the Perry Study over the years, I have experienced what seems to be a universal problem: Funds are not readily available for longitudinal studies, in spite of the critically important information they produce. One-time funding to start the Perry research was obtained only after a federal agency grant review board accepted the notion that a public school staff could actually conduct a research study on this topic. (I concede, however, that the concept of early childhood education was novel at the time and would have been risky for anyone to undertake and fund.) However, over time, we managed to fund the study both by soliciting contracts and grants and by reassigning our own staff. In 1999, the McCormick Tribune Foundation extended full funding for the required three-year period to complete the age-40 phase of the study.

How the Curriculum Got Its Name

The name "High/Scope Curriculum" evolved over time. Initially, the program was called the Cognitively Oriented Curriculum. I wanted to avoid its being labeled either as a free play/social development program or as a direct-drill/structured-teaching program. Also, while the name "High/Scope" was used for the adolescent camp program from its inception, the High/Scope Foundation itself was not founded until 1970. Thus, in the late 1960s, when we were involved in National Follow Through, Planned Variation Head Start, and our own Curriculum Comparison Study, the approach continued to be called the Cognitively Oriented Curriculum. It remained so until a High/Scope board meeting in the 1980s, when Amir Bhatia of the U.K. (now Lord Amir Bhatia of Hampton) asked why we called it that. He made a convincing case that the Foundation should use its own name on the curriculum and the various research studies. His strongest argument was that the collection of projects and the curriculum needed to be instantly recognizable as the production and responsibility of one institution, the High/Scope Educational Research Foundation. Since then, all High/Scope research studies and the curriculum references have been so named.

Creating the High/Scope Curriculum

Creating a curriculum is neither a straightforward, practical task nor solely an intellectual exercise. It is a matter of knowing what you want and then taking a stand. It requires a commitment to a philosophy of education meshed with sound theory and high-quality research information. It is a personal expression of beliefs and values. It requires much work, and the willingness to absorb criticism and tolerate experimentation. Finally, it takes time—to try things out, to observe reactions, to integrate new ideas, and to gather staff willing to think "outside the box" and trust the process of experimental development. Creating the High/Scope Curriculum began when I first decided to operate a special education early childhood program in 1960. Today, more than 40 years later, the curriculum is still under development. To be sure, it is a mature methodology with extensive national and international use, but it is still evolving, within the overall guidelines hammered out over many long years. This section discusses this process of development. The historical preschool curriculum itself and related research documentation are described in detail in the series of publications listed in the appendices, p. 277. The focus here is on the preschool educational approach; the curriculum as applied at the infant, elementary, and adolescent levels is described in other chapters.

The development of the High/Scope Curriculum began almost as soon as I decided to operate a preschool program. Knowing little about early childhood development other than what I had learned in a course at Oberlin College taken a decade earlier and the standard graduate courses in education and psychology at the University of Michigan, I thought it necessary to visit some existing programs to see how they were operating. The Detroit Public Schools had a late-afternoon preschool service program for inner-city children at one elementary school. Several interested special services staff and I arrived on a dark, late-winter afternoon to observe. Certain events from that experience made a lasting impression on us. When we arrived, the children were playing on their own while the teachers talked together or observed from the sidelines. After a period of time, the head teacher stepped in to direct a whole-group lesson on the concept of "circle." To understand the program's overall approach, we looked at a wall chart of the daily schedule, which indicated that the primary block of time was for free play. In addition, some time was designated for teachers to present large-group instruction in such areas as colors, shapes, and number recognition, such as we were observing. During these instruction periods, the program looked like a standard elementary school classroom. There was also a snack time during which each youngster sat down at a long table to eat a cookie and drink a carton of milk. As each child finished,

"Creating a curriculum requires a commitment to a philosophy of education meshed with sound theory and high-quality research information."

he or she stood up and said to the rest of the group, "Excuse me," and left the table. The supervising teacher, tall and substantially built with skirts almost to her ankles, stood with crossed-arms at the exit door and observed the children. When the last child was done, nothing happened; he continued to sit at the table. The teacher waited. Finally she asked, "Well?" There was a long pause, then the child slowly rose, turned to the now empty table, and said, "Excuse me." Without glancing at the teacher, he left the room. We were watching the "manners and morals" portion of the program.

Two observations dominated our staff discussions of this program: Why would children be given such undirected freedom to play as they wished, and then have teachers step in with such directive lessons? Why would a child benefit from saying "Excuse me" to an empty table which he, at least, saw as a strange obligation indeed? We hoped whatever curriculum we could create would be without these obvious contradictions for the child as well as the teacher.

Searching for alternatives, I turned to the literature to find some guidance on curriculum choices. Most of the information came from directors of university-based early childhood demonstration programs. They usually recommended a social development program (the children in their care tended to be middle-class youngsters from small families with little opportunity to play with other children). Their programs included large blocks of unstructured play and a focus on self-sufficiency skills such as training in toileting, hand-washing, coat-buttoning, and shoe-tying. Pauline Sears and Edith Dowley, directors of the model demonstration preschool at Stanford University, listed 10 major program concerns such as those above, but neither children's language development nor general cognitive skills were included. Terms such as "cognitive," "problem solving," or "academic preparation" were not mentioned by most of these program teachers, but personal care skills, social relations, and psychological adjustment were "in." New ideas for program elements, such as High/Scope's *plan-do-review process*, had not yet been proposed. (The focus on children's self-sufficiency skills is interesting to me now, because that was also the top-rated concern of both parents and teachers surveyed in most of the 15 countries participating in the Preprimary Project of the International Association for the Evaluation of Educational Achievement (IEA), a long-running study for which High/Scope has been the International Coordinating Center.)

Not much information came from where I needed it the most, research. Sam Kirk at the University of Illinois had completed a five-year study in 1958 of the impact of early childhood education on various groups of children with special needs and a range of etiologies. Indeed, his study was essentially the first in the early education movement of the late twentieth century. His major finding was that the experience didn't seem to help most of the various groups of youngsters, but those who came from disadvantaged homes did show some improvement. This outcome was very important to me, because those youngsters were the very group I hoped to assist. Excited by the prospect of finding an early answer to our curriculum search, I wrote asking what curriculum he used and requesting any documentation he could send me. His response was illustrative of the state of the field. He directed me to his book and to the *paragraph* on curriculum.

The High/Scope Curriculum was conceived, then, in response to what I *couldn't* find in the research of the time. Basically, I decided to follow the line of program development that I had been using in working with adolescents in residential summer camps. This philosophy was based on fully involving the learner with the adult as a learning partner and providing ample opportunities for creativity and initiative for both. The relationship had to be respectful and cooperative to provide a psychologically safe environment for the learner. Finally, while I was interested in content (after all, it was the lack of academic skills that was defeating so many of the youth I was seeing as a school psychologist), I was equally interested in the process used to learn content. With this background, I chose to draw from John

Dewey's educational philosophy and from the experiences of the Perry Study's teachers. The result was a focus on active participation by children with much hands-on opportunity provided by the teacher.

Finding Teachers

A major stumbling block to establishing the program was locating teachers. With the state staff certification requirements, it seemed we would never be able to operate. Required to hire only fully certified teachers with three areas of endorsement (regular elementary, early childhood education, and special education for the mentally handicapped), I almost gave up on the project because this rule was an impossible requirement. In the early 1960s, teachers with even temporary elementary certificates were hard to find for any open teaching staff position. The Ypsilanti Public Schools was as desperate to hire teachers as any system in Michigan. We even offered compensation that was 10 percent above the normal pay schedule for any teacher with special education certification. With persistence, during the spring of

"While I was interested in content, I was equally interested in the process used to learn content."

1962 I identified four candidates with at least two of the required certificates and supported their return to summer school to take enough courses to obtain temporary certification in the third area. Consequently, we opened in the fall with four staff—the only four I could locate and cajole into taking a risk on such an unusual project—who would be working with 28 children in a community center assembly hall. Our special education social worker, Norma Radin, supported the teachers' work with families, and our school psychologists, Byron Aldrich and Percy Bates, helped provide information on the children.

The project opened for the children in October 1962. Teachers had a daily noon planning time because they were all teaching together in one room with the same group of children. To my surprise, planning quickly became a chore for the teaching staff, and as a result it became a game of minimal thought, with them often reaching quick agreement: "Anything you want is okay, as long as I don't have to do it." Indeed, lunch planning time became Scrabble game time. They seemed to think that working together to implement joint ideas was too difficult; too much discussion and compromise were required. Making planning even more demanding and complicated, I added weekly strategy meetings to explore what child development research could contribute to the program. Such meetings necessarily involved both the teaching group and the project's psychological and social services staff.

This was hardly a propitious start for a new era in education of the disadvantaged! Tradition didn't bode well: Teachers rarely worked in teams, and the researchers didn't understand day-to-day classroom practice. The stress on staff in starting up a whole new program that many others thought would fail, conducting home visits in difficult family circumstances, working in a community hall where everything had to be packed up and stored under the stage each night, and my inexperienced project leadership, all combined to make a unified curriculum development effort difficult.

Then one day, six weeks into the program, it all changed. Big-for-his-age 4-year-old Victor threw his chair, a big folding one, across the room. That got everyone's attention, and the group seemed to suddenly coalesce—ready to act together to prevent such dangerous behavior. The choice of direction in finding a solution was critical, for in that decision we established the line of development of the High/Scope Curriculum. Was Victor a disturbed child in need of referral to a clinic or even removal from the program? Was the program in need of clearer definition for both children and teachers? Was there even a program in place that engaged the children in a manner that reflected our commitment? In a very real sense, young Victor was the instigator of the High/Scope Curriculum, for he experienced what we initially had to offer and found it lacking. Our choice was either to blame him or to reform our practice. Our decision

"A research study can't have a roving curriculum."

was to accept that program opportunities and management, not the child, were the problem. Thus, a major philosophical milestone for our work was achieved, one that characterizes all of our curriculum efforts since that time.

With a renewed sense of purpose, the teachers and other special services staff went to work on developing a unified curriculum. It was clear that what we wanted didn't fit in a continuum of rigid lessons or, at the other end, of wholly free play. Instead, I wanted teachers to have ideas that enabled children to play as they wished and allowed the teachers to talk with children to develop their language skills. (Indeed, I coined the term "verbal bombardment" to encourage the teachers to supply language for whatever a child was accomplishing. This intense focus on language was later abandoned when children complained that the teachers talked too much!) Our aim was for both teachers and children to be actively involved, not that I knew what that entailed in actual application. In the midst of the great social changes of the 1950s and 1960s, the view that poor minority children were failing in school because of poor genetic stock was being challenged. This general push for an activist curriculum on the part of both teachers and children was a major decision, fundamental to the development of the High/Scope approach. Once it was made, I, as study director, had the role of fully defending it. A research study can't have a roving curriculum.

Identifying Key Curriculum Elements

When we most needed them, we came upon a series of important curriculum ideas during the 1963–1964 school year. In the spring of 1963, I discovered Piaget while reading a review of J. McVicker Hunt's 1961 book, *Intelligence and Experience*. This major work integrated the research evidence supporting the central role of the environment in the development of intelligence and achievement. Hunt presented a summary of Piaget's research in some detail. That fall, both the project research staff and the classroom teachers attended a series of seminars totaling six days of introduction to Piagetian concepts. (I contracted with a Professor Gilmore from the Merrill-Palmer Institute in Detroit, who was familiar with Piaget's work, to conduct these sessions.) The staff and I were ecstatic. We now felt we had a well-defined theory that supported our environmentalist view of child development, one that was also compatible with the progressive education ideas of Dewey that we were loosely following. With Piaget's theories and Dewey's philosophy, we had a rationale for the "do" portion of our approach. Next, reading Sara Smilansky's reports on her systematic observation of children in Israeli outdoor play settings in which elements of planning were introduced, we focused our attention on what was to become the "plan" element of our program. Finally, a late fall consultation with Robert Hess, of the University of Chicago, resulted in the obvious addition of "review," to the proposed curriculum. As Hess pointed out, the children plan their work and undertake it, why not have them evaluate it? Thus, by the end of 1964, the now famous HighScope process to support the application of the scientific method by children in preschool—*"plan-do-review"*—was in place at least as a concept. Yet, it took years to work out the details of this process, whose value today seems so obvious.

In the spring of 1964, a major decision affecting project organization was forced by staff differences. This decision, like the one forced by Victor's disruptive activity mentioned earlier, dramatically shaped the curriculum. After the seminars on Piagetian theory, the staff as a whole felt we had found a base from which to organize the curriculum we were developing. The research staff (led by Constance Kamii, who later became a noted Piagetian scholar) felt that their better understanding of Piagetian theory and research qualified them to set the overall direction of the curriculum and to guide the teaching staff in organizing daily activities. They began to outline lesson plans for the week and to instruct teachers about theoretically correct and incorrect ways to promote children's development of cognitive skills. While the teaching staff, led by Donna McClelland (now deceased, Donna spent her professional career at High/Scope), welcomed the suggestions; they felt that they had a better understanding of the children and what experiences best fit within the daily routine and teacher-child relationships. They also felt these instructions were pushing them toward a program that was more directive than we had originally envisioned.

These positions proved to be irreconcilable. I tried various administrative adjustments, to no avail. As the tension became more pronounced, I had to make a difficult decision. Should I keep the talented and committed researchers on staff, or keep the capable and experienced teachers? One group was on the way out; there was no compromise—feelings and tempers were too strong. At this point, I formalized my position: The High/Scope approach would draw upon child development theory such as Piaget's, but the application of theory had to be tempered by advice from experienced classroom teachers. We would never be a classic, strictly Piagetian-based program. The research staff departed, and I replaced them with others who understood this delicate balance. The teachers stayed. Henceforth, the curriculum was to be pragmatic and applied while still relying heavily on sound theoretical principles. I continue to believe that the use of theory, even well-documented theory, must be tempered by the real-world wisdom of experienced staff. Thus today, the High/Scope Curriculum is an amalgam of related developmental theories hammered into usefulness by decades of teacher experiences in the classroom and on home visits. I have never regretted this decision nor questioned the results. When I see our approach being used throughout the United States and in over 20 countries by a wide range of ethnic, religious, and language groups, I see its broad accessibility as support for my decision to listen carefully to the teachers.

"By the end of 1964, the now famous High/Scope process to support the application of the scientific method by children in preschool —'plan-do-review'—was in place at least as a concept."

As the newly discovered Piagetian theory swept the country in the mid-1960s, what Piaget called "the American question" was asked: What can be done to accelerate cognitive development? With many in agreement that intelligence and achievement are formed by the environment, the next step was clear: "Now let's teach what is required to develop cognitive ability." Psychologist Celia Lavatelli produced a kit of exercises in each of the major cognitive development areas (seriation, classification, and so forth), so that teachers could systematically give children specific train-ing. In their reliance on prepackaged equipment and exercises, these approaches were like Montessori, but with modernized content. Publishers rushed to introduce competing prod-ucts with multiple claims. Even J. McVicker Hunt produced a series of training exercises with infants organized by Ina Uzgiris, one of his students.

"I continue to believe that the use of theory, even well-documented theory, must be tempered by the real-world wisdom of experienced staff."

My decision was to defend our position that children learn through the carefully organized engagement process we had de-veloped, especially when working with their own plans and im-plementing their own decisions. We did not buy the new prod-ucts nor develop kits ourselves. Research studies of the pro-grams using such systems soon reported negative or few results and the fad began to fade. This experience strengthened my re-solve to be aware of other areas of distraction: new theorists, new jargon, new gimmicks, and fads that might draw the cur-riculum away from its historic commitment to teachers and chil-dren learning together.

The early 1970s brought an important, much needed, and positive development in the High/Scope Curriculum. As teach-ers struggled to document their work and to produce guides both for training others and for supporting teachers new to the program, a need to describe the program's content became ap-parent. In the fall of 1967, we began the High/Scope Preschool Curriculum Comparison Study, and more professionals were in-terested in learning what we did in our program and how it dif-fered from the others. Bernard Banet, a staff member who was a doctoral student in child development at the University of

Michigan, conceptualized a way of organizing child growth needs into theoretical units call *"key experiences."* The key experiences were organized in ten categories: *language and literacy, creative representation, initiative and social relations, movement, music, classification, seriation, number, space,* and *time.* This organization gave the adults an intellectual basis for interacting with children, observing their play activity, and making program decisions. We also began to organize the teachers' observations of children to judge their progress, thus taking the first steps in creating what is now the Preschool Child Observation Record (COR), an observation-based assessment tool.

Is the High/Scope Curriculum a Play-Based Approach?

Unfortunately, the use of key experiences rekindled the argument between teachers who were committed to children initiating all activities and those who recognized that teachers have a role to play in introducing key experience-related activities children may be overlooking. Child-initiated learning was seen as opposed to teacher-initiated learning experiences (offering plan-do-review in a supportive style and various content ideas at small- and large-group times). As an open framework for daily activities, the curriculum has great flexibility, so this difference in approach may not be readily apparent. Some teachers tread lightly at group times. They observe children to understand them and to learn about their various interests, but they rarely act on the basis of that knowledge to introduce curriculum topics. Other teachers, who are aware of their opportunities to extend children's learning, tend to use their observations, along with their knowledge of the key experiences, to introduce ideas at group times or to extend child's plan-do-review efforts. The impact of these differences is subtle and the role of the teacher often looks essentially the same. However, the long-term difference of opinion among staff over these issues led to major turmoil in the program from the late 1980s to 1990, enough to actually threaten the curriculum's continued existence.

This problem is seen most clearly in a plan initiated to convert the curriculum into a traditional nursery school approach with lots free play. I became aware of a parent-infant education program developed at the University of Connecticut that seemed to neatly dovetail with the High/Scope approach. (Unable to obtain funding, we had dropped our parent-infant work in 1984.) The program needed a home because the chief investigator was leaving the university and there were still several years to go on their grant. The program trainer, Amy Powell, was the only staff member who moved to High/Scope, and she became a powerful voice among training staff. Her program for infants, solidly based on a Piagetian theory, did not use the High/Scope plan-do-review process, of course, because infants are too young for it. However, the program did employ child choice of toys (as we also recommend). Teachers played with the infants, babbling sounds and responding with words as appropriate and paced by the child. All were practices that High/Scope staff encouraged for parents and infants years before in the 1967 Ypsilanti Carnegie-Infant Education program.

What the introduction of this program resulted in, however, was a small group of staff who felt these simplified methods should be applied with the more mature preschool children. They ignored both the increased mobility and expanded language capacity of older children. Therefore, they encouraged staff in the demonstration school to drop the formal plan-do-review process and replace it with only talking briefly to children as they played—resulting in more of a traditional free-play situation. They developed drafts of material stating that the principal curriculum task of the High/Scope teacher was to "play with children." No other teacher curriculum responsibilities were relevant. In short, their approach advocated a play-based active learning environment and ignored the plan-do-review process and the 58 key experiences in child development as a teacher content guide.

The problem with this revisionist approach was that it threw the High/Scope Curriculum in with those who think that it is mainly genetics that determines the outcome of children's educational experiences and not the opportunities provided by the environment and the teachers. It would return High/Scope to the position of educators before the 1960s. Free play as envisioned by this group was child driven with a passive teacher as a responder. In short, the 100-monkey theory (given enough time, 100 monkeys can type out an Ogden Nash poem such as: "Many an infant that screams like a calliope/Could be soothed by a little attention to its diope" or perhaps with a little more time, Henry V's St. Crispin's Day speech from Shakespeare's *Henry V.*) This understanding of development is not the High/Scope assumption nor is the curriculum approach based on this position. I believe that while genetics plays a role in achieving educational success, its full expression is formed by the opportunities one has to experience a rich learning environment facilitated by others. (The sidebar on pp. 72–74 illustrates how I took advantage of one such learning opportunity while driving my grandson, Brian, to High/Scope's Demonstration Preschool.)

"I believe that while genetics plays a role in achieving educational success, its full expression is formed by the opportunities one has to experience a rich learning environment facilitated by others."

My role in the debate was limited; this all bubbled over when I was undergoing a year of chemotherapy for lymphoma in 1990. I was, however, aware of the meetings and managed to attend one to listen to the discussion. At the end of the meeting, I stated that these ideas might be of value, but not to us. We had made our commitment and we needed to stay with it. If there were staff who were no longer willing to adhere to High/Scope's core principles, especially to the emphasis on the plan-do-review sequence, they needed to seek employment elsewhere. The dominant spokespersons for the opposing view left the Foundation. The rest of the staff stayed, with some commenting they were glad I finally ended the debate. Like the earlier argument over whether teachers or researchers would direct the program, this attempt to redefine the teacher's role and the structure of the routine was a key turning point in our development. As the

"Driving Master Brian":
Supporting Children's Thinking

*In this personal account of experiences with his then 3-year-old grandson,
Brian, the author considers an important and challenging issue for those
using the High/Scope approach: How can an adult pose problems that
stimulate a child's thinking?*

A round 7:45 each weekday morning, I stop by my daughter's
house to pick up my grandson Brian for our daily drive to the
High/Scope Demonstration Preschool. If you've never experienced a daily 45-minute drive with a 3-year-old, you can't imagine the
pleasure this can bring. So many things to discuss—"I went with my
dad to Big Wheel and we got some new baskets for my room"; to
observe—"Hey Pa, the horses are still out in the yard in the cold. See
the steam [their breath]?"; and *to wonder about*. It's this last topic that
I want to discuss here.

About 10 minutes into our ride, we pass a microwave transmission tower, a rather small one, with only two satellite dishes and a
single blinking beacon on top of the 100-foot structure. The beacon
on top of the tower appears to be a warning signal for low-flying air-
craft. The signal is operated by a light-sensitive control and comes on
or off automatically. During the day it's usually off, unless it's dark because of bad weather.

For the first few months of the school year, Brian didn't notice
the tower, although it is fairly close to the road. One day, however, he
started the drive talking about a discovery he had made. He and his
mom had seen "flying pancakes" (the satellite dishes) the day before
on the ride home, and he couldn't wait to show them to me.

It was a grey, rainy morning, and as we drew near the tower,
Brian excitedly pointed out the flying pancakes to me. The red beacon at the top of the tower was blinking steadily. "I wonder why the
light is on," I said casually to Brian.

Brian immediately informed me why the light was on: "It's a little bit sprinkling," which it was. During our drives over the next several weeks, we often found the signal operating. Whenever we noticed this, I would "wonder" why the light was on. Each time, Brian
would offer an explanation: "It's a little bit winter," or, "There's snow
on the ground," or, occasionally, "Because it's a little bit dark."

Brian's curiosity was sparked by these discussions, and we soon
fell into a routine that became the high point of our daily trips. When
I picked Brian up in the morning, I would usually say, "I wonder
whether the light will be on today." Brian would then confidently

The author and grandson Brian at the High/Scope Demonstration Preschool (1996).

predict that the light would be on or off because of some generally observable condition, such as "winter." On dark mornings he would predict that the light would be on because it was "dark." After a while, Brian began to initiate our discussion about the light as soon as I picked him up.

Each morning, as we rounded the bend to the tower, Brian would lean forward eagerly to see if his guess had been correct. When his prediction was right, he cried out in delight. When his prediction was wrong, he was disappointed. But whether or not he had predicted correctly, I would usually then ask him *why* he thought the light was on or off. Brian always had an explanation: "It's winter," or "It's raining," or sometimes, when his guess hadn't been right, "He's sleeping."

Continued on p. 74

Brian's answers told me he did not yet understand that the degree of brightness outside determined whether or not the signal was operating. Then one morning in mid-January, Brian announced the light was off because it was "too light." After a pause, he added that it was "still a little bit winter." By February, he had dropped the false part of this explanation, and he usually predicted the condition of the light accurately, based on the brightness of the morning.

Of course, aside from the fun and suspense this small mystery provided Brian, a larger educational purpose was being served. *Each day, Brian entertained a problem, predicted an outcome, held his prediction in mind, and verified his position based on his direct observations.* I never saw it as my role to suggest to Brian that his predictions, or his explanations for them, might be right or wrong. I left it up to Brian to draw conclusions. Based on whatever else he was observing—winter, snow, rain, and so forth—he extended various working theories to explain the beacon's operation. Gradually, this allowed him to make the connection between the light being on or off and the degree of brightness outside.

Early on, I knew that Brian realized something was causing the beacon to turn on or off. But within this basic logical framework, he felt free to invent whatever theory seemed appropriate at the time. It would have been easy to give him a "rule" that would predict the operation of the light and then to drill him on it each day. But then he would have been denied the chance to make his own observations, discoveries, and judgments. And I would have missed that excited, wondering cry, "Pa, it's on!" as we came around the bend.

*Excerpt from Weikart, D. P. (1996). In N. A. Brickman (Ed.), *Supporting young learners 2: Ideas for child care providers and teachers* (pp. 23–26). Ypsilanti, MI: High/Scope Press.

leader, I felt I had to step in and make the decision that not all these new practices were compatible with our mission and traditions. While the curriculum could and should continue to evolve, it would lose its identity if it strayed too far from it roots.

In the sidebar on p. 76, there is a short presentation of the High/Scope educational philosophy as it exists today. You will note that the plan-do-review process (a child's version of the scientific method) continues to be a central element of the approach. This process frees the teacher to employ conversational language with the child because she or he genuinely does not know what the child is thinking or experiencing. It also offers an opportunity for teachers to use the concepts from the key experiences to expand and extend children's thinking in essential learning areas. While we are clearer today in our the curriculum statements, the same guiding principles have been present from the start. It is this collection of insights that has made the High/Scope Curriculum work—for decades.

> *"While we are clearer today in our the curriculum statements, the same guiding principles have been present from the start."*

The Role of New Curriculum Ideas

What are twenty-first century challenges to the curriculum? I think our field is full of ideas and fads based on personal beliefs rather than solid research. While personal opinion and a commitment to a belief system are important, especially when the ideas are based upon actual experience, research-based information is also essential. An illustration is the program developed by Reggio Emilia in Italy—a well-marketed approach that stems from a postmodern belief system. In this approach, research is irrelevant and outcomes are what you see in the individual child. Another example of unsubstantiated educational practice is the recent national enthusiasm for "brain research." Jumping from recondite laboratory studies to the average classroom may make a good corporate sales pitch (see the catalogs and workshops from the Jensen Learning Corporation's "The Brain Store"), but in his book reviewing this situation, neurologist John Bauer refers to these classroom applications of brain research as "a bridge too far." Neurological research offers great promise in understanding the chemical balances necessary for normal functioning and the possible pharmacological adjustments that might be required, but today it can hardly be considered a valid classroom tool.

I don't believe the currently available information from brain research has enough valid evidence to allow us to arrive at more than some basic conclusions: Protect children from head

The High/Scope Curriculum Approach Today

The keystone of the High/Scope approach is a commitment to engaging children and youth in their own education through the *plan-do-review process*. This program component is crucial because it encourages children to state their intentions, to carry out their ideas, and to reflect on what was accomplished or discovered. In this perspective, initiative, thinking, and language expression by the child are central to the education process.

Based on the scientific method (modified, of course, to reflect the thinking abilities of children at each level) the plan-do-review process builds an early foundation for logical thinking and problem solving throughout life. This process also fundamentally changes the teacher's role from one of directing groups of children and their learning by providing uniform lessons to one of observing the individual child's self-planned work, engaging in conversation about the progress of the work, expanding language (vocabulary) use, facilitating  problem solving, and planning activities based on key experiences that will extend the thinking of the child. As the child matures to the elementary school and beyond, the key experiences evolve into the more traditional academic content around which the child uses the plan-do-review process. Because the ideas, action, and language come from the child, the activities are always at the child's developmental level and are culturally relevant.

Through 40 years of careful research, the positive impact on children of this type of intentional learning is well documented. For children, learning to see themselves as responsible actors who can set personal objectives and are respected for it, especially at ages 3 and 4, has life-long impact on their thinking and behavior. For teachers, this type of classroom can be a delightful challenge. The expanded opportunity for positive child management, the commitment and energy children show in pursuing their own intentions, the response of parents to the enthusiasm of their children in learning, all make the use of the High/Scope approach a welcome change from more traditional approaches. Because the child determines the actual learning activities within a defined framework, the approach is useful across cultures and language groups as long as this type of independent thinking is desired.

injuries; recognize that growth is always occurring at all ages; keep young children well fed and active. Beyond this, it is necessary to turn to validated classroom practices such as those in the High/Scope Curriculum and others to provide effective education for children.

As new ideas are proposed and solid research is accomplished, we must continue to seriously consider the value and validity of the new information as it relates to recommended practices. A good example is information about the development of language by social class in a study by Betty Hart and Todd Risley. They found that the more language a primary caregiver uses with a child, the more language the child uses. Not a surprising finding, but a very useful one for infant and toddler programs, staff development, and parent counseling. This finding also supports the High/Scope teacher-child relationship in which conversation about the child's actual work is emphasized.

"It is necessary to turn to validated classroom practices such as those in the High/Scope Curriculum and others to provide effective education for children."

The High/Scope Perry Preschool Study was the first of a series of High/Scope research projects in early childhood education. It began in 1962 as my first longitudinal study, and it continues today with a three-year grant for the age-40 phase awarded by the McCormick Tribune Foundation in 1999. It is my hope, given the unusual nature of the participants and the astounding value of the findings to date, that the study groups will be interviewed again at ages 60–65. But that is something for a future generation of High/Scope researchers to decide. The age-40 phase examines the impact of early education on the events under way at midlife for this group of adults. It asks two major new questions: What are the participants' health issues? What is the evidence of family generational transmission of personal success and social stability? When this study first began, I had no idea of its importance to educational policy and its eventual use as a basis for many early childhood programs both here in the United States and in a number of foreign countries. Now that its value for policy and the education of teachers is known, we have even more of an obligation to both complete this phase of the study accurately and to disseminate its results widely.

3

Differential Curriculum Outcomes: Preschool Curriculum Comparison Study

I t is hard to convey the satisfaction, even power, that members of the Ypsilanti special services staff felt in 1966 as the work of the High/Scope Perry Preschool Study began to bear fruit with positive intellectual and behavioral outcomes. Successfully solving the initial problems of organizing and launching a project with a new curriculum approach gave us the sense that we could do anything. We didn't need the school system; we didn't need the state regulators; and we certainly didn't need outsiders to tell us what to do. With President Lyndon Johnson's War on Poverty announced in 1964 and summer Head Start beginning in 1965, it seemed as if the whole world was to be ours, or at least ours to offer our hearts and labors. We could do nothing about the war in Vietnam, but we could change education for poor children. At a spring meeting in Lansing, Michigan, to discuss the upcoming summer Head Start program, one of the speakers asked the audience of about 300 educators how many had worked with 4-year-olds before. In addition to those of my staff, about 15 hands went up. Early childhood education, especially for disadvantaged children, really was a new world. However, we were also realistic enough to accept the fact that few people outside of Michigan had ever heard of Ypsilanti. We had much more work to accomplish; a few years of success were not enough.

Based on our data from the High/Scope Perry Preschool Study, I assumed that preschool intervention "worked." Early preschool education could produce change in the future for disadvantaged children. From a research perspective, however, a new question had arisen: Is any type of early childhood education effective, or is it just the High/Scope Curriculum that could produce such positive outcomes? In brief, the question shifted from Does preschool education work? to Which method of preschool education works best? As when the Perry Study began, the field was full of belief systems, with hardly any information from vigorous research to guide a potential user. If we were going to make public policy recommendations, we needed more information.

"The question shifted from Does preschool education work? to Which method of preschool education works best?"

Establishing the Curriculum Comparison Study

Thus, a new research project was created out of the same need to inform policy that had been the impetus for the Perry Study. In the spring of 1967, we would complete the project part of the High/Scope Perry Study; it would then enter into longitudinal follow-up status. It seemed natural to plan this extension of the Perry research with the same strong scientific footing as we had the earlier phase and to begin a new project to compare curricula in the fall of that year.

This decision to start a new research effort coincided with a personal milestone; in the spring of 1966, I obtained my Ph.D. in education and psychology from the University of Michigan after six years of procrastination. Thus, I was ready to make decisions about new work. I would be starting out as an experienced researcher and not a "green" graduate student. (The actual event that served as a catalyst to invest the six months neces-sary to finish writing the dissertation that had remained dormant since 1959 was an invitation to speak at the University of Kansas Symposium on Disadvantaged Children. The other three presen-ters had their doctorates, and I was embarrassed by my self-in-flicted "Mr." status. I did go as Mr. Weikart, however, because I missed my completion deadline by two weeks.)

As we planned the new project, I knew it would be more complex and more demanding operationally than the High/Scope Perry Study. First, it would enroll both white and African-Ameri-can disadvantaged preschoolers. By 1966, the idea of operating a multirace classroom no longer was a problem for either parents or the school system. Second, the new project would not have a control group. We felt we had answered the question of treat-ment versus no-treatment in the High/Scope Perry Project. Third, I decided that to effectively address the research question of comparing curricula, each of the three different programs we operated would be completely committed to the highest quality that curriculum approach could offer. This meant staff training and support by individuals expert in the approach would be re-quired for each program. Fourth, no program could be our fa-vorite; all had to be treated equally in terms of operational money, outside visitors, consultant support, staff training, and so on. While we obviously were committed to the High/Scope ap-proach, a serious and honest effort would be made to implement each of the alternative preschool curriculum methods objectively.

Preparing the proposal for the project was a fascinating challenge. It is one thing to describe a single effort as in the High/Scope Perry Project; it is another to describe a multicur-riculum effort. Why were these specific curricula selected? What training did the teachers need to faithfully discharge the program obligations? How could we keep the programs from contaminating one another? Where would we find staff with the specialized skills and experience to implement different philoso-phies? The special services staff discussed these and other issues at length. With proposal guidelines from the U.S. Office of Education, notes from our meetings, reference books, typewriters, and the excitement of youth, Ron Weigerink from the Perry Study research staff and I retreated to High/Scope Camp. Taking up our posts in the formal dining room of the old mansion, building a glowing fire in the fireplace, heating coffee on a hot plate, and throwing the curtains open wide to view the expanse of grounds, we settled in to write the ideas in a final form for submission. I recall our sense of triumph as we marched around the antique dining table collecting our finished product and assembling the final copies. We knew we had the right ideas for what the future would require when the early childhood field expanded. Various theoretical models needed an unbiased head-to-head comparison. Our only uncertainty was whether the High/Scope approach would hold up to such a comparison.

Selection of Curriculum Approaches

The search for curricula to be included was an interesting one. Each had to be theoretically different so as not to be just variations on a theme. Of course, the High/Scope approach was one of those selected. It focused on helping children think, solve problems, and use language to express their ideas through the plan-do-review process in a supportive learning environment established by the teacher. It was developed sufficiently to be documented; the data available at the four-year point looked promising; and it represented a unique amalgamation of theory and practice. Besides, it was ours. We had trained staff to implement the approach.

The second curriculum was the traditional approach toward play and social development espoused by university laboratory schools. It focused on children's social adjustment and self-sufficiency through free play and traditional activities such as story reading time, discussions of the weather, and help in developing personal skills. Teachers trained in this method were available (it was the basis of the national Head Start curriculum approach), and there were many books and other materials for teachers to use.

Selecting the third approach was a little more difficult. We obtained our lead for the third approach from Maya Pines, a national education writer, who had published an enthusiastic piece in the *New York Times* about a direct drill program called DISTAR being offered at the University of Illinois by two men, Siegfried Engelmann and Carl Bereiter. When Pines visited our Perry Preschool program, she encouraged us to see what they were doing, because it contrasted sharply with our approach. With this admonishment in mind, several staff members and I made the trip to Champaign-Urbana, Illinois, to view the program. While there, we visited four additional early childhood experimental model programs. Merle Karnes, who was undertaking a comparative evaluation of all five programs, oriented us to the research aspects. While not witnessing any of the extreme disciplinary behavior Pines reported (for example, shutting kids in the coat closet or direct physical punishment), we were impressed by Engelmann's obvious commitment to his mission and his determination to produce a complete basic skills curriculum for disadvantaged children in reading, mathematics, and language. The approach appeared to represent the behaviorist school: "If you want them to know it, tell them until they can repeat it to you." Our only question was, Does it work? And, as with many of these direct instruction types of programs, it seemed to. The children passed the daily tests of what they were expected to learn. Year-end tests had yet to be given in this program. However, Englemann and his wife had written a book five years earlier, titled *How to Give Your Child a Superior Mind*, that proposed using these methods in the home. The approach was well documented; there were consultants who could train our staff; and its theoretical approach was clearly very different from High/Scope's.

"We knew we had the right ideas for what the future would require when the early childhood field expanded. Various theoretical models needed an unbiased head-to-head comparison."

I believed we should have a fourth approach, something unique or unusual. I considered the Montessori approach as a possibility, but decided not to include it due to a lack of formal research on its effectiveness in spite of years of operation beginning in the nineteenth century. Also, there didn't seem to be many teachers who met public school certification requirements who were using the program. The cost of establishing the classroom with all the required materials, which had to be imported at that time from the Netherlands, would have been prohibitive within our budget. Another option we considered was one of the Scandinavian approaches in which children spent their time outside in all kinds of weather. The class would have a meeting point in a county or city park and then use the outdoors for a classroom all year. While this approach would have been very "1960s," I finally decided that American parents, children, and teachers would find it difficult to sustain, given Michigan's weather. In addition, the usual problems were present: lack of trained teachers and no research. With the spirit of adventure subdued, I let the idea pass.

So, we selected three programs instead of four. From the three selected, it was clear we had a range of theoretical models represented. I developed the following diagram to represent the practical differences in the approaches.

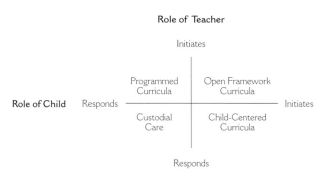

This organizational model was developed to allow us to categorize each approach through observation rather than teacher report. When teachers and staff discuss curriculum, the language used is often without clear meaning. When systematic observation is used, actual child behavior is the basis of the description.

Using this observation model, the three selected programs could be categorized in the following ways.

1. Teacher initiates: Child responds. The DISTAR direct teaching approach represented this quadrant. In DISTAR, the teachers worked with small groups and gave (initiated) specific instructions, presented information to be repeated, or asked a question requiring a precise answer drawn from the materials. The child's job was to respond with a correct answer. (When the teacher pointed to the word "cat," the role of the child was to respond with "cat." If the child did not, then the teacher repeated the lesson until the child got it right.) Working in small groups of six to eight children, the pace was rapid and demanding. Lessons focused on reading, math, and various language skills, all offered through the same tight instructional method. Learning was verified through class worksheets and multiple-choice tests.

2. Child initiates: Teacher responds. Our second model, the traditional social play approach, fit best within this quadrant. Children were invited to enjoy playing within a classroom rich in materials, a sharp contrast with the DISTAR classroom where no play materials were provided. Children played in small groups or individually, as they desired. The teacher read stories, introduced cooking activities, and planned field trips to the farm, fire station, police station, and around the block to the bakery. On the whole, the children carried out (initiated) their own activities with the teachers playing with them and helping (responding) as requested or necessary for safety. Learning was reported through teacher narratives of child classroom experiences.

3. Teacher initiates: Child initiates. The High/Scope approach represented this quadrant. As in the social play approach, the importance of child play (initiating) is a key principle of this model. However, the High/Scope method assigns the teacher a major role (initiating) in helping the child structure that play. Through the plan-do-review sequence—a central element of each day's routine—the child develops an explicit intention and, after carrying out that plan, is asked to think through what happened and use language to discuss results. The teacher initiates involvement by making conversational comments and asking divergent questions in order to understand what the child is doing, but avoids quizzing children by asking questions with obvious answers (for example, commenting "I wonder how you made that car" rather than asking "What color is that car you made?"). The teacher is also responsible for observing the child and initiating key experiences in child development, especially at small-group time, that one or more children may not be routinely including in their play activity (for example, encouraging the child to recognize and maintain steady beat by patting either to nursery rhymes or simple songs). Learning is verified through systematic observation of the child's accomplishments.

4. Teacher responds: Child responds. The study did not include a program from this quadrant. There was little reason to assume a program in this area would produce any improvement. Indeed, a study in Turkey by psychologist Cigdem Kagiteibasi found such programs to be detrimental to the child. I later saw programs of this type in developing countries where the charity operating the service limited its objectives to improved health through nutritional supplements; between meals, children were "parked" around the walls of the room until the next feeding or nap time. While such programs did provide a health benefit, they also appeared to be neglecting a major opportunity for enhancing the child's intellectual and social development.

As in the High/Scope Perry Preschool Study, classroom funding for the Curriculum Comparison Study came from regular state and county sources for special education. While this limited us to disadvantaged children, they were the ones we wished to serve. The state, of course, still required that the teachers be certified in three areas: special education, elementary education, and early childhood education. This requirement was made even more difficult, during a period of chronic teacher shortage, by the need to employ teachers proficient in the various curricula to be studied. After an extensive local-area search,

I was able to employ all six of the teachers who applied for the project. In a very real way this was a fortuitous event, because the project avoided the criticism that the classrooms were operated with a highly select and unusual group of teachers who did not reflect the general teaching field.

Operation of the Project

Compared to the intense activity involved in starting up the High/Scope Perry Preschool Study, this new project was, literally, fun. All of the teaching and research staff already knew what was required to operate a project. New staff were quickly integrated into the effort. We knew the steps for community surveys necessary to qualify study samples for possible participation. The school system gave us the use of two old-style, one-room schoolhouses just outside of town for our classrooms. The traditional nursery school model was housed in one. The teachers set up the classroom and stocked the necessary equipment. The High/Scope approach and the Direct Instruction approach shared the other building, with the High/Scope program operating in the morning and the Direct Instruction program in the afternoon. All child equipment and supplies necessary for the High/Scope approach were stored in bins or on shelving units with wheels. After the High/Scope program was finished for the day, these were all turned to the wall so the direct instruction classroom would have only the tables, chairs, and blackboards that were required for their program with no distractions from toys. Project vans picked up the children from each program with each of the drivers serving as a teaching aide in the classroom of the children they transported. Thus, children did not mix on the way to or from school, though they might within the home community.

Each pair of teachers was trained in the program they taught. The two teachers in the nursery school program had master's degrees from the University of Michigan in early childhood education. They received an occasional consulting visit from an expert in their field for review and discussion of class-

room issues. The two teachers in the direct instruction classroom were both speech teachers with classroom and speech
therapy experience. They requested the DISTAR program since
they felt their small-group teaching experience melded well with
that approach. Training consultants from the program at the
University of Illinois came to insure authentic replication of their
model. The most frequent visitor from this group was Jean Os-
borne, because of her specialties in language
and reading, although she helped out in many
ways. The two High/Scope approach teachers
were experienced in the High/Scope method
and had contact with a High/Scope staff consultant, Donna
McClelland, for review and discussion of classroom issues.
(McClelland had been head teacher in the High/Scope Perry
Preschool Study.)

*"Each pair of teachers
was trained in the
program they taught."*

We took many steps to insure that the programs varied
only in curriculum approach. So many comparison projects fail to
have such equality in operational detail and therefore leave an un-
clear legacy. Through use of random assignment, we insured that
the groups of children were equivalent initially so that differences
later would be the result of program impact and not some extra-
neous selection factor. We used equally experienced and certified
teachers for each program and then made certain they were
trained to meet their program standards. We used equivalent
classroom space and spent as much on each youngster, because
variations in these areas could skew the results. All programs
were given outside consultants to insure they had independent
viewpoints and assistance available. Transportation was provided
equally so all selected children could attend. Teacher meetings of
all project staff did not refer to curriculum issues. All had an equal
number of visitors. In short, everything possible was done to
insure the programs were equivalent, except for curricula.

We verified these efforts in two ways. First, in 1968 and
1969, we invited 12 nationally known experts in child development, language, behavioral theory, and related fields to spend
two days examining the programs: E. Kuno Beller, Marion Blank,

Courtney Cazden, Joseph Glick, Edmund Gordon, J. McVicker Hunt, Lawrence Kohlberg, James Miller, Todd Risley, Leonard Sealey, Irving Sigel, and Burton White. They visited in groups of four in the fall and the spring. They observed each program for a half day and wrote comments on their observations. These observations authenticated that the programs accurately represented the theories upon which they were based. Our second verification effort used direct observation of the classrooms by the research staff. This may sound like a normal idea now, but in the late 1960s, it was a foreign concept. However, encouraged by education professor Ned Flanders of the University of Michigan, we applied a time-sample technique that confirmed that in each program children spent time as would be predicted from the guiding curriculum principles.

The staff approached their assignments with vigor and enthusiasm. With the study now well known at least in our part of the country, we had hundreds of visitors. (With three programs to observe, each operating from a different theoretical perspective, it made for a good field visit.) Our system was to give visitors a quick orientation at our headquarters and then take them to observe the High/Scope classroom, especially to see the plan-do-review process. Then a stop was made at the traditional nursery school classroom, with visitors usually arriving when some small-group activity was under way for some children while others were engaged in free play. After lunch, the group visited the direct instruction classroom and then returned to headquarters for a debriefing. As can be imagined, there were many excellent discussions and debates as the contrasting curriculum ideas were actually seen in practice.

One of the most interesting visits occurred during the second year of the study. I was called and asked if I would personally host a delegation of heads of university-based early childhood programs from about the state. I said I would be honored. The day arrived and all six program directors arrived. We went through the visits, offering impressive demonstration programs (true to their theory) for them to see. All the teachers were pleased that they came to visit. After what I thought might be a stressful day, we gathered back at headquarters for tea, cookies, and conversation about the project. Yes, they liked the traditional program; the teachers were outstanding. The High/Scope approach was a little of a puzzle—why would you hold up the children like that to make a simple plan they quickly forgot? But, the teachers were good with the children and there was a sense of purpose to the classroom. But what was that drill program? How could you subject children to such rigid conditions? Where were the toys? Weren't they allowed any play time? Such comments built up like a buzz of mad hornets until one grey-haired lady, tears in her eyes, reached around a friend of hers sitting between us and swatted me hard with her weapons-grade purse! Things got very quiet; the visitors said what a nice day it had been, thanked me for my hospitality, and left. No mention was made of the anger or the wild swing with the purse. Later, with other visitors, we stressed the *experimental* nature of the project very clearly and very early in the day! This incident brought home to me how much the early childhood field operated (as it still does) on belief systems far removed from validating data. Even if I didn't believe a program would work because it didn't follow my personal commitments, the task was to remain objective and study its application and outcomes. To develop effective practices, the field must be driven by actual outcome information and not personal biases.

> *"To develop effective practices, the field must be driven by actual outcome information and not personal biases."*

Major Findings

The first of two central findings of the High/Scope Preschool Curriculum Comparison Study is that any high-quality program (good teachers, adequate resources, good attendance, home visits, good supportive services) will produce similar educational results and outcomes. The specific approach used does not make a difference. Everyone benefits. This outcome was a very great surprise. The different theories predicted differential outcomes.

National Curriculum
Comparison Study Outcomes

National Head Start in 1969 decided to ask the same questions about model effectiveness that our study was asking, but on a national basis with a number of models implemented. This decision to operate an effective study of theoretically different curriculum models came at an important time. Back in 1967, the National Follow Through program had asked the same question at the elementary school level. However, few projects outside of these national efforts were undertaken, and none used random assignment of the sample to treatment groups where all participants had an equal chance of being placed in the treatment group. The national study provided few answers. A 20-year follow-up by High/Scope in Fort Walton Beach, Florida, and Greeley, Colorado, found a slight indication that children in Head Start did better than children who did not attend, and Head Start children who had the High/Scope approach did slightly better than Head Start children in regular programs. Overall, the outcomes were minimal and nothing like those of the various High/Scope studies.

However, the second major finding, which became clear only through long-term follow-up, is that social behavior outcomes dramatically vary by choice of program employed. Children enrolled in the High/Scope approach and, to a slightly lesser extent, in the traditional nursery school method obtained significantly better social success and community adjustment. Those in the direct teaching approach displayed higher crime rates and other signs of educational and personal problems, suggesting that such approaches are inappropriate for young children. (Key references for the High/Scope Curriculum Comparison Study are listed in the appendices on p. 285.)

As we have made these findings known, those supportive of Direct Instruction methods have been very aggressive in attempting to refute the findings, as might be expected. Engelmann and his associates, now at the University of Oregon, have been especially vocal in attacking the study design (for example, significant differences on small samples are not really significant)

∼

and project staff. To show the extent of the anger, in a personal e-mail to a cluster of professional fiends, one individual described those who supported the findings as "retardates who drool on their clothing."

Of course, the political force of the federal administration in 2002 is to push for the direct-instruction style of teaching because of the concern for "basics." How minor is the role of sound research in political and policy decision-making! For many, especially those not in the early childhood field, it is their beliefs that matter most. To paraphrase President Ronald Reagan, "Trained staff are not really essential at this preschool age when grandmothers have done it for years." One illustrative event occurred during a discussion I had with the state treasurer of Georgia. The state was contracting for large-scale training from High/Scope in the mid-1990s. I was at a meeting to discuss the possible expansion of the work, and I was finding that the state would probably not do much more with High/Scope. Why? "You know the evidence and you know how well received the High/Scope training is in the state. What is the issue?" I asked. The treasurer responded that the state senator who was chairman of the budget committee had a grandchild who attended a Montessori preschool program. This grandchild really liked to go to school. Therefore, the senator was unlikely to expand the evidence-based High/Scope service because he knew Montessori worked just fine.

"How minor is the role of sound research in political and policy decision-making! For many, especially those not in the early childhood field, it is their beliefs that matter most."

The High/Scope Preschool Curriculum Comparison Study started out to answer a basic question: Which method of preschool education works best? Clearly, we could not test all the various curricula available at the time, so representatives of different theoretical approaches were selected. We found that most early education approaches have a cadre of believers, but they have assembled mostly field stories and other anecdotal evidence in support of their models. I don't believe many programs have undertaken the difficult task of conducting the research needed even to validate their approach against a no-program condition, let alone against other methods. This study is a beginning because it compares representative programs. And the results indicate that the early childhood field needs to examine all approaches much more seriously because they are not all alike. Some approaches may be effective in limited areas while failing to support key aspects of important areas of children's development. For me personally, these findings validate High/Scope's commitment to using evidence-based outcomes as a basis both for our own programs and for our policy recommendations.

4

Infant Education: Parent-to-Parent Programs

During the period of excitement created by the release of the early findings of the High/Scope Perry Preschool Study, especially those related to the increase in measured intelligence of the participating group, ideas for other programs began to surface. One of the most significant of these related to the home visits that had become such an integral part of the High/Scope Perry Preschool Study. Such a parent-education program was unique in the education field at that time. Because of the insistence of Norma Radin, project social worker, we had provided 90-minute weekly home visits to help the parents understand how their children were developing by participating in program activities and to encourage them to provide related activities at home. While the major focus of the home visits was the child's development, the wide range of problems that the mothers faced also often became a topic of discussion during the visits. While we later discovered (in the High/Scope Preschool Curriculum Demonstration Project) that such home visits do not determine child outcomes (each curriculum approach provided home visits; program outcomes for the children were very different), I was impressed by the moral statement these visits made: Because you are entrusting your child to us for education, we will provide as much information as possible to you and listen

~

closely to issues that concern you. We, the educators, are experts in our field; you, the parents, are experts on your family and your family's culture.

As staff discussed these issues in regular meetings, specific questions gradually emerged: Suppose we operated a program with home visits only, no preschool? Would mothers accept this? Would such a program be effective? Originally, we viewed the home visits as ancillary to the preschool experience, but not as the whole service in and of itself. During this time, a teacher in the Ypsilanti special services classroom program for the blind, Delores Lambie, became active in our discussions. She had strong feelings about the importance of the family and the respect that outsiders, especially experts who worked with parents, needed to extend to them. Lambie had worked extensively with the parents of her blind students and this had given her special insight into the issues that were involved. As she pushed these ideas, another important research question became obvious to us: If early childhood education for 3- and 4-year-old children produced the positive results we were finding in the High/Scope Perry Preschool Study, could we not obtain even better results if we started earlier, in infancy? Thus was conceived the concept that evolved into the Ypsilanti-Carnegie Infant Education Project, a home visit program for mothers and infants. It was one of the first in the nation to be undertaken by a public school staff.

"The Ypsilanti-Carnegie Infant Education Project, a home visit program for mothers and infants, was one of the first in the nation to be undertaken by a public school staff."

The Ypsilanti-Carnegie Infant Education Project

The project began with a standard experimental research design. Infants in disadvantaged families were recruited at 3, 7, and 11 months of age and randomly assigned to one of three groups: (1) a group receiving treatment from professionals of different backgrounds with an organized program; (2) a group receiving treatment from community volunteers; and (3) a group receiving no treatment. The second group served by community volunteers could not be sustained. The problem was not the lack of family cooperation but that the volunteers found it too difficult to maintain the demanding schedule of weekly visits. Short-term was fine; long-term did not work. Thus, the study essentially became a treatment versus no-treatment comparison. Dolores Lambie accepted the role as project director, and she began a study that would have a very uncertain history over the next three and a half decades.

Steps in Launching the Project

In launching the project in 1965, the first step was to employ a small group of home visitors to find out if mothers would accept visitors coming into their homes for consultation about their children without any outside service (such as preschool) being provided. During the school year of 1966-1967, a brief 12-week home visit program was operated with preschoolers to see how the mothers responded and to work out issues such as scheduling teachers, arranging staff meetings, and solving problems that typically occurred during a visit, such as interactions with husbands and male visitors.

"Few visits to any family were simple or easy."

These normal-sounding statements cover some enormous pain. Few visits to any family were simple or easy. For many of the families, a visit from an adult from a powerful institution such as the schools was a major event and a major disturbance in the delicate relationship the man and woman had created. For example, in one family, the husband decided that the home visits were upsetting the household order he was used to. His wife was receiving attention and support that bypassed him. One day, Dolores Lambie arrived for a scheduled home visit only to find the mother in tears and her husband and a male friend playing a loud game of cards in the living room. The mother did not want to have the visit: "Please come some other time." Dolores looked inside and noticed that the kitchen floor was covered with water. The mother finally related that as she was cleaning up in preparation for the visit, her husband came in and said she was not worth being in the program. Then he dumped the pail of water all over the floor so she could not meet with the home visitor. Dolores told the mother that she understood what had happened and asked if she could help mop up the water. The mother permitted her to come in and together they cleaned up the floor. Dolores then conducted the visit at the kitchen table as if nothing had happened. Much to her surprise, the husband and his friend stopped making loud, derogatory comments from the other room and came to the doorway to watch. Eventually, the husband sat down at the table. In later sessions, the husband occasionally joined in and seemed to demonstrate more respect for his wife.

Locating Funds to Operate the Project

Absolutely no state money was available for this type of project, and submitting a grant request to a private foundation was new ground for me. I had applied for and received a federal grant for the High/Scope Perry Preschool Study in 1963 and had just submitted a grant request for the High/Scope Curriculum Comparison Study, again to the federal government. So I had a little experience in the grant-seeking business. There were a lot of questions to answer: A foundation? Which one? Where were such institutions? How did one apply? From this initial confusion somehow I learned of the Carnegie Corporation of New York. (I wondered why, if they were a foundation, they called themselves a corporation.) "Good idea, we'll apply to them." Without contacting Carnegie for information on how to submit a grant application (that's how innocent of the process I was), we prepared a grant request. It was fairly brief, but did have strong sections on how the project would be run, information on our trial program efforts, and details on why we believed such a program might make a significant difference in the lives of disadvantaged

children. Request prepared, cover letter written, New York address discovered, I mailed the grant papers off in high hopes in
September 1967. During the preparation, I did have the good
sense to never mention the word "infant," only using the ages to
be served—3, 7, and 11 months—and the words "young child."
(Because I had never heard of a program in education serving infants, I was afraid to use that term because it might completely
close off any chance of obtaining the necessary funding.) So,
without any applications in preparation to other foundations
should our Carnegie one fail, we eagerly waited for a response.

As though such things were the way of the world and not
an extraordinary exception, I received a telephone call from Barbara Finberg, a project officer for Carnegie Corporation, some
time in November. She asked if she might visit our project and talk
with us about the grant request. Thrilled with the possibility, we
eagerly prepared for her visit. We lined up a family who had been
in the trial program so Finberg could see the home conditions and
understand the issues we faced; an all-project staff meeting was
organized at lunch time that day to permit a wide-ranging discussion of our experience; time was set aside with the researchers to
discuss sampling and analysis issues; and an appointment was
made to visit with Paul Emerich, the superintendent of schools,
for any discussion Finberg and he might wish to have.

The day arrived; all went as planned. We had a good discussion of issues; the research plan seemed fine: "Oh, you are
working with mothers and infants!" Finberg said, without batting
an eye. The home visit elicited many unusually precise observations from Finberg, and then we went to visit the superintendent. After the secretary said we could enter, I ushered Finberg
into his office. The superintendent was seated at his desk, and
before I could even make the introductions, he blurted out, "I
wish you would take your money and go back to New York! We
are a public school system, not a research institution!" To describe my feelings at this unexpected outburst is impossible:
defeated, defensive, deflated, discouraged, angered, embarrassed, and furious are some of the words that come to mind!

Yet Finberg proceeded as though the superintendent had never uttered a word. Seeing that I was incapable of coherent speech, she graciously introduced herself and soon after we departed. What was there to say to her? Knowing we had lost the grant, my staff and I did what we could to salvage the day, and I managed a graceful run to the airport. To my total surprise, in early December we received the Carnegie grant, and we launched the project in January 1968. I never did receive an explanation from Emerich for his belligerent attitude. He later parted ways with the Ypsilanti School Board and took a job in a larger school district in Iowa. Barbara Finberg went on to recommend Carnegie Corporation funding for several major High/Scope projects over the next 25 years. The year after her retirement from Carnegie Corporation as executive vice-president, she accepted an appointment to the High/Scope Foundation Board of Directors.

High/Scope Infant Videotaping Project

At the end of the Ypsilanti-Carnegie Infant Education Project, we found that working with parents and infants in their homes did produce significant growth on the part of the children. This development showed up especially strongly in language development in contrast to the control group. I believed we had some data to back the initial hypothesis that early intervention with infants would be an effective way to compensate for the difficulties faced by economically disadvantaged children. With this information to buttress our position, I applied for a second grant from Carnegie Corporation. Dolores Lambie felt we were ready to expand our program and train staff in other programs in the area as to what we had learned. The project group also concluded that what was needed were teacher training materials to illustrate how to work with parents and infants in the home. Carnegie Corporation agreed and funded us for a three-year training documentation and materials development project. What we submitted was a proposal to film home visits to collect raw information and then to create training films to illustrate

Home visitors in action during the High/Scope parent-infant education programs

such things as questioning style, choice of toys, effective interactions with babies when they make sounds and begin speech, discussion of parenting issues, and so forth. To reduce the costs of the project, we agreed to film the visits in 3/4-inch video format. Not a good decision! While it reduced costs, the footage was in black and white. Standard 16mm film in color would have greatly assisted later work, especially because video soon shifted to a color format. Thus, while the project produced some magnificent training videos, we were hard-pressed to use them. Later we transferred many of them to the more modern format, but the lack of color remained a handicap.

Nevertheless, shooting the videos was a fascinating adventure. The various pieces of equipment were very bulky, so we purchased a van to transport all the cameras and video decks. Representative families were selected to participate based on their willingness to be taped and their general interest in the services they would receive. While a teacher conducted a home visit, the camera man, using one camera and one sound man, moved about to gain the best perspective. The tape ran full time, there was no on-site editing (we wanted the teaching staff to do that later). A second assistant took care of the tape deck and lights, supporting the video staff in whatever way was necessary. Parents thought the sessions were fun and often invited neighbors over to witness the event. On one occasion, a father ran to a neighbor's house to have them turn on channel 3 so they could see his wife and child on TV. Of course, that wasn't possible. While I'm sure we're all more technologically sophisticated now, such misunderstanding of technology is probably just as prevalent.

Unexpected Results

As we collected follow-up data on the original sample and carried out the training materials development project, we began to plan for extending our work into other communities. Trouble loomed, however, as we analyzed our follow-up results collected one year after the close of the project. To our shock, we found no significant differences between the experimental and control groups. They performed essentially the same on retesting. We were stunned. Did this mean such early intervention didn't make a difference? Had we run a major project that produced no great outcomes? This was 1972, and there were no other parent-infant home visiting projects that had reported data. We were at a loss to explain our findings.

Barbara Finberg, still our Carnegie Corporation project officer, assembled a review panel of outside experts to look at our work: the initial project, the follow-up findings, and the progress on the training materials project. The panel consisted of Robert Egbert, former director of National Follow Through and dean of Teachers College, University of Nebraska; Ron Lally, Syracuse University Infant Day Care Project; and Henry Ricciuti, infant development professor at Cornell University. After two days of extensive discussion, the panel recommended to Carnegie that they not fund extending the work to other communities. The initial data looked great, the training materials project was innovative and of great promise, but because of the failure to obtain even a one-year duration of significant results between groups, they felt there was little reason to try to extend our practice to other communities. This recommendation was a major blow. My cockiness, even arrogance, was in full flower due to the success of the High/Scope Perry Preschool Study, the dramatic findings of the High/Scope Preschool Curriculum Demonstration Study, and even the continued progress being made in the adolescent work at High/Scope Camp. To fail with the Ypsilanti-Carnegie Infant Education Project was both a professional and personal shock. While of little comfort, this finding of no results was to be repeated for the next several decades in many other parent-infant projects with some small exceptions in health such as

"Had we run a major project that produced no great outcomes? This was 1972, and there were no other parent-infant home visiting projects that had reported data. We were at a loss to explain our findings."

David Olds's home visit program by registered nurses. But of course I didn't know this at that time. I saw this as a personal failure.

What to do? The staff were still excited about the work, and other agencies in other communities had expressed interest in working with us. We began to rethink what we were doing. During this period, Dolores Lambie left the Foundation and Judith Evans joined our group to direct the parent-infant work. Together, we decided to adapt our model to train local supervisors who could then train women from their communities, each of whom would work with a few parents and infants. This process would lower a community's costs, allow more local women to be involved, leave trained persons in the community, and permit small social-service agencies to cooperate in project dissemination. A small community near Lansing, Michigan, became the location for this project, and it became known as the High/Scope Parent-to-Parent Project. Funding was obtained from the National Institute of Mental Health and the Lilly Endowment, and we moved on. Our rationale was not that we could solve the development problems of economically disadvantaged children but that we could reduce the stress that families faced in childrearing and thereby help both the parents and their children. We argued that more was happening than we could measure with standardized tests of child development. Weak evidence for a group of researchers, but it was enough to allow us to rationalize continuation in an area I felt was of unusual importance. I was allowing my belief system to overcome my commitment to basing decisions on hard data.

"We decided to adapt our model to train local supervisors who could then train women from their communities, each of whom would work with a few parents and infants."

The plan also included a follow-up study at the end of second grade for children in the original Ypsilanti-Carnegie Infant Education Project. One last hope I had was that the general web of support the project provided, plus the increased capacity for verbal interaction seen in the mothers, would gradually have a significant impact on the children so they would be better able to function and achieve. Some researchers call this a sleeper effect. While hard to justify because a strong program should produce effects that can be seen all along, it opened the door for us to look at the sample again. High/Scope researcher Ann Epstein took the assignment. She developed a home cookie-baking task that provided a standardized opportunity to see mothers from the original study interacting with their now 7-year-old children. Standardized test scores from the schools were also collected. Focused parent interviews were conducted. Basic findings indicated trends in favor of the treatment group, but there were no significant differences. The door seemed closed both to evidence to support the work and funds to permit it to go forward.

A breakthrough came in late 1976 during one of my visits to Europe. I was invited to speak about High/Scope's work at the Max Planck Institute in Berlin. While in Europe, I arranged to visit the Bernard van Leer Foundation in The Hague, The Netherlands, an international foundation financially supported by ownership of the Bernard van Leer Companies. The Companies made oil barrels and other metal and plastic containers. From the profits, the Foundation funded child development projects in every country that their Companies had manufacturing plants. While the Van Leer Companies had plants in the United States, little project funding was undertaken here. My visit was fortuitous, because I arrived with my parent-infant community-based education model in hand just when the Foundation was looking for a way to expand its work in the United States. Great projects are born of such coincidences. (At least I have experienced several such opportunities.) The van Leer Foundation approved the High/Scope Parent-to-Parent Dissemination Project for a three-year funding cycle, which also included a three-year renewal (although I didn't know that at the time). With Dutch guilders in hand (exchanged and paid in U.S. dollars, of course), we began to extend our work to new communities.

Parent-to-Parent Dissemination Project: Community Implementation Model

The main focus of this phase of the parent-infant project, from 1978 to 1984, was to develop service programs in different communities serving different populations. Toledo (Ohio) Public Schools worked with parents and their handicapped children; Dayton (Ohio) area Head Start worked with women of their community; the Great Lakes Naval Base in Chicago provided services to military families; and the Northeast Kingdom of Vermont provided services to teen mothers. These were exciting times. High/Scope staff traveled to these various communities and facilitated the use of the parent-to-parent approach, introducing training materials we had developed over the previous 10 years. There was always the nagging worry about the lack of sound research, and this did dampen our enthusiasm somewhat. However, the anecdotal field reports, and the obvious progress of the women involved in both delivering the service and receiving it, allowed us to feel we were making a contribution.

Toward the end of this six-year service period, two significant things happened. One was that the van Leer staff began to ask if these sites could take over the training of other agencies in their regions. We weren't too sure about this idea. The sites were very specialized and focused only on their defined service populations. Furthermore, as I had discovered in my own work for Ypsilanti Public Schools, local agencies are focused almost entirely (as they should be) on local needs. Having staff train persons from other agencies, even if the agencies were paying for the training, would take staff energy, time, and attention away from wrestling with local issues. Thus, our efforts to encourage several sites to take on broader responsibilities were interesting and commendable, but not successful. The van Leer Foundation assisted by providing start-up supplementary funding. However, as that funding went directly to the site, bypassing High/Scope, we had little direct influence.

~

The second event was the election of U.S. President Ronald Reagan, and the significant decrease in government social funding to increase funding for the military buildup during his presidency. This effort greatly reduced funds for projects on the margin such as our parent-to-parent work. Thus, when the van Leer money ended in 1984, I could find no other funding source to keep the parent-infant work going. Nonetheless, it seemed to me that we had achieved a great deal by keeping the parent-infant work going with a coherent plan and a logical sequence from 1965 to 1984 on the thin thread of evidence that we had used to support it. But it was over. It would not be until the late 1990s that the nation would suddenly find some value in infant growth and development through the publicizing of findings on early brain research, and that infant education would be promoted again. Still without much if any research to support such programs or clear assessment procedures to evaluate them, infant education began to receive some major national attention both from policy and funding viewpoints. Unfortunately, as I write in 2002, there is still very little solid information to guide the work. The main support for the thrust, as it was for High/Scope 25 years earlier, is that it seems logical and the participants seem to get something from the opportunity. The fact is, though, that in our research studies the randomly assigned control groups did just as well (without support) as the treatment groups. This is not part of the policy thinking at this time. We all find it hard to abandon our belief systems.

A final point to this work developed in 2000 and 2001 when we were given the chance to review our work once again. The van Leer Foundation was interested in discovering the impact of the projects they had funded over the last several decades. Their effort, although on a smaller scale, mirrors what United States policymakers are asking about the nation's long-term investment in various programs for the poor. For the last 25 years, the government has provided in excess of $1 trillion for programs to enable the poor to move out of poverty. Yet, the recent census data point to even more people living in poverty.

The van Leer Foundation wanted to know what seemed to work, what failed outright, what lessons were learned that might provide a basis for future funding policies and decisions, and what recommendations should govern the Foundation's current funding policy. From this background, our interest in conducting a long-term follow-up study was readily accepted by the new van Leer staff, and we were approved for a small grant that would enable us to return to the four training groups mentioned earlier to see what remained of our original efforts and what implications could be derived.

Much to our surprise, we found individuals at each site who were still using much of the training and training methodology from the earlier project. Although some of the initial problems and misperceptions from the earlier project still influenced them, they also recognized the great benefits. For example, one group of staff remembered how rigid the High/Scope training model was to them. It was only after the training, when they were free of our direct influence, that they felt they could come up with innovative strategies they believed were relevant to their staff. Of course, our staff reports at the time had found them rigid and unwilling to adapt, and our staff pointed out how happy they were that after the training ended the trainees started to come up with innovative strategies to meet their local needs. This miscommunication happened among professionals, so imagine the room for misunderstanding when working with parents from the community.

This final grant enabled us to bring to a close 35 years of a parent-infant program development cycle. We had tried a variety of ways to test the logic that intervention with disadvantaged families would significantly help the development of infants and children. We were unsuccessful, so either we were using the wrong methods, or perhaps in-depth intervention, other than for general health and welfare, is not necessary for this age group. There is strong evidence that most of the developmental needs of infants are typically met by mothers and caregivers within most environments. It is only at later ages, two and three years, for example, that added stimulus may be necessary to enable children's more mature abilities to emerge, such as developing a rich vocabulary, playing and singing music, doing more than simple counting. Looking back on our work, I believe that we built our program from our direct experiences with children and families. We responded to the family needs as we understood them. The work clearly preceded other work in this area by years and was accurate enough to find some of the research outcomes that others are just now uncovering. A list of the major parent-infant studies and brief summaries of their findings are presented in the appendices on p. 289. The references provided offer further information on High/Scope's work in this area. Some of these summaries were prepared by Ann Epstein who has been involved in High/Scope parent-infant work since the mid-1970s and now directs High/Scope's early childhood department.

"This final grant enabled us to bring to a close 35 years of a parent-infant program development cycle."

The answer as to what to do next is not obvious. Ideas for new styles of services, such as linking child care and parent education, as outlined in our final 2001 monograph, may be of importance. One thing is certain—women are going to continue to join the paid workforce and, as a result, high-quality infant care remains a critical need in the United States. A second need is certain, too—private- and government-funded family services are still needed to help poor children and their families lay the foundation for greater life success. While preschool education can be effective by itself, harnessed with better infant development programs it might prove even more so. This area of infant development remains a challenge for future generations of curriculum developers and researchers.

5

High/Scope's Elementary Program

While we were beginning our work in parent-infant home visiting in 1968, I was also challenged to extend the High/Scope approach to the early elementary school grades. Typical of the way Congress works, both houses had passed a massive elementary school reform bill authorizing billions of dollars for new programs for disadvantaged children, including the National Follow Through Project. When it came time for appropriations, however, the majesty of the congressional vision was reduced to the political reality of what funding was actually available. This new federal effort was designed to extend Head Start–style programs into the early elementary grades nationwide to improve overall school program quality and maintain the children's Head Start gains. Robert Egbert, then dean at Teachers College, University of Nebraska, was appointed director of National Follow Through in 1967. Because he had obtained a relatively minor amount of money to demonstrate what a major program might accomplish, Egbert converted the initiative from a general funding program into a research and demonstration effort. Accordingly, he asked model program developers to demonstrate their best efforts by undertaking sponsorship of specific public school sites across the nation, and he contracted with independent research organizations to evaluate these efforts.

~

Although Follow Through operated in various forms from 1968 to 1995, it unfortunately never achieved its potential for successful school reform. Nevertheless, our model sponsorship in Follow Through laid the groundwork for our subsequent efforts in elementary education.

Participating in the National Follow Through Project

From the outset, our participation in the National Follow Through Project was a challenge. In the fall of 1967, Laurel Schieffer, a field worker from Michigan's Office of Economic Opportunity, contacted me. Schieffer described the potential of this new federal program and suggested that because of my work in the High/Scope Perry Preschool Project, we should apply to be one of the model sponsors. I was in good humor. The early Perry results had stimulated us to bank on investment in our parent-infant work. If preschool education could produce such positive outcomes, wasn't earlier intervention the best method of reform? Why, I asked Schieffer, would I want to devote energies to trying to initiate reforms at the elementary school level with all the accompanying difficulties: teachers set in their ways, principals committed to standing fast, and an overwhelming commitment to focus narrowly on reading and math skills? As director of special services for the Ypsilanti Public Schools at that time, I was well aware of the realities of the elementary school situation. Nonetheless, in early December 1967, I received a phone call from Egbert's Washington office asking me to attend a meeting on January 4, 1968, and present the High/Scope model (still called the Cognitively Oriented Curriculum at that point). I agreed to go and, in my ignorance, presented a paper to National Follow Through staff and assembled potential sponsors from around the country with what probably wasn't the best idea I've ever had. My topic

"The majesty of the congressional vision was reduced to the political reality of what funding was actually available."

was why I thought the National Follow Through Project was inadvisable since I believed the focus of reform should be on infants and parents and not on public schools. My first big trip to Washington, and I spent my time advising a group of educators not to do what they were being paid to do! After the meeting, I returned somewhat sheepishly to Michigan and decided to keep a low profile. Then telephone calls began to pile up from both Schieffer and Egbert urging me to reconsider my stance. With much trepidation, I finally committed High/ Scope to participate in National Follow Through in May 1968.

By coming into the program late, we missed out on obtaining representative sites because we did not attend a major meeting earlier in 1968 at which participating school systems selected potential model sponsors. Thus, instead of starting out with at least 10 sites as did other model sponsors, we began with only 3. In the summer we added 2 more sites—latecomers like ourselves—and eventually we did end up with 10 sites. This slow start-up was to plague us throughout the study. For example, unlike the other sponsors we were assigned more sites with low socioeconomic populations within the range served by the National Follow Through Project. In the overall research, those sponsors who had worked with the higher socioeconomic sites, even in this limited-range sevice provision, had better long-term outcomes, regardless of model. By being "slow starters" ourselves, we were teamed up with some school districts that approached the work without much enthusiasm. This attitude changed during the project, but it affected our start-up activities.

First Steps in Setting Up High/Scope's Follow Through Project

Looking back, I am struck again by how naive I was in deciding to undertake such a major effort as Follow Through model sponsorship. Just establishing an organizational structure for the project was an interesting and challenging experience! The first problem I encountered was that my boss from the Ypsilanti

Public Schools was unwilling to accept the contract from National Follow Through. (I did not create the High/Scope Foundation until the spring of 1970, so we were still operating as part of the school system.) After extensive discussions with Al Myers, director of special education at Eastern Michigan University, I accepted his invitation to establish the project as part of his department. While this made for a complicated management situation, it permitted the work to go forward. Now I had staff working for two public entities—each with different benefits, work rules, and work schedules! My solution was to ignore the differences and focus on project needs. When the High/Scope Educational Research Foundation was officially established on July 1, 1970, the Follow Through Project was moved to the new organization and these staff operational issues were resolved.

The second challenge was the need to hire appropriate staff—individuals who would be willing to work on High/Scope model adaptation and also travel at least a week a month to our distant sites to provide consulting to classroom teachers. For this job I needed individuals with classroom experience at the elementary school level, who had knowledge of the content areas appropriate to the age levels, who could work in support of classroom teachers, and who had some administrative experience so they could present the project to the local superintendent. My "dean" for these initial years was Marion Erickson, a highly successful classroom teacher and special education expert. With her vast experience and her senior position, Erickson oriented new staff, guided curriculum development, and worked successfully with local sites. Other staff hired had backgrounds in speech correction, special education, elementary education, and school psychology. An interesting interview took place during the search for staff: A recent Ph.D. graduate from Indiana University spent the day with us as part of the job interview process. Late in the morning I asked a Follow Through staff member, Roger Rugg, to go with the small group hosting the candidate for lunch. I wanted Rugg to use his speech therapy background to explain to me the problem our candidate seemed to have in articulating some speech sounds. After lunch, Roger returned to issue his eagerly awaited report. The lunch had been a great success, the discussion had gone well, and Roger told me I hadn't recognized the candidate's pure Hoosier accent (even though his accent certainly was close to my own Ohio farm pattern)! Embarrassed but undaunted, I hired the man, not because of his accent but because he had the skills and special training needed to be part of our team.

A third challenge was to develop an appropriate adaptation of the curriculum processes used at the preschool level to an elementary educational setting. In 1970, I divided the High/Scope Follow Through staff into curriculum development teams, each focusing on a

"We tried to focus on the traditional needs of these early grades using published materials, but delivered through the High/Scope lens."

High/Scope approach scope-and-sequence for reading, math, and language content areas. While a great deal of material was produced, all of us came to the realization that curriculum development for these content areas from a blank sheet of paper was beyond our expertise, and I abandoned that approach. Next, we tried to focus on the traditional needs of these early grades using published materials, but delivered through the High/Scope lens. Thus, we introduced the plan-do-review process and developed an appropriate teacher questioning style, one that was more conversational rather than lecturing and asking test-type questions. Because much of the actual classroom material used by the different school systems was very directive, we encouraged the use of more flexible systems that better supported the open classroom model we endorsed. For example, we recommended using Cuisinaire rods in math studies to encourage children's hands-on, active involvement, and we recommended adoption of the Nuffield Foundation reading and science series from the United Kingdom. By 1988, we also encouraged use of Addison-Wesley's *Math Their Way* and *Explorations.*

We began to document our positions in a series of staff publications conceptualized by High/Scope's Charles Wallgren, who was then directing the project. Staff member Gary

Sapanich documented group conversations and debates, and another staff member, Charles Hohmann, turned these into an overview of the approach. Frank Blackwell of Ramsgate, Kent, U.K., an experienced British educator and author, consulted with us on the production of a series of texts on key curriculum topics: classroom environment, science, language and literacy, and mathematics. Blackwell continued as series consultant and later wrote three additional science books to round out student activities in that area. Jane Maehr, a High/Scope staffer, conceptualized the language and literacy book. Phyllis Weikart and Elizabeth Carlton, High/Scope movement and music consultants, took the movement and music program Phyllis had been developing over the years and created teacher guidebooks for those areas. Both Charles Wallgren and Charles Hohmann were careful reviewers of all these materials. When computer technology became more user friendly and appropriate software programs began to appear, we supported their adoption and use in High/Scope classrooms. Staffers Warren Buckleitner and Charles Hohmann created a software review system to help classroom teachers new to this process select educationally appropriate software programs for classroom use.

"It was difficult to proceed and succeed in this area of education."

But it was difficult to proceed and succeed in this area of education. The traditional curriculum was too entrenched in many places, and we were too unsure that what we had to offer was best for the children. However, it was a time of gaining insights and making changes both for us and for the institutions we were attempting to advise. We did find value in maintaining our active learning approach and encouraging teaching staff to use the fundamental High/Scope open framework process to engage children meaningfully in various curriculum areas within the context of their site's needs and requirements. Our current position on elementary education is summarized in the sidebar on pp. 118–119 by Charles Hohmann. (Charles Wallgren recently retired after serving High/Scope for 27 years in various capacities.)

Implementation of the High/Scope Follow Through Model

A routine administrative Follow Through site visit illustrates the extent of the curriculum problems we faced in our model sponsorship. This particular program was located in a very rural, geographically isolated midwestern community. (This site was a joy to visit—and very inexpensive! As I remember, in 1970 a room was $6 a night at the most expensive motel and $4 at a less expensive motel. Housing was so cheap we even considered buying a small place for our staff visits, but with motel accommodations available at that price, why bother?) The school principal and I met as part of our administrative review of the work being accomplished. He was very concerned about the High/Scope Follow Through classrooms; indeed, he was irate! The classrooms, he told me, were out of control and the teachers were not teaching children the basics. (I squirmed and thought how difficult it was to work through a traditionally administered school.) The principal decided to show me exactly what he meant. I was pleased that he was willing to put the discussion on a factual level, because I knew from my classroom visits to his school that the teachers and children were doing very well. We walked, or should I say, I walked (he stalked) down the hall to the High/Scope third grade class. He swung open the door and stomped inside with me close behind. The children were busy working in small groups in all areas of the room. "No teacher in sight," he huffed. "See," I pointed out, "how busy the children are, how focused on their work?" But he responded that the teacher wasn't in charge; he couldn't see her. Then he saw her. She was under a table with a group of children laying out a series of tracks (for a weight object experiment). "What a noise level! Where is the discipline? How can I let this go on?" he exclaimed.

I asked the principal if he would show me a non-Follow Through third grade class as an example of how he believed classrooms should be conducted. Gladly. We walked down the hall and

$\sim$

High/Scope's Elementary Approach

The cornerstone of the High/Scope approach to early elementary education is the belief that the plan-do-review process of intentional learning is fundamental to the full development of human potential and that such learning occurs most effectively in settings that provide developmentally appropriate learning opportunities. This fundamental belief has guided the development of High/Scope's elementary education approach from its inception. Evolving over more than two decades of research, curriculum development, field study, and professional training efforts, the High/Scope approach to elementary education strengthens and extends the natural maturational and intellectual development of all children.

In elementary classrooms using High/Scope's approach, children and teachers form a partnership to support children in significant areas of intellectual development and to support them as they engage in important social interactions with other children and adults. In all students, the High/Scope approach promotes independent thinking, a "can-do" attitude, and an active, inquisitive imagination. While each child will develop these attributes at different rates and in varying degrees, the High/Scope approach is designed to foster self-confidence and social competence in all children—skills that are necessary to function in today's society, where life-long education, on-the-job training, teamwork, and problem solving are increasingly important. When fully implemented, the High/Scope educational approach yields long-term economic and social benefits both for the youngsters involved and for all members of society.

The High/Scope Elementary Curriculum has adopted many of the practices of the highly successful and effective High/Scope Preschool Curriculum. The effectiveness of High/Scope's educational approach has been documented in research studies over a span of more than 30 years.[1]

Of course, the High/Scope Elementary Curriculum differs from the preschool program in that it is designed to meet the needs of older children in the context of public school expectations for the elementary grades. The High/Scope elementary curriculum model is designed to help children's intellectual development in the following areas:

- Language, logic, mathematics, and science
- Spatial, temporal, and physical-motor skill development
- The creative arts
- Social studies and social-emotional development

Because young children respond best to direct sensory experience, manipulation of materials and physical motor activity play crucial roles in helping them form concepts, generate ideas, and produce symbolic representations. To promote these aspects of the learning process, the High/Scope Curriculum establishes a classroom environment organized around inviting learning centers stocked with practical yet appealing materials, supplies, and equipment. Moreover, the daily schedule provides frequent opportunities for children to work with materials and equipment as they devise projects of their own choosing, make thoughtful efforts to solve problems (encountered on their own or through teacher-assigned tasks), and share the results of their efforts with teachers and other children through speech, writings, drawings, or other forms of communication. Children express their intentions and plan courses of action by carrying out their intentions, creating products, offering solutions to problems they may encounter, working independently, and talking freely. Finally, they reflect on their experiences by reporting on what they have learned. They are comfortable among themselves and with adults, see to their own needs whenever possible, and respect the needs and wishes of others.

To achieve this knowledge-construction process, the High/Scope Curriculum offers a set of learning objectives known as key experiences in such areas as language, mathematics, science, movement (physical/motor development), and music. The developmental continuum illustrated in these key experiences provides teachers with a framework for sequencing instructional materials, formulating daily plans, and assessing and tracking the children's individual and group progress. The teacher-student interaction involved in these High/Scope key experiences— teachers helping students achieve developmentally sequenced learning objectives while also encouraging them to set many of their own goals—distinguishes High/Scope's curriculum from others. In addition, by recognizing that learning is also a social experience involving reciprocal interactions among both children and adults, the curriculum builds in numerous opportunities for children to engage in social processes with friends, families, and the community. Many opportunities exist for small-group and one-to-one interaction among children as well as for child-adult interaction. To foster development of spoken and written language, the curriculum includes many opportunities for children to use their verbal and written communication skills.

[1]Bond, J. T., Smith, A. G., & Kittle. J. M. (1976). *Evaluation of curriculum implementation and child outcomes* (Annual Report, Vol. 2, Pt. I). Ypsilanti, MI: High/Scope Foundation; Weikart, D. P., Hohmann, C. F., & Rhine, W. R., "High/Scope Cognitively Oriented Curriculum Model," in W. R. Rhine, Ed., *Making schools more effective: New directives from Follow Through.* NY: Academic Press, 1981; Schweinhart, L. J., & Wallgren, C. R. (1993). "Effects of a Follow Through program on school achievement," *Journal of Research in Childhood Education, 8*(1).

entered a silent room: desks in neatly spaced rows; teacher seated in front at her desk reading a picture story for a science lesson about a tree, learning the words "root," "trunk," and "crown" as the lesson of the day. As I gazed about the silent room, I saw some bored-looking children with their hands raised, but wilted at the elbow, several other children looking out the windows, and a few others actually with their heads on their desks. The teacher droned on. When we left, the principal pointed out how proud he was of the discipline represented by the straight rows of desks and the silence in that classroom. And I could only think about how many times this midwestern classroom scene was repeated throughout the country—where true learning is traded for the coin of discipline. Active learning settings may be noisy—but it's the noise of children eagerly embracing ideas, making choices, following through, talking about their discoveries with their peers and teachers. They are gaining a love of learning that lasts a lifetime.

The early years of our Follow Through Project operation were times of great social change throughout the country— schools, public facilities, and housing were becoming racially integrated. These changes challenged deeply held beliefs and were experienced very intensely in the South at one of our sites. With court-ordered school integration in the mid-1960s, the county schools where we were to work underwent major changes. All-white private schools were set up to serve white families who had pulled their youngsters out of the newly integrated public schools. The county school board (all white) "discovered" that they had a surplus of school buses and they sold those to the new private schools along with much classroom equipment at greatly discounted prices. When we arrived, the school board had managed to buy some old school buses from a dealer to transport the public school children, who happened to be black, but there was little equipment and few supplies for daily projects. Many storage closets in the public classrooms were actually empty.

The lack of materials was a special problem for implementing the High/Scope approach because of its emphasis on hands-on manipulatives. After a year of working with the coordinator in charge of the program, the parent council, and the teachers to solve the problem, the need for more direct action became obvious. It was clear that all of our equipment and supply requests were being ignored by the central administration, even though funds were allocated for this purpose in the Follow Through budget. A special meeting was arranged with the superintendent, the administrative coordinator of the program, a member of the High/Scope Board of Directors who lived in the South, and me to discuss the issue and find some resolution.

"Active learning settings may be noisy—but it's the noise of children eagerly embracing ideas, making choices, following through, talking about their discoveries with their peers and teachers. They are gaining a love of learning that lasts a lifetime."

Why could supplies and equipment not be purchased when the funds were in the federally approved project budget? After a difficult and testy discussion of the problem, the superintendent finally burst out in full regional drawl to ask me if I knew what they did thereabouts with a squeaky wheel on a wagon? Relieved that we were finally about to solve the problem, I replied that I didn't know. He said, "We take it off the wagon, boy! We take it off the wagon!" I was stunned. In Ohio, where I grew up in farm country, the story was that the squeaky wheel got the grease. Now here in the rural south, the story had a unique twist, the wheel got the ax! The meeting ended on this negative note, but eventually we did get the supplies we needed.

Changes in the National Follow Through Project

Follow Through was a program of the 1960s and was destined not to survive in spite of valiant efforts by model sponsors and active federal officers. As the program matured through the 1970s and 1980s, federal support gradually diminished. Perhaps key to this reduction was the fact that the evaluation never was able to report clear results that outside experts could agree upon. Tension always existed between the sponsors and the series of research groups employed one after another to assess program effects. This gradual turnover in research groups indicated the internal difficulties involved in assessing the work of the model sponsors. Follow Through was a complex project with limited capacity to create adequate experimental and contrast groups, conflicting views of education among the model sponsors, and the need to meet daily practical demands of school districts to operate programs for children. Combine these difficulties with the federal requirements for program management, and the program was like an off-key choir!

"Follow Through was a program of the 1960s and was destined not to survive in spite of valiant efforts by model sponsors and active federal officers."

Meetings organized by the evaluation groups were often confrontations between model sponsors. Especially difficult were the discussions of measures of achievement. Tests of rote learning by multiple-choice achievement tests were easy to find; tests of complex problem-solving and language usage were simply not that available. Groups that focused on teacher-directed learning such as DISTAR from the University of Illinois (later at the University of Oregon) were quite happy with a test called the Wide Range Achievement Test for all grades. This simple test required children to exhibit specific knowledge of letters and numbers, word recognition, and arithmetic. Groups such as Bank Street, the Open Education School Movement, and High/Scope preferred tests that at least opened the door to opportunities for displays of children's comprehension and integration of knowledge. Because the contracted research teams had few options, the tests employed to evaluate the project typically used multiple-choice questions to obtain factual information. This debate was to roil the sponsor meetings for decades. At one meeting, to the astonishment of the sponsors, one group of researchers from Harvard University stated that they really were looking forward to *"playing"* with the data. This comment was made about the outcomes of the major life work of some sponsors. Most felt we deserved better treatment and consideration.

◠

All these difficulties eventually led to a number of reviews of the whole process by consultants hired by outside groups to examine the information collected by the various federal contractors. These included the Ernest House and Eugene Glass report funded by the Ford Foundation and the Walter Hodges report sponsored by the model program sponsors themselves.

During this period, Robert Egbert stepped down as director of the national office and a nonresearcher was appointed. Feeling more and more at sea, in 1973 the sponsors organized an association to both speak with the national Washington office about our general interests and concerns and to combat the increasing impetus in Congress to drift away from supporting Follow Through.

I was elected chairman of the sponsor organization. The sponsors held their annual meeting each fall at the High/Scope Retreat and Meeting Center in Clinton, Michigan, in order to review general issues in our relationship both with federal contractors and Washington officials. Representatives of these groups also attended the annual sponsor meeting along with other experts in education and child development. While the schedule of meetings was tight, the casual setting was conducive to many informal interactions as well. For example, after lunch we would often take walks in the surrounding fields and forests, canoe, play volleyball, spend an evening pressing apple cider with fruit gathered that afternoon from the orchard, and enjoy hay rides on wagons drawn by an old Ford 600 tractor. These informal gatherings played an important role in forging a spirit of cooperation among model sponsors and helped Follow Through mature as a truly national effort. This common focus and spirit of unity also helped us explain the project to the U. S. Congress in terms of a national effort rather than as a series of discrete programs. From its high point of involving about 23 different sponsor groups and 154 public school sites, Follow Through gradually was reduced to a much smaller project. As Follow Through shrank in size and influence, model sponsor groups focused more on completing reports and trying to understand the lessons learned.

~

High/Scope's Follow Through Research

Research on the High/Scope approach at the elementary school level has been difficult to achieve. In National Follow Through, contrast groups (groups of children who were similar to those in the High/Scope–supported classrooms but did not have a chance to be assigned to them) were hard to identify and difficult to track. Also, research on the elementary school programs participating in National Follow Through was the province of federal government contractors. Nevertheless, although operating on limited resources, since the end of National Follow Through in 1992, High/Scope has conducted project-monitoring research follow-up studies on its model (including establishing control groups for comparability). In 2001, Larry Schweinhart and Charles Smith of the High/Scope Research Department compiled information from 10 schools in different parts of the country on child outcomes from the end of the High/Scope Follow Through training for up to five years later. (Different types of information were available from different schools.) The findings are impressive:

1. Six schools in the group, with samples averaging 142 children, on the whole achieved a 9.7 percent higher rate of children passing state reading achievement tests than the contrast schools: a 10.7 percent versus 1 percent increase.

2. The same group of schools reported a difference of 17.5 percent on the state mathematics achievement tests: a 25.7 percent versus 8.2 percent increase.

3. Three schools, samples averaging 141 children, on the whole achieved a 6 percent higher rate of children passing state reading achievement tests than the contrast schools: a 9.1 percent versus 3.1 percent increase up to five years after High/Scope training ended.

4. For the same period of follow-up on the state mathematics achievement tests, the three schools reported a difference of 11.9 percent: a 10.2 percent versus –1.7 percent increase.

~

5. In four of the schools where data were available, discipline referrals during the period of High/Scope support decreased by 48 percent.

6. A survey of 28 teachers about their perceptions of their classroom experience in three schools found that 76 percent of the teachers were positive about the High/Scope effort with only 4 percent negative. The remaining 20 percent were either neutral (12 percent) or did not respond (8 percent).

Information such as this indicates that the High/Scope model, when appropriately implemented, achieves success. (A list of references related to our elementary program development and research is provided in the appendices on p. 297.) Since these studies, others have occurred. (Visit the High/Scope Web site, *www.highscope.org,* for the most recent studies.)

Other High/Scope Elementary School Program Recognition

A number of organizations have recognized the work of the High/Scope Foundation at the elementary school level. In 1992, High/Scope submitted its Follow Through research findings to the U. S. Department of Education's Program Effectiveness Panel for review. The Panel judged the school performance outcomes of children enrolled in the High/Scope model classrooms and approved our approach as an effective program based on these positive academic achievement outcomes. Also in 1992, High/Scope applied for and received funds from the U.S. Department of Education's National Diffusion Network to operate as a service provider. These project funds allowed High/Scope staff to provide training to hundreds of teachers who were not part of the National Follow Through Project. The National Diffusion Network ended in 1996, but in 1998 the High/Scope elementary school approach was accepted for inclusion in the U.S. Department of Education's *Catalog of School Reform Models.* The research on effectiveness was reviewed again, and the model was listed in the 2001 second edition of the catalog.

Another important elementary school effort has been our work with the Bureau of Indian Affairs, Office of Indian Education, which began in 1992. Deciding to bolster the quality of education offered to Indian children and families on various reservations, OIEP decided to implement a three-part strategy: working with parents of infants and toddlers in their homes, providing adult education while providing preschool center-based programs, and improving elementary education. To accomplish these goals, the Office selected the Parents-as-Teachers model program for the parent-infant work, the National Center for Family Literacy to provide the adult education and preschool program (which uses the High/Scope model), and the High/Scope Foundation to support elementary school program development. High/Scope started with five reservation sites in 1992. Because of its positive acceptance and successful evaluations, the project gradually expanded to 38 schools in 2002. The Office plans further expansion over the next several years to reach almost all reservation schools. Further, High/Scope's work with Indian populations has been sponsored by the Charles Stewart Mott Foundation of Flint, Michigan. With this funding, High/Scope has provided teacher training programs for leaders in Indian preschool education at several southwestern sites through a multiyear project.

"In 1998 the High/Scope elementary school approach was accepted for inclusion in the U.S. Department of Education's **Catalog of School Reform Models.***"*

Foundation staff also have provided training to teacher trainers in various aboriginal tribes in Canada under the direction of Health Canada.

Lessons From the High/Scope Elementary Education Experience

What lessons have we learned from these years of experience in elementary education? One obvious lesson is that it is very difficult to try to make change happen in public elementary school settings. While we met many outstanding and dedicated individuals, both teachers and administrators, the adherence to traditional approaches (with the teacher imparting knowledge by lecturing in front of students sitting quietly at their desks) is very strong and not surprising. A range of research literature, including the results from our multicountry IEA study (International Association for the Evaluation of Achievement), indicates that traditional beliefs will always guide teacher behavior more than education, degrees, experience, and age. Where we were successful, it was because the participating teachers believed in what we were attempting. Thus, lesson one is that school reform will require a battle to win the hearts and minds of the teachers during the training process. Without a strong belief in what the reform can accomplish, teachers and administrators will not support a new program.

Training of teaching staff involves much more than providing information in a single-week, summer orientation workshop. The local teaching staff and High/Scope con-

"School reform will require a battle to win the hearts and minds of the teachers during the training process."

sultants would complete the very necessary work of presemester training, believing things could hardly have gone better. Yet, in visiting the classrooms a month later, they would find little evidence that the teachers were implementing what we thought they had learned—even when they seemed to be completely willing to try the alternative, reform-minded program. Thus, lesson two is that effective teacher training provides extensive opportunities for consultants to work in parallel with teachers in the classroom so that the theoretical elements of the new approach can be gradually absorbed and applied by the teacher in his or her actual setting. This practical learning occurs only through ongoing discussions about the children in the classroom and problems encountered there. The teaching and learning that occur in college education courses and other off-site training for most teachers are a good foundation, but interactions with a trainer in the actual classroom setting enable teachers to assimilate information in a concrete and meaningful way.

The third lesson is best related through one of my personal experiences. While visiting High/Scope's New York City Follow Through site, I was stopped in the hall one day by a fourth grade teacher. I could see immediately that he was going to be rather belligerent. He said that he thought the High/Scope program was supposed to teach children to take responsibility for themselves and their actions. I assured him that was indeed our hope. He replied that he knew better. He had told all his children (who came from a High/Scope Follow Through third grade classroom) to line up against the wall and to keep one of their hands on that wall while they waited for their turn in the lunch room. They couldn't do it. They kept taking their hands off the wall. They were not responsible enough to carry out his directions.

"Our goal is to assure the long-term engagement and success of children in using their language, math, science, social studies, and related knowledge and skills as thinking and problem-solving tools."

I couldn't take time at that point to discuss the difference in the meaning of *responsibility* and *obedience,* but the episode illustrates the difficulty that trainers have in introducing new curricula organized around nontraditional assumptions and goals. The third lesson, then, is that learning to think differently about the process of educating children is not a matter of providing teachers with new definitions as much as it is a matter of helping them change the way they actually work with children so they can see for themselves that real, constructive change is possible.

The fourth lesson relates to the widespread belief that learning to read, write, and do arithmetic is the primary goal of the early elementary school experience. All other educational areas are secondary, so any curriculum that hopes to offer other advantages to students must first be successful in these academic areas. There is little doubt that using directive teaching methods to push children to score better on multiple-choice tests will work in the short term. However, our goal is to assure the long-term engagement and success of children in using their language, math, science, social studies, and related knowledge and skills as thinking and problem-solving tools. Because of what we observed firsthand in our longitudinal research on different styles of teaching and learning, I know that the child development approach of programs such as High/Scope's, properly executed, can produce both the short-range and even more important, the long-range results we all desire for children.

High/Scope has not solved all the problems we've encountered in working at the elementary school level. In our efforts to date, we have explored the efficacy of a variety of approaches, but we continue to recognize the value and importance of supporting active child engagement through the plan-do-review process and through meaningful teacher-child conversations and interactions. Schools using High/Scope's approach show what can be done when teachers work with children as partners in the active learning process. We need to continue working on these critical issues.

6

International Work

We live in a global community with interlocking networks of communication, extensive tourism, exchange of technical knowledge, international trade agreements, and sharing of intellectual property, including entertainment, research, and health information. Many differences exist, however, such as the Dutch penchant for using declarative sentences, and the English affinity for ending many opinion statements with "... don't you think?"—giving rise to many subtle and not-so-subtle differences in attitudes and beliefs. When the many religious groups and language clusters are counted, differences can be profound. The treatment of women in some Moslem countries represents a very different world view than that of the Judeo-Christian West. Health practices in the traditional societies of East Asia or Africa differ significantly from the standard practices of Europe and America. Even logical thinking, as exemplified by the scientific method (and in the High/Scope approach by the plan-do-review process), clash with some of the thinking processes of persons in India or China and in the great sweep of ancient Eastern cultures. With such great differences, can an educational method developed for one population work elsewhere?

High/Scope answers this question not by promoting our point of view but by responding when groups from the far reaches of the globe request our help. The world over, adults want their children to succeed in a global economy, whether they are aboriginals of northern Canada ("What your [High/Scope's] teachers do is what we want *our* teachers to do"), an Iraqi minister of social welfare during the Iraq-Iran War ("Our men are at the front; we need our girls to think for themselves like they do in your class-rooms"), or Chinese parents with children in a High/Scope day care center in Singapore ("We didn't realize that our children had so many things to say"). These people believe that an open frame-work curriculum, such as High/Scope's, may give their youngsters new opportunities for knowledge. This chapter traces how the High/Scope Foundation became involved in a number of geo-graphic regions in service to the goals of parents, teachers, and community leaders.

Beyond Ypsilanti

The first formal exposure of the High/Scope educational ap-proach outside of the United States came about almost as a re-sult of a joke. It was February 1970. Since the Foundation would not be launched officially until July 1970, in February we were still employees of the Ypsilanti Public Schools. At a month-ly staff meeting of the Preschool Curriculum Comparison Study, I was leading a discussion of how we should celebrate the com-pletion of the three-year preschool program study. While the re-search follow-up would go on for years, the program itself was slated to end officially in late May 1970. As only those who have experienced such informal and spontaneous brainstorming ses-sions can attest, the responses ranged from the slightly obscene to the impossibly hilarious to the thoughtfully possible. Finally, Linda Rogers, one of the High/Scope teachers, suggested that the project should take us all to Europe for a well-earned vaca-tion. After the boisterous cheers and laughter at such a prepos-terous-impossible-beyond-consideration-where-would-the-money-come-for-25-staff idea stopped, we began to think. Per-haps the staff could earn the money. We already offered an an-nual Ypsilanti conference each spring to interested educators, which began in 1963 with the start of the High/Scope Perry Preschool work. Why not just expand that idea and take "the show" on the road? The staff meeting ended with a promise to keep the idea alive and continue to explore possibilities.

After further consideration over the next several weeks, I concluded that the idea had merit, but to successfully execute it would involve a number of steps. We would offer our regular spring conference in Ypsilanti, as planned. We knew the approximate income from that event. Next, we would work with friends in Seattle, Washington, and present our conference there as well. This additional program dissemination would generate additional income. Finally, working through an English psychologist who had visited our program in the late 1960s and had offered to help if we ever needed a British contact, I arranged for Goldsmiths College to be our sponsor in London. I would take all the project staff—bus drivers, classroom aides, program teachers, program consultants, researchers, and indeed, anyone who served the program—and go to London for a working visit that would include a conference presentation and several observations of British schools. Our original "pie-in-the-sky" plan worked!

With cooperative Ypsilanti School Superintendent Ray Barber to bless the adventure and brand-new passports in hand, we were off to London for our final project presentation and first High/Scope exposure overseas. Our British hosts arranged for us to stay in the Bloomsbury, a tourist hotel in the Russell Square area of London near the West End theater district. Lecturer Len Marsh of Goldsmiths College arranged space for our conference presentation, disseminated information about the event, and made our presentation possible. He also gave us a range of contacts for English school visits as part of our weeklong program. We organized the conference and presented repeat sessions, with staff of each curriculum model presenting their different theoretically based approaches and discussing what they had learned during the project, and the research staff discussing assessment instruments and what data were available at that time from the project. We were heady with a sense of success and pleased with the questions participants were asking.

What we missed, and what I learned years later, was that the American style of suspending educational beliefs to conduct a research study was beyond the expectations and experience of most of the British teachers in our audience. We further confused them by presenting three operationally and theoretically different preschool education approaches. (What did these Americans mean, what did they believe, and, if they believed it, why conduct research on it?) When conference questions and discussions were considered along with what we learned as we observed in a range of London early education and primary classrooms, a whole new world opened up for High/Scope staff.

Indeed, the conference had several important outcomes. It was a significant event in the lives of the High/Scope staff, especially individuals who would never have had an opportunity for international travel. (Two English-speaking-only classroom aides extended their trip and flew to Paris for the weekend before coming home, independent of the group, an extraordinary act of courage and confidence on their part.) It also introduced many young British teachers and college lecturers to High/Scope, though the early confusion about the three approaches would come back to haunt us 15 years later. (When I returned later to offer High/Scope teacher training, I found that all three models had become blended as "the High/Scope approach.") Finally, the experience brought home the fact that other national groups had different approaches to education; for example, the public embarrassment by their teachers—in classrooms and all-school headmaster assemblies—of individual students experiencing academic or behavioral problems; the signs on exterior walls at school gates telling parents to stop and not enter school grounds. Yet, through these experiences I forged important relationships with U.K. early childhood educators, and these contacts led to a number of speaking engagements for me in which I was able to publicize our approach and findings. As interest gradually grew in the High/Scope educational approach and its accompanying research, I was emboldened to offer a Training-of-

Trainers program for British early childhood staff, and this step launched what is now a major curriculum movement throughout the U.K. (This will be discussed in a later section of this chapter.)

International Service: A Focus on Latin America

Actually, my experience working as an international consultant was very gradual and was based on requests from a number of countries who wanted to implement our program in their settings. Indeed, I did not develop a formal international strategy until after 1985. Before that time, my international service was more in line with my early experience setting up training in the U.K.—the result of making speeches and related presentations.

My first major overseas consultation took place in 1970, not in the U.K. but for an early education research project that was operating in Cali, Colombia. Dr. Leonardo Sinnistera, a pediatrician and nutritionist at Cali University, Arlene McKay, a clinical psychologist, and Harrison McKay, a research psychologist, had organized the project, which was funded by the Ford Foundation of New York. The goal was to study the impact of early childhood education and nutrition on children aged 2–5 in a program offered for various lengths of time. The program provided children with four years, three years, two years, and one year of early childhood education along with supplemental feeding to one group. The study compared the development of children randomly assigned to a supplemental feeding and education group or no feeding–no education or supplemental-feeding-only groups. I was asked by the Ford Foundation to consult with Arlene McKay on the development and implementation of a curriculum for the project's early childhood education component,

"I was emboldened to offer a Training-of-Trainers program for British early childhood staff, and this step launched what is now a major curriculum movement throughout the U.K."

and I worked with the project about twice a year for three years. I had the privilege of working under two Ford Foundation country representatives, Ralph Harbison and Emily Vargus, as well as with the talented project staff.

During my first visit, I saw that the program for the children was a fairly formal, group-centered, teacher-directed approach. The program had started six months earlier and all the children were now around 3 years of age. Reading books were used to drill letter names, rote counting was common, and children sat on chairs and waited for the teachers to tell them what to do next. As the impact of malnutrition on the children was still evident even to my untrained eye (blond or reddish hair from lack of protein; distended abdomens from lack of calories), the children's passivity seemed a natural outcome of their health history. Nonetheless, working with Arlene McKay, we decided to apply some ideas from the High/Scope educational approach to see if these children could reach a higher level of thinking and exhibit more active behavior. Thus, on the next to last day of my week-long stay, the teachers stacked chairs and tables to one side in each instructional space and placed blocks, toys, art materials, and puzzles on the floor or close at hand. Although somewhat anxious, the teachers were willing to try this new approach. When the children were first settled in their customary space (the 60 children were divided into groups of 15 with two teachers for each group), they were very confused; this new setting was not within their experience or expectations. Then the children were invited to play with whatever they wished. No effort was made to help them develop a plan as in the full High/Scope method. (Planning by young 3-year-olds is mostly providing them with choices anyway.) The goal was simply to see what the children would do so the staff could decide if they would like to adopt a more active approach to education. After a short while, most of the children were actively engaged, and their teachers, while still not certain,

"The goal was simply to see what the children would do so the staff could decide if they would like to adopt a more active approach to education."

were impressed. With great intensity and focus, one girl, Eloisa, built a tower of blocks that was taller than she was. Her accomplishment, along with the general enthusiasm almost all the children exhibited in their new setting, encouraged the staff to ask for more information on how to provide even more of these opportunities within their program. They had no idea that children could work so hard or so effectively. They were impressed that all the children were busy and not just waiting for more instruction.

Over the next three years, the High/Scope approach was adapted to the setting by implementing the key curriculum elements. The plan-do-review process was the most important addition. In the last year of the program, some 240 children (60 from each experimental group) were being served in a beautiful open-air tropical school, with high-roofed, palm-thatched classroom buildings and bamboo dividers partitioning the classrooms. They had

Eloisa's choice was to build a block tower taller than she. Its complicated structure and that it remained standing when she finished were important factors in helping the teachers understand that children are capable of difficult work without direct, minute-by-minute supervision.

excellent equipment and, although most of the teachers had little formal education, they were well trained in delivering a modified High/Scope Curriculum. All the now 5-year-old children were also well versed in the approach. Unfortunately, about three months into the final school year of the experiment, a visiting mother allowed her child to play with her cigarette lighter; the

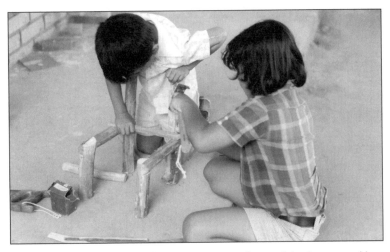

The children took responsibility for the construction of most of the classroom tables and chairs after their thatched-roof school building burned to the ground. These two boys, one the experienced "consultant," carry out their plan to build a chair during the class work time.

The teacher and the boys who built a chair discuss the process during the small-group review time.

result was that the complete complex burned to the ground. No children were injured and all research data were safely housed in another building. When I made my last visit, the school had been moved to an abandoned supermarket that had been donated by the owner. All classroom materials were "found"—scraps and surplus supplies donated by the community. Most of the chairs and tables were made by the children themselves. Indeed, during one work time, two boys planned to make a new chair. Their mentor was a third boy of their same age who had made several himself. He helped the two boys for a short while, demonstrating the hammer grip and how to hold the wood correctly.

"Children everywhere have sufficient energy, interest, and responsibility to play a major role in their own education as long as teachers support and insure that the full range of necessary materials and experiences are available."

Then he said, "I got to go, but if you need me, I'm in the math area and I can help you some more." Then without cockiness but with confidence, he walked off. The two boys went on to make their chair, completing their plan and explaining the process to the teacher and their small group during the review period.

The Cali experience was the first at applying the High/Scope approach in a foreign setting with another language and another culture. It taught me several important lessons. First, it demonstrated that teachers, even those with relatively little formal education, can learn the approach with competent inservice supervision. Second, it showed that because the curriculum uses an "open framework" for classroom activities and experiences, it can be adapted to other settings—even settings that are dramatically different from ours. Third, it reinforced a basic concept of the High/Scope approach—that children everywhere have sufficient energy, interest, and responsibility to play a major role in their own education as long as teachers support and insure that the full range of necessary materials and experiences are available.

For most of the 1970s, High/Scope's international work was conducted in Latin America and the Caribbean. Another important early international project took place in Peru—working with mothers and infants and training preschool staff—made possible by UNICEF (United Nations International Children's Education Fund) assistance. A UNICEF contractor made a dramatic 16mm color film about the preschool work in the high mountainous region of Peru, at Puno, located on Lake Titicaca. The film depicts a male teacher, trained in the basic High/Scope approach, working with about 60 children and clearly implementing an adaptation of the High/Scope plan-do-review process. It shows 4-year-old children carrying out their plans such as building outdoor fires in rough clay stoves to bake potatoes. It also illustrates how the children's parents were involved in keeping the school operating and supplied with materials. All the children and adults wore bright knit hats with ear flaps to keep the sharp, clear rays of the sun off their heads at that 12,000 foot (3,810 m) altitude.

Another opportunity to work in Latin America involved an evaluation of a parent education and child nutrition project in Venezuela. As in many Latin American countries, such a project was sponsored by the country's First Lady, and it opened our naive eyes to the problems of doing careful research with individuals who do not understand how to collect objective informa-

"The project opened our naive eyes to the problems of doing careful research with individuals who do not understand how to collect objective information."

tion. For example, in an effort to assess the quality of the nutritional data we were receiving for analysis, we made a field visit to one of the health and nutrition data collection centers out in the Andes. The young doctor who operated the center was asked to review the information he had collected just that morning during his rounds when documenting the food intake of a project participant. (Such food-intake records are a standard practice in nutritional studies.) He read aloud the report from one mother he had just interviewed regarding what her 4-year-old son had eaten that morning for breakfast. He said, without a doubt in his voice or manner, "The mother reported that her son ate eggs, bread, pork-bacon, beef, potatoes, rice, beans, milk, oranges, and a banana." We asked if a dirt-poor barrio woman had access to such a rich and varied diet for her son, and we were assured that the data were correct. As a result of a number of these types of occurrences, we, as evaluators, were forced to question the accuracy of the information being provided for analysis, and we were not able to give as complete and accurate a final report as the project wished.

One sad incident occurred while reporting the final outcomes of the evaluation to the First Lady at the "White House," as the Venezuelans call their president's residence. The primary Venezuelan data supervisor for the overall project was an asthmatic. During the initial day of meetings, other women in the group, smokers all, enjoyed teasing her by blowing smoke into her face and hair. The data supervisor was visibly distressed by their behavior, but seemed unable to curtail it. On the second day of the meetings, the government project leader announced that the data supervisor had died during the previous night of an asthmatic attack. Those of us from the Foundation were stunned. As outsiders, we had been in no position to step in the day before, but when hazing behaviors so obviously wrong are witnessed, perhaps the sense of "outsider" should not prevail. While this kind of bullying incident undoubtedly has parallels in all cultures, our failure to intervene was due to our sense of "otherness." As guests in a foreign culture, we literally didn't know what the social rules were.

Indeed, working in other countries means that the normal signals used to judge and govern behavior are different, and Foundation staff often found themselves in problem situations where a lack of "street smarts" or knowledge of the local social system produced difficulties. Another example of this occurred in Panama. One High/Scope staff member lost his passport, credit cards, and money when he was robbed on the street by a well-known national boxing champion. No one would stop, interfere with, or report such a celebrity. When I joined our staff member two days later, I was able to use my passport to vouch for him at the American Embassy and obtain temporary travel documents. In Colombia, two weeks before, another staff member and his wife were set to return to the States after a year's stay when the Foundation-owned jeep was stolen. In that country, a whole system was in place to "ransom" your car back. But because of the short time before departure, the usual system of advertising and hiring a "broker" to act as middleman could not be completed, even though we made initial contact. Peru offered another such experience. Inflation is a problem we Americans fail to understand because our country generally experiences relatively low rates. At the end of a project in Peru, US$7,000 in local currency was left in a bank account, because taking it out of the country seemed too elaborate a task and further work was planned there. When we finally came back to use it three years later, the "value" of what was left was barely enough to pay for one night at the Sheraton Hotel in Lima. So much for, "It's too much trouble."

There were some major successes in providing the various services High/Scope offered in Latin America. Through contacts made (during the Cali project) with Dr. Fernando Monkeberg of the University of Santiago in Chile (who had served as the project's nutritional consultant), I was invited to speak to a number of groups in Chile. I made several visits there even during the hyper-inflation days at the end of the Salvador Allende regime. I worked with Sylvia Lavanche and Emy Suzuki at the Catholic University of Santiago to enable use of the High/Scope approach in their teacher training programs. They organized a two-month training seminar, staffed by two High/Scope trainers, to help support early childhood development programs in Chile.

In another effort, the Foundation worked with the United States Agency for International Development (AID) to build several preschools and provide staff training on the Carribean island nation of St. Kitts/Nevis. The AID project also enabled us to provide early childhood staff training in Ecuador, Peru, and Bolivia. After such projects were over, I often wondered if a long-term impact was achieved. So I was pleased to hear in May 2001 from early childhood educator Janet Brown of Jamaica that the High/Scope Curriculum still looked like the High/Scope Curriculum on Nevis, even though 20 years has passed since the initial training.

After more than a decade of work in Latin America, I arrived at some basic conclusions. First, developing nations are anxious to work with anyone who can provide both services and the funds to underwrite those services. A formal agreement may be signed with all good intentions, but the cooperating agency or governmental unit most likely will not be able to fund the program. The agency can supply the letters of cooperation and participation, but a foreign agency (USA, Canadian, European, Japanese) must supply the funding. Second, people in other countries have very different work styles, sense of time, and views on what it means to carry out agreements.

Here is an example to illustrate one of these types of cultural differences: sense of time. I was asked to address a fairly large group of graduate students in education, sociology, and psychology at a major Chilean university. The time for my speech was set for 10:30 a.m., and this information was included in every announcement placed around the university campus. My translator and I arrived in plenty of time. Our hosts showed us about the campus, even walking by the large lecture hall where I would be presenting. Close to 10:30, the host suggested a second cup of coffee, and I began to get nervous—I would be speaking in only a few minutes and we were making no moves toward the lecture hall. Then, at about 11:00 a.m., my host decided to introduce me to the president of the university, and we chatted for a while. About 11:40, my host suggested we start for the auditorium. We arrived one hour and 15 minutes late, and the hall was packed: no empty seats, no standing room. I gave the lecture and answered the usual questions, and then we all adjourned for a pleasant lunch hosted by the president and the trustees. No one seemed to be bothered by the delays except me! I never learned why my talk

"People in other countries have very different work styles, sense of time, and views on what it means to carry out agreements."

was delayed. If no students had shown up for the lecture and they took the time to "round up" some, then why were so many attending? Was the announcement of the lecture wrong in location or time? Or was there a tacit understanding that lectures begin when a majority of folks feel comfortable arriving?

Another conclusion I came to is that a nonprofit organization like High/Scope, which is dependent on grants and contracts from other agencies to conduct its work, would have to work where the groups being served could raise their own resources and cover the costs of the High/Scope service. Even when working with aid agencies in Latin America, funds for projects proved too difficult for us to raise. High/Scope was headquartered in the United States, and we were primarily interested in providing early childhood education programs, but health, nutrition, and community development were the major funding concerns of these aid agencies. With these lessons in mind, I turned to Europe as a possible place to be of service.

Shifting Focus: High/Scope in Europe

The work in Europe began, as it had in Latin America, because of lectures I gave at educational conferences and opportunities I had to talk with government officials. In the late 1970s, I was invited to Germany to present findings from the High/Scope Perry Preschool Study at the Max Planck Institute in Berlin. It was my first real exposure to European research conferences. (So few of the reports included any statistics that I felt out of place with my charts and test-retest data.) What was really important about the trip for the work at High/Scope, however, was the opportunity for me to stop by the Bernard van Leer Foundation in The Hague, The Netherlands. Discussed more fully in the section relating to parent-infant studies, this visit led to funding for a series of studies I undertook in the parent-infant field. Invitations followed for me to lecture in Denmark, Norway, The Netherlands, Portugal, and the United Kingdom. While all were enjoyable and offered opportunities to disseminate our work, the contacts I made in the United Kingdom proved to be the most important, for they laid the groundwork for the establishment of the first licensed High/Scope international institute.

Establishing the British institute, High/Scope U.K., required a number of steps and years of effort. Indeed, my initial steps were more focused on organizing training in the High/ Scope approach than on establishing an institute, because that concept had yet to be developed. In the early 1980s, after High/Scope staff began to organize a systematic Training-of-Trainers program in New Jersey at the request of the state director of special education, I had the opportunity to give several speeches about our work at national conferences and to university audiences. I recall my first major lecture, about 1981, presented in Manchester, England, and organized by Teachers and Lecturers in Training Early Years Workers (TATYC). I spoke to an audience of over 800 British early years teachers. (At that time, the various British accents were still strange to my ear—even the billboard advertisements didn't make much sense to me. British pubs calling themselves "free houses"? What? They give away their beers? Verb forms were wrong: "Barclay's Bank have a new estate plan for you." Various sayings didn't make sense to me: "At the coal face." "At the end of the day." And some things the British thought of as dreadful, such as their train service, were miracles to a midwestern, USA-reared citizen.) When I came to speak, I talked about the High/Scope approach and compared it with several other approaches, using data from the High/Scope Curriculum Comparison Study. The applause was polite but brief and then on to morning coffee (not the tea I thought would be served). A number of participants were familiar with High/Scope from our experience visiting there in 1970 and asked whether specific training programs were available. It was because of these queries that I began to plan a High/ Scope Training-of-Trainers program for the U.K.

My first task was to find the funds necessary to pay for the seven-week program. In the States, participants would find their own resources to attend the training program, while the funds we raised would pay High/Scope's costs in providing the services. I produced a brief write-up of the training program and called on U.K. foundations and trusts that I thought might be interested in funding such an enterprise. Now, if you can imagine it, here I was, arriving with a proposal to fund a U.S. organization to offer a training program in the U.K. Of course, I answered many questions: Who wants such a service? Why would teachers in the U.K. with many more years of educating children under five wish to learn anything from the USA? While we speak a common language (mostly), your materials are based on children, teachers, and experiences in the United States. What makes you think that anything you do can apply to the U.K. situation? Can your ideas help us solve the problems we are having in our inner-city schools?

Once we worked through these and similar issues, the discussions turned to more practical matters related to funding, recruiting, and scheduling. After several such visits to various foundations and government offices, I realized that fundraising in the U.K. was very different from what I had experienced in the States. The foundation and trust endowments were, on the whole, much smaller than those with which I was familiar. Few groups were interested in funding the entire training program (about US $80,000 at that time) and were not used to funding such large projects in any case. After a round of discouraging meetings, Frank Blackwell, the retired English school head, writer, and international program supervisor for the van Leer Foundation, who was serving as my advisor, suggested I meet with a few individuals who seemed genuinely interested in deciding what to do next. That meeting was held in autumn 1981 at Kites, a Chinese restaurant near Russell Square in London. Attending were Rosemary Peacock, Her Majesty's inspector (HMI) for the national government, Anthony Tomie, project officer of Nuffield Foundation, Elsa Dicks, secretary of Voluntary Organizations Liaison Committee for Under Fives (VOLCUF) and the group thinking of coordinating our work should we receive funding, Ron Davie, executive director of the National Children's Bureau, Frank Blackwell, and me. The food was very good; the conversation, very discouraging. The group did not believe I had done enough legwork to be able to initiate a training program at that time. I was discouraged because I could only work on the idea when I had an invitation to visit Europe to speak or consult, and because I felt I had already done all the legwork that any reasonable proposal should require. While Blackwell consoled me and the others encouraged me, it still meant I had to undertake a great deal of additional work.

With the group's dictate, I focused on several funding groups: the Gulbenkien Foundation (U.K.), the Aga Khan Foundation (U.K.), and the Nuffield Foundation. The first two organizations expressed interest in funding the work while Nuffield was interested in funding an independent evaluation of our training in Britain. The Gulbenkien Foundation has its main headquarters and funding center in Lisbon, Portugal, where it undertakes a broad range of work, especially in the arts. The director of the London office was willing to fund part of the project if I could find major funding elsewhere. The Aga Khan Foundation has a worldwide presence with a majority of its funding going to help Ismaili groups in Pakistan through assistance in agriculture, health, and education at all levels. In addition, in each nation where there are Ismaili immigrant groups, national foundations are active, both to raise money for the international effort and to support local projects. When I approached Amir Bhatia (now Lord Amir Bhatia of Hampton), chairman of the Aga Khan Foundation in the U.K., I received a most sympathetic welcome. He expressed a great interest in early childhood education and in the research base that supported efforts to expand high-quality services. He set up meetings with his board of directors, government officials, and corporate leaders to discuss the issues. While none of these meetings produced immediate results, I did make inroads in publicizing this proposal. Bhatia told me that I could count on the Aga Khan Foundation to fund a portion of the work if I could obtain some of the funding from other groups (a familiar refrain). After a year or so of meetings and negotiations, Bhatia said that I could count on obtaining most of the funds from the Aga Khan Foundation. It was time to get on with the work; his fund commitment was firm. With that money in hand, I obtained additional funds from the Gulbenkien Foundation, as promised, and we began to recruit participants through VOL-CUF. The irony of the whole matter was that the amount of money the Aga Khan Foundation provided to initiate the project would have paid for the entire project if it had been granted when I first asked! (Such is the impact of inflation and currency exchange rates.) Nonetheless, I had learned a great lesson in the workings of another country and the problems of cross-national fundraising.

An interesting event occurred about this time: I received a visit in the States from a self-appointed delegation from Britain who wanted to take a careful look at the High/Scope program in operation at our headquarters in Ypsilanti, Michigan. The group spent several days observing the demonstration classroom, reviewing our research outcomes, and discussing educational philosophy with staff. At the end of the visit, they expressed cautious optimism that a successful training program might be possible in the U.K. This visit turned out to be of great help in creating acceptance for High/Scope in the U.K. For example, one visitor, Peter Haslip, was a lecturer at the Bristol Polytechnic Institute. After his visit, he incorporated information about the High/Scope approach in his course, thus introducing many student teachers to our program. Another visitor, Maude Brown, an early childhood advisor from Bristol, felt that it would be important to introduce the High/Scope approach into the under-fives programs in her area, and she organized a number of special meetings for teachers and orientation sessions for administrators in Bristol.

I had another interesting and illuminating experience a few years later when I was visiting Bristol to conduct a training workshop. I called Maude Brown's office from London the day before my arrival to confirm arrangements, and her secretary answered the telephone. I asked if I might speak with Maude Brown. The secretary kindly informed me that there was no such person at that office; would I like her to transfer me to the main switchboard? Stunned, I asked if I had dialed the wrong number and again said Maude's name. "No such person is here," was the reply. Finally, I asked for the early childhood advisor who worked out of that office. "Of course," she replied, "that would be Maude Brown. She is in and can take your call." (I guess I only thought I spoke English!) Two days later, I had a similar experience when I phoned Pat Stace, another educator I was working with, at her home in Milton Keenes to schedule my visit to her training classrooms. When her husband answered the telephone, I asked for "Pat Stace." He had me repeat the name several times and finally told me that I must have the wrong number. Remembering my Bristol experience, I then asked if the woman who supervised preschools was there. He put down the phone and called, "Pat, there is someone calling who is looking for the preschool supervisor," and Pat came on the line. What happened in these two instances, I can't say. To me "Maude Brown" and "Pat Stace" seem like simple names to pronounce. And even if I was not enunciating with the proper "a" sound in both names, it was close enough that a secretary or a husband could make a good guess, I would think. I relate this story because it illustrates some of the minor difficulties encountered in working in various cultures and language groups. If we could miscommunicate at this level, what were we missing at a more profound level?

Launching the High/Scope U.K. Institute

In 1988, after three rounds of U.K. training led by High/Scope staff trainers with funds raised through tuition and other support, some of the most active participants asked to do their own training with High/Scope's approval but without High/Scope's direct involvement. The push for this request came from a major British children's social service agency, Barnardo's. The agency's field staff in northeastern England were very active in the application of High/Scope in their early childhood care centers, and they were recommending more use of the approach throughout Barnardo's U.K. programs. With this major organization's interest to propel us, discussions were held with Michael Jarman, director of Barnardo's, Nora Dixon, head of research for Barnardo's, Elsa Dicks, VOLCUF, Frank Blackwell, High/Scope senior advisor, and me regarding the establishment of a High/Scope U.K. Institute that would provide official High/Scope training. Barnardo's offered a beautiful facility in Penge (greater London area), basically rent-free for the new group. They also offered a sizable multiyear grant to help cover initial overhead expenses while the Institute was developing funding for its services.

To accomplish such a new venture, a strong and lengthy licensing agreement was prepared by High/Scope staff and lawyers for review. Included were provisions for accounting for funds and monitoring management. Also, in an effort to recover some of the costs expended on the institute development, a five percent fee on gross training income was included. The agreement may have looked fine to American eyes, but not to the British. No way would they proceed under such arrangements. To the committee's credit, they recognized that High/Scope was offering a major "gift" of intellectual property, but they felt they had no capacity to add such a financial obligation to their task of establishing an independent institute. As a result of these discussions, High/Scope withdrew its request for a percentage of gross training revenues. I wanted the Institute to become well established and be an effective force in the British education scene. The amount of revenue to High/Scope would be small in any event. The concept and implementation of the institute was the important development at this point. The agreement was signed in 1990, and the High/Scope U.K. Institute assumed the responsibility for representing High/Scope in the British Isles. Our first overseas service agency was underway!

Research on High/Scope in the U.K.

The London-based Nuffield Foundation is an important research support and curriculum development group in the U.K. Anthony Tomi, project officer, was interested in studying the effects of High/Scope's training project on classroom programs and child development. Nuffield offered to fund an independent evaluation of our early training work in Britain. Accordingly, proposals were solicited from several research groups, and the one from Oxford University's Cathy Silva and Teresa Smith (lecturers in early childhood development) was accepted. Silva and Smith planned to use observation and interview procedures developed in a 10-year-long early childhood study led by psychologist Jerome Bruner in which they had participated. They also planned to examine the work over a three-year period to track its development as well as its impact. I welcomed this independent evaluation of our program by an experienced and respected British team. I was confident that we would have a positive impact and that this would give High/ Scope a strong base for its work in the U.K.

> *"I wanted the Institute to become well established and be an effective force in the British education scene."*

The Nuffield Foundation research study of the early years of our work in the U.K. was very important. While I was confident that the High/Scope approach would be as effective in Britain as in the States, transferability was a question that required validation. Awarding the grant to two experienced Oxford researchers whose work I respected, suggested that the effort would be comprehensive and objective. Over the three years of the study, the reports were all that we could have hoped for. The first-year report included extensive questioning of the approach and the basic philosophy. We were too organized a program for some of the professionals from the historic British Play Group Association. One trainee said that our approach "wouldn't let parents cut legs off tables so they could be on the floor." Another commented that we offered nothing new to the British scene because they had years of early education experience and were well aware of Piaget. But others were impressed with the program's organization of information and support for genuine teacher-child interactions. One participant even went so far as to comment that the High/Scope approach allowed her to do what she always wanted to do with children but couldn't.

By the second year, many of the first-year complaints and issues were replaced with questions about how to get more training, ways to inform parents about what was happening, and how to answer colleagues' questions. In the third year, the report was much more supportive, with indications of effective training and classroom application. In addition, Sylva supervised an interesting doctoral thesis done in Lisbon, Portugal, by Maria Emilia Nabuco. The project conducted a five-year study on the long-term impact of three curricula, patterned after the High/Scope Curriculum Comparison Study. In this application, the High/ Scope approach was contrasted with a directive program and a traditional play program. On most measures, the High/Scope approach proved to be more effective than either of the other two curricula. Thus, the Nuffield Foundation's early interest in research was unusually helpful in documenting the effectiveness of the High/Scope approach in the U.K. and spawned some interesting studies elsewhere.

> *"While I was confident that the High/Scope approach would be as effective in Britain as in the States, transferability was a question that required validation."*

An unusual event occurred during these early British efforts. During the third year of work, a letter appeared in the *London Times Education Supplement* decrying High/Scope's program in Britain. It was "written in haste whilst on the way to Heathrow Airport" by a woman living in the New Jersey (United States) area. She pointed out that it was a tragedy that while the High/ Scope approach was being rejected throughout the United States, it was making inroads in the U.K. Surprised (to say the least) at this misrepresentation, I attempted to contact the letter-writer. First, I went through the college that she gave as her affiliation. No luck. Then, I went through various regional and national professional associations. No luck. No one had heard of her. Finally, I wrote the editor of the *Education Supplement* to ask for the address that the newspaper had. The response was, *mea culpa!* They had printed the letter without verifying the name and address of the sender. Ah, but good things came from this experience! I was treated to lunch by way of apology; but no retraction was made as, the editor said, that would draw attention to the untrue issues raised in the letter. (By whom she didn't say.) Later, in the States, I read a discussion about curricula that included information about the High/ Scope approach. The fictitious *Educational Supplement* letter was quoted as part of the critical negative evidence presented in the article. Once any information, even false information, gets into print it is regarded as true by many and is used to support another conclusion now made false. My strategy was to let our evidence speak for itself.

Establishing International Institutes in Other Countries

To establish an international institute, we now have certain procedures. An official agreement is signed with High/ Scope Foundation that outlines the operations, responsibilities, and various legal arrangements that are part of the process. The mission of each institute is to promote the use of the High/ Scope educational approach within its national borders. To accomplish this mission, each institute has a director, at least two staff consultants endorsed by High/Scope to train teacher-trainers, adequate support staff, and a board of directors or advisors. The actual structure of an institute depends on the traditions of the host country and whether it is part of a larger entity such as a university or national agency or has free-standing legal status.

Since 1988, High/Scope Foundation has established a number of cooperating institutes in various foreign countries to allow local experts to direct and support the application of the High/Scope educational approach in their locales. In 2001, these countries included the United Kingdom, Republic of Ireland–Northern Ireland, Singapore, Indonesia, The Netherlands, and Mexico. Institutes are also planned for Chile, South Africa, Morocco, Brazil, and Turkey. During the Iraq–Iran war, we worked in Iraq through the United Nations Development Agency, providing staff training and consulting visits, but since the Gulf War, we have not been involved in Iraq.

The institutes have been developed in various ways as a result of various relationships. Our institute in Mexico, for example, came about because a young behavioral psychologist was making a tour of various American preschool programs. Roberto Barocio became fascinated with what he observed in the High/Scope demonstration classroom and wanted to know more. After participating in a Training-of-Trainers program, he organized several others in Mexico City and began to work toward establishing an institute. Now, the High/Scope Mexico Institute trains early childhood teachers and supports other Spanish-speaking groups interested in the High/Scope approach. A for-profit educational business training corporation in Singapore became involved conducting High/Scope training in both Singapore and Malaysia, and became our High/Scope Singapore Institute. High/Scope Indonesia began by obtaining training from High/Scope Singapore, completing the training requirements at High/Scope headquarters in the States, and becoming the second for-profit national institute. High/Scope Kaleidoscoop, The Netherlands, came about because I was serving as a consultant to the Averroes Foundation, a Dutch government-funded QUANGO. (A QUANGO is an independent, nonprofit agency funded by the government to do work as assigned by the government. It has its own independent board of directors.) Institute staff received their training by traveling to the United States to participate in a High/Scope Training-of-Trainers program. Kaleidoscoop also contracted with High/ Scope U.K. to provide several Training-of-Trainer programs in The Netherlands.

"The mission of each institute is to promote the use of the High/Scope educational approach within its national borders."

~

Institutes are developing in Chile at the Catholic University in Santiago and in South Africa. In South Africa, a group of 27 early childhood service organizations, representing most of the nation, have organized a network to manage a High/Scope South Africa Institute. The initial training was provided for four candidates each year for three years in London by the High/Scope U.K. Institute and funded by the Nuffield Foundation. In 2001, Kululeka, one of the largest children's charities in South Africa, contracted with High/Scope to provide a Trainer-of-Trainers program to their key staff. With this work, the South African Institute will have at least four staff-level endorsed trainers and be ready to work throughout the country.

Of special importance was the development of the cross-borders Republic of Ireland–Northern Ireland Institute. During a conference to celebrate the implementation of High/Scope preschool education in Northern Ireland and the Border Counties (those counties currently in the Republic of Ireland but historically part of Ulster), I suggested that the Irish might prefer to establish their own cross-borders institute rather than be served from London. The conditions specified were that it had to be "all Ireland" and be run equally by individuals from both sides of the border. Siobhan Fitzpatrick, executive director of the Northern Ireland Preschool Play Association (NIPPA), took the initiative to build the organization. Interest was generated in the Republic through involvement of the Irish Preschool Play Association (IPPA), Hilary Kenny, executive director. Outside government groups such as the Library (education) and Health Boards became interested. Major voluntary groups such as Barnardo's (Ireland) expressed interest. With this backing, I approached High/Scope U.K. to "release" Northern Ireland from their license so it could participate in the all-Ireland group. I had no idea of how much anger and resentment this request would cause among the English board members (not among those from other parts of the U.K.). The series of angry meetings that ensued reminded me somewhat of the civil rights encounters of the early 1960s in the United States and the turmoil generated when cities tried to apportion federal funds for projects or change zoning requirements or expand teaching staff to be more representative of the community.

However, Michael Jarmine, High/Scope U.K. board chairman, Serena Johnson, executive director of High/Scope U.K., Siobhan Fitzpatrick, executive director of NIPPA, and Elis McKay, proposed executive director of the new High/Scope Ireland Institute and a High/Scope endorsed trainer, all met with me at the Imperial Hotel in London off Russell Square to discuss the issue. At that meeting, the need was recognized for an all-Ireland Institute and for enabling the High/Scope U.K. to withdraw gracefully from northern Ireland so that neither its image nor its finances would be damaged. Both parties agreed to a course of action. The High/Scope Foundation undertook to help with the British financial issues. High/Scope U.K and the High/Scope Foundation also provided the trainers for the first High/Scope Ireland training program. With this agreement in place, staff from both the fledgling Irish Institute and the mature U.K. Institute have worked to make both programs a success. In the end, mature British statesmanship and historic Irish flexibility repaired the damage done through American ignorance.

"The High/Scope model can be transferred successfully because it provides a flexible framework that fits different teaching styles and different cultures."

By taking on the challenge of working in other countries and cultures, I believe we have answered the question posed at the beginning of this chapter: Can model programs developed and validated in one country be successfully implemented in other countries?" We have learned that the High/Scope model can be transferred successfully because it provides a flexible framework that fits different teaching styles and different cultures. Encouraging children to think and to relate what they have learned is a high-level goal of almost all educational programs in all countries. Because of this, the High/Scope Curriculum can be successfully applied in almost any setting and country whose leaders and citizens believe that children should be prepared to live and work in a global economy as independent, thinking adults.

7

Fundraising for Projects and for Endowment

One of the main functions a president or executive director of an institution performs is insuring the continuity of the work and services by securing the necessary resources to sustain them. More simply put: *Find the money!* For a public entity, this step is usually accomplished by negotiating with elected officials or boards responsible for the allocation of public resources or by simply accepting tax revenue. For a nonprofit institution like High/Scope, it means asking for money from individual donors, submitting proposals to foundations for funds to operate specific projects, creating ways to package and sell the intellectual capital the group has developed, and responding to requests for proposals (RFPs) issued by local, state, and federal agencies. As a general rule, the broader the range of sources, the more likely an even flow of revenue can be maintained. During my years at High/Scope, we depended on all of these funding sources.

The funding pattern of a cross-generational project, illustrated in the sidebar on pp. 158–159, is typical of funding efforts to the extent that it represents the torturous path that each new undertaking requires. Widespread mailings to foundations and corporations without an initial contact and discussion are rarely effective, even when the grantors ask for an explanatory letter

Funding a Project—One Example

In the late 1990s, several High/Scope staff members became interested in a cross-generational program, Generations Together, that was operating in nearby Dexter, Michigan. Several leading local Dexter businessmen had learned of programs that provided day care services for both the elderly and preschoolers. They decided that their small southeastern community had a need for such a program, so they organized a nonprofit 501(c)3 entity to establish and operate one. They appointed an executive director, Lee Tracy, and launched Generations Together. From the outset, this community program offered joint services to both age groups. The director designed the day care program to provide a stimulating environment for the elderly and an opportunity for children to work closely with older adults. It was also designed to encourage the elderly adults to take special interest in specific children and to be honored with recognition of their unique experiences as seniors. Tracy and many of her staff were familiar with the High/Scope approach, and she applied it in their setting. Previously, the Foundation staff had visited a similar program run by High/Scope endorsed trainer Diane Williams Woodruff in another small community—Olathe, Kansas. So there was extensive interest on the part of staff in the High/Scope Early Childhood Department for both providing support for the curriculum implementation and evaluating the novel approach of the program operating in Dexter.

In 1998, after a series of discussions, a proposal was prepared by Ann Epstein, Early Childhood Department director, and submitted to a number of funding sources, including the Charles A. Dana Foundation, New York; the Retirement Research Foundation, Chicago; ITT, New York; General Mills, Minneapolis, Minnesota; the World Heritage Foundation and Borman Fund, Southfield, Michigan; and the Taubman Foundation, Bloomfield Hills, Michigan. While such a "scattergun" approach seldom works, it seemed appropriate for this novel application. Epstein assumed that several foundations would be interested and contact her, but after review, each funding source rejected the proposal. It languished for lack of a possible funding agency as well as lack of High/Scope Foundation staff effort.

Three years later, in the spring of 2001, I was attending a Community Foundation for Southeastern Michigan orientation presentation on a new matching grant program that supported the development of Green Ways (public trails and nature areas). In that presentation, several pinch-hitting Community Foundation staff described their day jobs as program officers for specific interest areas. One staff member, Katie Goatley, was responsible for funding health projects for

elderly populations from a tobacco settlement fund called Healthy
Youth, Healthy Seniors. Bingo! Here was an obvious possible connection to our languishing cross-generational project. In talking with
Goatley after the orientation for the Green Ways initiative, she pointed out that our idea was not an exact match with their view of health
projects they intended to fund. On the other hand, she noted, it was
novel and well within their general interest area and they needed
something that struck out in a new direction. Epstein followed up
with her, adjusted the proposal to better match the Community
Foundation's requirements, and submitted it for review in July 2001.
It was funded in December of that year.

first. There is too much room for confusion over what words
mean, how the program will actually function, and what is
meant by an evaluation. On the other hand, funding obtained as
a result of a requested submission is rarely rapid. The example in
the sidebar illustrates the need for flexibility on the part of High/
Scope staff, and the advantage of always seeking interconnec-
tions whenever and wherever any staff member may be, even
when the event is focused on an entirely different topic. Finally,
the cross-generational funding experience illustrates the need for
persistence: The project idea was generated in 1998; the proposal was rejected by several foundations in 1999; the funds finally
came through at the end of 2001 because of a chance encounter
with project officers at a community foundation, after which
some adjustments had to be made by both parties to complete
the process. The cross–generational experience also illustrates
that good ideas can be funded.

Fundraising Strategies: Foundations and Corporations

For High/Scope, the most important source of money initially
was a mix of grants from foundations for research projects and
federal government contracts for curriculum development and

dissemination projects. My strategy for contacting foundations was to visit the offices of those interested in projects with a national focus. I used the Council Foundation Center's guidebook to learn about each institution. I would peruse the book for names and possible groups that might have the same interests that we did, a difficulty at the time because most foundation executives could not even spell the word "early childhood education." I asked myself a series of questions: Were the projects being funded by a particular group related at all to our areas of interest? Were significantly sized grants awarded? Did anyone at High/Scope have any links with the organization? Had an executive director or a project officer attended any speeches I or another staff member had made? Had there been a casual contact at a meeting, conference, seminar, or elsewhere that could open the door (as in the Community Foundation example)? Cities that offered the best funding prospects were New York, Minneapolis, Chicago, San Francisco, Los Angeles, and Miami, although I also discovered potential funding institutions in other locations. Most of the foundations had a local or otherwise limited geographic interest that made them difficult to tap, even when our interests overlapped. For example, the Woodruff Foundation in Atlanta, Georgia, is a foundation with vast resources but it only funds groups with projects in Atlanta or sometimes elsewhere within the state, but rarely anywhere else. Another large foundation, The Robert Wood Johnson Foundation of Princeton, New Jersey, is focused on medical issues, making geographic location irrelevant. Successful relationships are built only when there are both mutual interests and geographic compatibility between the seeker and the funder.

Corporate philanthropy is typically even more geographically focused because corporate funders pay special attention to cities that have a concentration of their workers, business locations, or national headquarters. Indeed, at one point I felt that I had discovered a fundamental truth when dealing with corporations: If the location of the project could not be seen from the executive dining room windows of the corporation, it was unlikely to be funded. And, of course, that makes good sense. A corporation wishes to serve the community in which it is located. Its workers live there, the quality of life of the local community is important in recruiting new staff and holding on to current workers, establishing a local reputation as a good citizen is important, and a community expects support for its special needs from the corporations operating within its borders.

Raising project money from any source is always an interesting adventure. Indeed, it is a voyage of discovery. I would set up an appointment with a foundation officer in some major city. Usually this appointment was the result of a telephone call I made to talk about my pending visit. Of course, we both knew I was trying to raise money, but that purpose was seldom stated. The officer would warn me that their priorities were under review and all their available funds were committed until the next ice age. I would assure the officer that

"Successful relationships are built only when there are both mutual interests and geographic compatibility between the seeker and the funder."

I just wanted to discuss general education issues of mutual interest, and I just happened to have some time available during whatever trip I was planning. During the initial visit, it was sometimes appropriate to discuss a project I was thinking about, but many times it was not. I could almost judge my potential for success by how long the initial meeting lasted. If it was a meeting to introduce High/Scope and describe our range of work, a good meeting would last one and a half hours. However, if the discussion seemed to dry up in 45 minutes, I knew I was out of luck (this time). In general, two criteria had to be met for possible funding. First, the foundation officer had to be interested in the project, or I had to create that interest. (Sometimes establishing such an interest required several years of meetings.) Second, there had to be mutual personal respect for the process to go forward. If there seemed to be no personal "chemistry" between the players, nothing would happen. Two of my most memorable fundraising ventures are described in other chapters (with the Spencer Foundation in Chapter 2 on the High/Scope Perry Preschool Study and with the Carnegie Corporation of New York in Chapter 4 on the parent-infant work). In this chapter, my examples illustrate the range of experiences and efforts I was involved in over the years in raising funds from foundations for various High/Scope projects.

One of my most unusual experiences involved asking the Lilly Endowment to fund our preschool training work. I had heard that the Endowment was expanding its areas of interest as a result of new federal requirements for yearly charitable disbursements. I believed my task was an intriguing challenge because they had not worked with us before, they were a very large fund, and they were interested in funding a new field—early childhood education. I wrote a general letter of inquiry asking where they were in their planning and if I might come to their office in Indianapolis, Indiana, to discuss our work and some plans we had for dissemination. I heard nothing back, other than hearing through the grapevine that they were overwhelmed with the challenges of start-up. I gave up hope of hearing from them, but decided to wait another month or two and then write them again. Just a week later, though, the High/Scope reception secretary brought me a letter from Lilly. "Ah, instructions," I thought. I opened the envelope and took out the single item it contained—a check for $100,000! I looked closely inside for a letter, a note, but there was nothing else enclosed. After recovering from my astonishment, I wrote a letter, still to their general address, and thanked them profusely. Then, almost shyly, because I didn't know what else to do, I asked if they would like a proposal to substantiate the work we intended to accomplish. I soon received a reply: The new director of the early childhood effort, Joe Howell, had been a classmate of mine at Oberlin College and he was well aware of my early childhood work. Oh, yes, and please do send in that proposal.

Things are not often this easy. Sometimes, it takes years for the interests of a grantor and High/Scope to finally merge because many factors must be brought into alignment. Working with

Nicholas Goodban of the McCormick Tribune Foundation is a good example. Goodban is in my special group of serious and intellectual foundation officials who have a broad range of interests. While he was at the Joyce Foundation in Chicago, we met about once a year for lunch when I happened to be in Chicago. While there did not seem to be a match between what the Joyce Foundation was undertaking and what High/Scope needed, Goodban had many good ideas and made cogent observations. I always learned a great deal from talking with him. After a number of years, Goodban moved to the McCormick Tribune Foundation as their executive director. There, his board of directors gradually became interested in early childhood education, including research on program effects. Consequently, things changed dramatically in our relationship in the fall of 1997. One of Goodban's project officers called and asked if we had obtained funding for our age-40 follow-up of the High/Scope Perry Preschool Study, which Goodban and I had discussed over the years. Their board was interested in obtaining more evidence about the effects of early childhood education. "No, we have not even started looking for funding," I replied, "but the proposal is ready and it is time for us to make such a request." We submitted the proposal, and the Tribune Foundation officer conducted a site visit during which she peppered us with solid questions and suggestions. We adapted the proposal to meet her concerns as much as possible. We asked for $400,000 to fund the three-year effort. Just before the proposal went to the board for approval, the program officer called and asked if we could begin with only $100,000. With nothing in hand, that amount sounded fine: "Yes, go ahead." After the board meeting, the program officer called with the outcome: "No funding, sorry. The board members have other things on their plate."

"Sometimes, it takes years for the interests of a grantor and High/Scope to finally merge because many factors must be brought into alignment."

A year passed; now it was fall 1998. The phone rang. Larry Schweinhart, director of research, talked with the program officer who asked him to submit the proposal again, just as is, no changes. (An easy "yes" on our part!) "Would $200,000 be all right this year?" the officer asked, surprising us. We did not understand the request, given the experience of the previous year, but "yes" was certainly the excited reply. After the subsequent board meeting, the project officer called to tell us that the board did not fund the project at the requested $200,000 level, fulfilling our worst fears. However, she continued, "We want to fund the entire project at $400,000, and if you need more money to complete the work, please come back to us." I was ecstatic. To have what I think of as my most important contribution to the early childhood field fully funded for the mid-life study was an enormous load off my shoulders.

Both these examples were not that common in my fundraising efforts. More typical were chance meetings with a foundation official or program officer at a convention or a seminar. We would arrange to meet sometime in the future to discuss what mutual interests High/Scope and the particular foundation might have. A meeting would follow with the understanding that nothing High/Scope was doing was probably of any interest to the program officer. ("However, would you please send some information about High/Scope?" I always would.) Then about a year or so later, another meeting would occur and, yes, there was some mutual interest. ("Why don't you write that project idea up, nothing fancy now, and send it in for review?") Usually funding in some format would arrive later after a very humanlike gestation period of nine months. A good example of this is my interaction with a foundation in New York. (The firm policy of this foundation is that they remain completely anonymous.) I met one of their project officers at a national meeting of both grantors and grantees, called the Independent Sector. There was absolutely no discussion of either our work or their foundation's interests; just an exchange of business cards. Taking a chance, I made an appointment with the officer when I was again in New York, something this foundation rarely allows because their policy is to call you and not to accept institutional requests. The brief meeting included a short discussion of High/Scope research and our Curriculum Comparison Project Study—it was a discouraging 45 minutes. A year later, another chance meeting occurred with the same individual at the same national conference, and there was another follow-up meeting in New York with more general discussion. Almost a year after that meeting, another project officer from the foundation called to request a proposal on the Curriculum Comparison Project Study, and they funded the next three years of the follow-up. They have funded nothing for us since.

"To have what I think of as my most important contribution to the early childhood field fully funded for the mid-life study was an enormous load off my shoulders."

These funding experiences are fairly typical of my 40 years of experience in developing projects and funding them. As I look at it in retrospect, it makes sense. High/Scope was active in program areas involving social and educational change. The 1970s and 1980s produced great shifts in public opinion as to what might be possible for public schools, especially for early education (our major area of interest). In discussions with foundation officials, I had the opportunity to acquaint them with some of the advances in the early childhood education field. As their foundations closed out old lines of work, I was offering a possible new one connected to a strong institution. So, the major societal changes of the 1970s and 1980s were a great help to High/Scope in obtaining funding from foundations and corporations.

Fundraising Strategies: Government Agencies

During the early 1970s, the other major source of High/Scope funding was local, state, and federal program contracts. As the number of these agency requests for proposals (RFPs) increased, staff began to discuss the advisability of bidding on these types of federal contracts to support an increase in the activities of the Foundation. During the pre–High/Scope days of the 1960s, the main sources of government money were state funds for classroom operation and federal money for Follow Through and Planned Variation Head Start work. When we became independent in 1970, all staff realized that we had to expand our contacts and increase our range of work. Dennis Deloria, who headed up the Research Department, suggested that we should go after federal contracts. He felt our longitudinal project work gave us the necessary research background and our field training efforts (such as Follow Through) gave us experience working at a distance in other locales and with other education groups. In 1974, we succeeded in our first major bidding effort by obtaining an award from the Head Start Bureau to conduct an evaluation of Project Developmental Continuity. It was exciting to prepare the bid, organize the necessary field support, recruit an advisory committee, and do all the other planning work involved in developing a major five-year project. We later bid on a range of such projects, only gradually realizing that federal research contracting was a very specialized area that was tied closely to a complex mix of contacts and friendships between contract houses such as Abt Associates, SRI, Rand Corporation, major university department staff, and government officials. When High/Scope bid on a project, it was from our perspective, and our resulting submission often took us out as a serious contender. For example, we often "corrected" the RFP when our experience indicated that the proposal request had missed an essential issue. We also seemed to bid "high," even though our cost structure was lower than the contract houses. So, in many ways we reduced our possibility for success by our own actions. Each government agency wanted what it asked for, not our interpretation of what it *should* want!

One interesting experience from the 1970s was our bid for evaluating the Head Start Bureau's Parent-Child Center program. I thought we had a chance because of our research with infants and parents, however we lost the bid to Educational Testing Service (ETS). When I saw their bid, I understood. Not only did they bid lower (apparently planning on supplemental grants during the work to complete it), but they had famous names in all positions. I was depressed because I thought we could do a good job and we cared about the program; yet, I was impressed by the obvious quality that such a team would bring to the beleaguered program. About six months after the contract was awarded, I was attending a national conference of the Society for Research on Child Development when an eager young Ph.D. approached me and asked if I could give him some suggestions. He had read reports on our parent-infant work and felt it provided important information. After some discussion of very basic issues, he sighed and said he really needed help. He was directing this huge Parent-Child Center evaluation at ETS and had little to go on. I was dumbfounded. This lad was to stand in for all those famous names who got the grant! Now he wanted me to give him help. I certainly gave him some, but I certainly was angry. Not at him, but at the system that created such outcomes. Bid with famous names and bid low; replace with new faces and ask for supplements to execute the work. While we continued to apply for those types of contracts, and still occasionally do, we select our targets very carefully—making sure they are close to what we do—and we seldom respond to general RFPs. As a result of these experiences, I had an idea that I felt might both circumvent some of these issues and add strength to direct service organizations.

Fundraising Strategies: Using Contracts to Strengthen Institutions

Over the years, I began to realize that much of the research money obtained from the federal government in Washington went to commercial contract houses that bid on any project remotely related to their area of expertise. If the subject became "hot," they would add staff in that specialty and continue their successful bidding practices. These groups would receive funds, build staff and expertise, and attend conferences to present their results. None of the billions of dollars in research funds went to build early childhood institutions in the nation that could both accumulate knowledge in a special program area and develop the skills necessary to evaluate outcomes. In short, a program like Head Start was not receiving the benefit of the funds expended in research on it. Furthermore, since the information collected was of little relevance to local projects, they paid scant attention even to information that might have been useful to them. The contract houses, on the other hand, gained both the dollars and the experience, and they packed up and left when the contract was completed. It seemed to me to be a terrible waste of resources.

This observation led to an idea: Why not set up a Head Start Research Cooperative? Our goal would be to bring research information to local Head Start agencies on issues of importance to people at that level. Local directors, not Washington officials, would constitute a committee to identify project study issues; funds would be spent within agencies to develop local skills and expertise; and results would be interpreted and disseminated by the committee and its staff. With the encouragement of the acting Head Start Commissioner, Clennie Murphy, a special project was established with 10 diverse Head Start centers that represented a range of regional and ethnic participants and with High/Scope providing the research expertise and executive secretary services for the group. The ten center directors constituted an executive committee that made all the administrative decisions for the project. Each research study was to be set up on a four-year cycle. The first year, the committee defined a Head Start problem or issue about which they wished information. High/Scope was responsible for incorporating that issue into a practical but scientific research design. The second year, local data collectors were trained and data were collected. The third year, the data analysis was completed by

"None of the billions of dollars in research funds went to build early childhood institutions in the nation that could both accumulate knowledge in a special program area and develop the skills necessary to evaluate outcomes."

~

High/Scope in cooperation with the participating Head Start agencies, and the reports on the outcomes were prepared and circulated among the committee. The fourth year, the committee reviewed the findings and prepared presentations as teams for various Head Start conferences and other outside groups. As the plan moved forward, after four years, one of each of the steps would be present in each year, as the cycle of research was played out.

This type of project was designed to provide a number of important outcomes. It insured that the question under study was relevant to the Head Start programs. It trained the directors to think about information in a different way so they could better understand the issues affecting their services and more accurately question program practices. It produced staff with research experience at the local agency level because data collection and analysis were accomplished in cooperation with High/Scope researchers. It provided research and evaluation training to local Head Start programs on an ongoing basis. It gave Head Start directors significant information to share with other directors, a much more powerful advocacy group than outside researchers. Finally, it poured money into strengthening local project sophistication and strengthening the skills of staff who remained in the community instead of contracting with an outside group of persons who left the moment the contract ended.

It was a wonderful project that lasted just long enough to complete one four-year cycle and prove powerful as a research design. Watching the Head Start directors from the committee present their work to their peers was a lesson to me in the value of local initiatives. Then the national 1980 elections occurred. Head Start staff changed in Washington, and new contracts were given out to the same old contractors who had failed to impact the field before. While the status quo offered little of value in my opinion, this small Head Start initiative had the potential to revolutionize the way Head Start used research information and conducted its programs.

Of all the projects outside High/Scope–developed work, the Head Start Research Cooperative was my favorite. It had all the ingredients necessary for providing good, sustainable programs and sound research. It was democratic, because the participants asked the questions, reviewed the information, and organized their presentations to outside groups. It produced sound research, because High/Scope was free, within obvious limits, to design the studies as close to good science as possible, egged on by the executive committee. It provided strong staff development both for the teachers participating and for the directors who explained the findings to outside audiences. While there was always the danger of becoming self-serving and contaminating the research, the risk seemed worth it for the payoff. As we struggled to keep the Cooperative funded, we suggested that a series of these groups of ten be established around the country to broaden the advantages to Head Start. The Head Start Research Cooperative costs were $15,000 per year per center (10) and $20,000 per year for the research executive agency. An extraordinary program could be built for the nation's children for $1.7 million a year with 10 groups involving 100 centers supported by 10 different research groups. This amount was a fraction of the total research and training budgets that rarely helped the actual Head Start programs. Ah, my favorite idea, one of many I could not fund.

> *"Of all the projects outside High/Scope–developed work, the Head Start Research Cooperative was my favorite."*

Fundraising Strategies: The High/Scope Endowment

In 1992, it became apparent that unless High/Scope created some independent sources of income, many of our ideas could not be developed nor services sustained. A frightening experience in 1985, with the forced layoff of many staff due to a reduction of grants, was a stark reminder of High/Scope's frailty as an institution. While we were accumulating a surplus in assets through careful management of earned income from High/ Scope Press sales and teacher training revenue, we needed to develop an endowment dedicated to preserving our core functions. Thus, in 1992, from a base of about $3 million in total assets, I set a goal of $10 million in net asset value to be reached by 2000. While the ambitiousness of this goal allowed the High/Scope Board of Directors to enjoy some moments of amusement at my expense, I felt we had to reach it to insure the long-term future of the Foundation and its services.

In the spring of 1993, a major opportunity arose when we learned of a special program sponsored by the Kresge Foundation and the Community Foundation for Southeastern Michigan, called the van Dusen Challenge. This program was specifically designed to enable nonprofit organizations to initiate or expand endowment funds. The program offered training for participating agency staff, especially in deferred giving, required that we hire a development officer to guide the effort, and supplied a small grant to enable us to get started. The program required that the funds be raised within a three-year period and, if the goal was met, the program would match $1 for every $3 raised. With our hat in our hand, we submitted an application to participate at the $3 million level for $1 million match with the program to start in April 1993 and finish in April 1996. We were approved, much to my surprise. Although we met all the criteria, we really were not a direct service group and we had extensive connections to agencies outside Michigan. (Also, to our surprise, we later learned that some other agencies approved at the same level were major Detroit institutions such as the Detroit Institute of Arts and the Detroit Zoo. Fortunately, we did not know that at the time of our application, so avoided feeling totally out of our class.)

How could we raise $3 million when we only had a few in-house staff donations up to this point? Such assets as we did have were obtained the hard way—we earned them. First, we were fortunate to have David Bruno as head of the Adolescent

Department on our staff at the time. He strongly urged that we participate. He had raised money for Oberlin College and was an expansive thinker about such possibilities. He put us in contact with David Clark and Jeptha Carroll. Clark was retired from Oberlin and Tufts University after 20 years as a development officer. Carroll was a retired president of the Nord Family Fund of Lorraine, Ohio. Both men agreed to conduct a series of interviews with selected individuals around the country who knew High/Scope and discuss what our endowment fundraising prospects were. Their basic finding: A possible chance for High/Scope to be successful—with much hard work. Clark, under Bruno's urging, agreed to work more directly with us as an advisor, especially in organizing planned giving opportunities. We hired a series of local individuals to staff the Foundation's new development office, and we got to work.

I should say, while the board supported the endowment drive, they had decidedly mixed opinions about it. These ranged from "It's too great a commitment" to "If High/Scope has an endowment, will that not take the edge off the aggressive search for funding?" Nevertheless, with survey and lukewarm board endorsement in hand, we began. It was a voyage of innocents!

Key to our success was the work of many individuals, but first among those was the sophistication David Clark brought to our efforts. While we were preparing the van Dusen application for the Community Foundation for Southeastern Michigan, Clark brought us a proposal that High/Scope accept property as a means of funding a charitable remainder trust. The donor family knew Clark because of his key role in the development of the Kendall-at-Oberlin retirement community. The family wished to move into Kendall and, by donating their California Pacific Palisades home, such a move would be facilitated. It was proposed that High/Scope create a trust, value to be established by the appraised value of the house ($1.2 million), which would pay a fixed amount each year as long as either donor lived. Even thinking about the proposal was difficult for me. Not only would this be our first deferred gift, but High/Scope would have to fund

~

the trust from our own resources until the property could be sold. There were a lot of questions: Could we accept property in another state? Could we legally do business there—that is, sell the house after we received the title to it? Did we have the resources to fund the trust at the agreed level, regardless of the actual amount for which we could sell the house? Would we be able to invest the money wisely and obtain the income needed to make the trust payments for the lifetime of the donors?

So much of this was new! Clark moved to obtain the appraisal and the board approved the decision. It was obvious that if we wished to both qualify and succeed in the van Dusen endowment effort, we would have to take on such ventures. We accepted the arrangements and submitted our proposal to the Community Foundation, with our first major trust already in place to indicate that we could accomplish our goals. (This unusually bold step was probably instrumental in the approval we received from the Community Foundation for the $3 million level of effort.)

It was a risky venture indeed. Soon after we received title to the house and before it was sold, the 1994 Los Angeles earthquake occurred. There were mud slides along the coast highway and fires burned out of control in the area to the north. Needless to say, we were unable to sell the house for the pre-earthquake appraisal, though it was undamaged. It was finally sold to the only individual who made an offer, and it was sold at less then the appraised price. Over the years since, the trust has paid the donor on time, every time. We had the great bull market of the 1990s to compensate for the 1994 Los Angeles earthquake losses. The trust has increased in value, and when it "matures" (as the philanthropic field so gently refers to the death of the last beneficiary), it should provide significant endowment support to High/Scope's direct service programs for children and youth.

The fruits of the campaign also included gifts from individuals of stocks and cash. Trusts were established for three major donors. We took in several houses and over 500 acres of farmland as bargain sales. (A bargain sale is a gift where the nonprofit institution is permitted to buy a property for less than appraised value. The institution immediately sells the property to gain the underlying value and pay related costs. Thus a $200,000 home donated for a $150,000 payment is a bargain sale. The donor takes the $150,000 in some form—cash, trade, trust—and takes a tax write off for the $50,000 gift.)

This idea of a bargain sale was completely new to us and a little frightening. Before the campaign started, the board turned down an offer of a Cincinnati, Ohio, riverfront property bargain sale where the owner was willing to sell at $160,000 a property that sold shortly after our refusal for $240,000. The board felt it was risky and, well, dishonest. During the three years of the Challenge, the board learned about many possible ways to transfer personal wealth to a nonprofit institution, and bargain sales were one of them. Finally, however, the last month of the drive still found us about half a million dollars short of our goal. We knew that without obtaining the entire amount, none of the matching van Dusen funds would be available. A board member saved the day by arranging a complicated major gift for the amount required during the last week. On the next to last day, I called three cash donors and asked for $25,000 total or about $8,000 from each so that we would be certain to exceed the amount required. I brought in my checkbook; I was not going to let some amount that I could handle make us fail. All donated. We made our goal by the Friday deadline of 5 p.m., and the Community Foundation provided the $1 million match as agreed. We had an endowment and were on our way to our $10 million asset goal.

Since the initial van Dusen Challenge effort, the Foundation has continued to build the endowment. Several major trusts and a major land donation have contributed to the growth. In our small world, the funds come about in unusual and unexpected ways. A $1 million 20-year trust was obtained by the Foundation because of an informal speech I made at a dinner meeting 10 years earlier. Another at the same funding level came about because the family knew our development officer, Michelle

Aloia, as a child. Indeed, that was an interesting situation. The UPS shares the family wished to donate were held as options by the husband. Because the corporation was going public, these options could be transferred only during a limited time period, and that window closed at 5 p.m. on a Monday. The family did not receive all the information they needed to make a decision until the last minute, and then they called our development officer on Friday. Indeed, a last-minute effort was required. Arrangements were made to meet at High/Scope headquarters over the last weekend that the stock could still be traded. The wife traveled from Illinois; her husband drove down from a moose-hunting trip in northern Ontario, Canada; and Clark returned early from a trip to New Jersey. The forces gathered, and the trust documents were developed by Clark and agreed to on Sunday. Attorneys were faxed copies and their approvals came in Monday morning, then the documents were signed. Michelle Aloia took a commercial flight Monday afternoon and made the bank deadline in Philadelphia to register the transaction with about a half hour to spare. All breathed a sigh of relief.

"One key to our development of trusts has been the organization of the High/Scope Trust Advisory Committee to accept and monitor these funds."

One key to our development of trusts has been the organization of the High/Scope Trust Advisory Committee to accept and monitor these funds. The Trust is chaired by Dale Embry, a principal in the MeadowBrook Investment Advisors (and one of my sons-in-law). It has members from accounting, law, real estate development, and corporate operations. Clark is the senior trust official and takes care of the actual paperwork involved. This committee offers the donors a broad range of experience and the opportunity to know who is advising on the management of their money. Interestingly, most of those considering donations to the Foundation have little interest in using traditional vehicles such as bank trust departments. Given the record of success obtained, the process of working through the High/Scope Trust Advisory Committee seems to be a sound one.

$\sim$

Funding High/Scope's Projects

Over the decades, two basic trends have influenced High/Scope's ability to fund projects. First and foremost, the content of what High/Scope does has usually been groundbreaking. When we first began our parent-infant work, for example, it was not an area of much interest to grantors. In the health area, of course, there was much interest, but not in providing parent education to enhance infant growth and development. The same was true for early childhood preschool programs for disadvantaged children. Thus, the potential group of grantors for these efforts was always small. We always seemed to be ahead of the curve. In the 1960s, we asked, Does preschool education work? Few grantors were interested in answering this question. What leadership there was came from the federal government's Head Start implementation. Since foundations were not interested in talking about early childhood development, the Carnegie Corporation of New York took a real plunge into the future by funding our early work with parents and infants. In the 1970s, we were asking the question, Which theoretical model of early childhood education is most effective? But foundations were just beginning to fund some local preschools and educating themselves about the field. So the idea of exploring differential model effects was not of interest to them then. In the 1980s, High/Scope was actively training specialists to implement the High/Scope approach around the country in response to the need for high-quality programs. But foundations wanted to fund operation of early childhood education programs for poor children in their geographic area only, and they seemed to assume that one preschool program was the same as any other. By the 1990s, it appeared that our interests and those of the funding agencies were drawing closer. High/Scope was focused on improving program quality by training a national leadership group of local educational consultants

"Finding funding for High/Scope activities has always had a 'take a chance, believe in us' flavor."

176

This 1977 photo shows representatives of the Harry E. Bagley Foundation of Detroit, Michigan, visiting the High/Scope Demonstration Preschool, which was purchased with funds provided by the foundation. The visitors were hosted by the author (at right) and the preschoolers.

who could supervise teachers in the field. Between national Head Start and a wide range of preschool programs initiated by the states, there were almost enough programs to serve disadvantaged children, so foundations were less interested in funding individual children in individual programs. It seemed that the recognition of the need to apply high-quality, validated model programs had yet to take hold. Thus, finding funding for High/Scope activities has always had a "take a chance, believe in us" flavor.

The other change affecting High/Scope funding has occurred within the foundations themselves. The foundations we approached in the 1970s had a general range of interests, such as child health, adolescent education, and the like. They welcomed innovative ideas from any source. While the program officers were far from passive, they listened well and judged the idea against its chances for operational success, the effectiveness of our design, the quality of staff who would implement the work, and other such criteria. Thus, my strategy of dropping in and discussing ideas with project officers was particularly effective because the opportunities were there. By the 1980s, I believe foundation boards had become disillusioned by the results of their funding decisions. That is, they realized they had helped here and there but had effected few systemic changes. As a result, they altered their funding strategies, developing specific interest areas that gradually narrowed. Program officers often accepted requests only for specific types of projects—for example, Spanish bilingual programs with migrants. This limited funding for research and development programs. At

"Sometimes, it is not necessary to have evidence that new ideas are good ideas; unfortunately, it is enough that they are new."

this point, the foundation project officers themselves began to propose research and service project agendas, directing rather than responding to the work of the field. (This was not always a detriment. For example, the Dewitt-Wallace Readers Digest Fund required us to add a service-learning component to our summer leadership development program for adolescents. As it was finally implemented, this component strengthened our program.) But this direct involvement in projects progressed to foundation officers actually designing programs and requesting bids from organizations to participate. The Carnegie Corporation's multistate middle school program is an example. Sometimes a foundation would actually approach communities and offer money if the community would follow the foundation's design. The Edna McConnell Clark public schools program followed this path.

There are good reasons for foundations to assume direction and guidance over grantees. First, there is simply more money available—more in the foundations' endowments that must be spent and more money at both the federal and state levels. For example, when we first received Carnegie Corporation of New York funds in 1967, their endowment was slightly over $100 million. In December 2000, the Corporation had an endowment in excess of $1.9 billion, this in spite of paying out 5 percent of gross value each year as required by law. These additional dollars often chase a limited number of new ideas. The 2001 interest in brain research is a good example of information from extraordinary progress in a highly specialized field jumping track to direct application to education and parenting. Sometimes, it is not necessary to have evidence that new ideas are good ideas; unfortunately, it is enough that they are new.

Second, so many ideas that appeared on first blush to have great potential simply have not worked. From the Boot Camps for first offenders or Scared Straight as crime prevention programs, to D.A.R.E. as a drug prevention program, to the many parent education programs to help disadvantaged infants, many foundation investments simply have not paid off. Once burned, it is natural that foundations should try another approach. Bill Gates contributed $100 million for world health. Ted Turner contributed $1 billion to the United Nations for special projects. Some foundations are giving communities large amounts of money to work with ideas that the community feels are appropriate to ameliorate local conditions: the Casey Foundation, for youth; the Kellogg Foundation, for community development; the Annenberg Foundation, for public education. But these approaches are also fraught with problems: Who owns the project intellectually? Can you actually hire people in education and social services to innovate? Is it the opportunity provided by the grant program money or is it the underlying initiative of innovative individuals that makes programs effective? When there are matching funds required, as in the Annenberg $60 million per community projects, it seems all other community philanthropic activities stop because money is committed to meet the match. So, High/Scope has sought other ways to insure that its services are sustained and available. These ideas are discussed in the chapters on High/Scope Press and on High/Scope's training programs.

~

What I Learned About Fundraising: A Summary

Looking back at my fundraising efforts in seeking grants from foundations and corporations and contracts and grants from government agencies, I can say that High/Scope has generally been successful. The basic principles I followed:

1. *Create a new idea to help solve problems that children and families face.* These ideas are most valid when they grow out of direct experience melded with theory. For example, the motivation for early childhood education, as expressed in the High/Scope Perry Preschool Study, grew out of the difficulty I faced as a school psychologist working with disadvantaged youth. The need for change was pushed down into the preschool years when I could not develop curriculum reform in the elementary schools. The program adopted the discipline of theory to structure the curriculum developed for the classroom and parent visits. Adherence to a theoretical approach limits choices by staff, but it permits and facilitates in-depth understanding of the program, opens the door to systematic training, and permits judgment of both child growth and program quality.

2. *Be persistent in developing financial support for the idea.* There is little reason for any foundation or government agency to be an exact match for a proposed project. Usually, a prolonged search is required to obtain funds. Most foundation and government project officers have not gone through the experiences that have led to the proposed program. They do not understand why the approach has a chance to solve a problem that the schools or society face. The organizing theory behind the project may not represent their personal viewpoint. Perhaps even more important, the individual and institution proposing the work may not be well enough established

to be recognized and accepted as a reliable grantee. Thus, persistence is required to orient the project officer to the individual making the request, the project, and the institution.

Both for me personally and for High/Scope, all these forces were in play, especially initially. "Now, what high school was that?" was a frequent response upon first contact, when I named my institution. My initial inquiries were followed up by a series of meetings that gradually educated the project officers about our proposed program and educated me in the workings of the funding organizations. In my experience, from the first "No, we don't get involved in that subject area" to an expressed willingness to accept a proposal was about 12 to 18 months. Funding typically occurred nine months later, with the entire process taking about two years overall. It should be emphasized that obtaining financial support is a long and difficult process. It takes real effort not to become discouraged.

3. *Once the work is funded, carry it out in as professional a manner as possible.* Achieving this goal is essential for further funding to be made available. For example, High/Scope's work with adolescents was enabled by a series of grants from the Knight Foundation of Miami, Florida. The first several grants were small, one-year awards; the stated purpose was to test our ability to deliver. Finding that we could execute our work, a much larger three-year grant request was approved. Such steps do not make things easy, but do make projects possible.

4. *Make the findings from the work as well known as possible.* The publication of a report from the project describing both the research and the content of the program is very important. Other professionals need to know what happened and why. Conference presentations, participation in seminars and work groups, discussions with the news media, and preparation of short summaries in layman's

terms are all important components of this dissemination process. When foundations look at new project ideas, they are influenced by the publicity and impact a program has achieved as it relates to their broader mission.

5. *Make the next project an outgrowth of what was learned in the first.* Project officers appreciate continuity of work, extensive development of ideas, and, above all, honesty in the recognition of the true outcomes of the first project. No matter what the researcher might believe, if the project is well done, the results are facts. Progress can be made only by accepting the outcomes. In my case, two projects illustrate this need for program developer integrity. First is the Parent-Infant Education Project, which produced outcomes I did not expect or desire. End-of-project data verified our support for such a program and the funding agency was anxious to expand the work. So far, so good. Then, first-year follow-up and five-year follow-up found no significant evidence of impact on either the parent or the child. Stunned, we floundered, argued, and tried to explain away the data, and in general did all we could to avoid the facts. It was a well-run project that obtained data clearly refuting our beliefs. The Carnegie Corporation project officer read our report, looked at the data, and stopped the funding; we were unable to continue the original line of work. In order to salvage something, I altered the program focus to helping parents in stressful settings. This enabled us to obtain funds from other sources for a "softer" area of parent development. Later, as more work was done in the field by other researchers, we discovered that our findings were typical of the field; most parent education projects in support of infant development produce limited results on most measures.

The second project was the High/Scope Preschool Curriculum Demonstration Project, which initially produced data that verified the equality and importance of any well-run early education model program in helping children succeed in school. Only later, in long-term follow-up, was firm evidence found that curriculum methods *do* matter. After the first year of formal schooling, all three methods of educating preschool children produced equal academic results. In this case, we had identified success in service provision, but no differentiation in approach. This equivalence of academic success continued throughout the participants' schooling. As time passed, however, children participating in the Direct Instruction method showed a significant lack of social skills and abilities. This finding was verified through further follow-up over the years, and much of High/Scope's work in teacher training, assessment instrument development, and consultations with international agencies and foreign governments is based on the implications of these findings. In this case, the project laid a firm foundation for future development after a surprising initial finding.

Funding projects is an acquired discipline—holding in check one's most cherished dreams and forcing them into well-conceptualized, written statements. Establishing a dialogue with a foundation or agency project officer provides a reality check on what is really understood and possible. At times I fretted and complained about the lack of understanding of our work and our potential contribution, but the process of obtaining funding is an important one, especially for the young professional. Over the years, I was fortunate to have intelligent and curious project officers who were willing to bend the rules at times and willing to take chances on out-of-the-mainstream ideas proposed by untried researchers from an untested institution. From such early support, High/Scope has gradually built its reputation and its services to children, youth, and families.

~

8

Financial Development and Management

L ike it or not, every institution needs to secure funds to
operate. High/Scope is no exception. In the years since
High/Scope's founding in July 1970, the reality of the
need to obtain funds has been a constant check on the idealism
and energy of both the staff and me. Building a funded budget
from zero dollars each year came as a shock after the public
school experience (where public school taxes provided a steady
basic level of income, no matter what). Over the years, major
changes were required in raising resources. But first, a history
of events…

Funding the Work—The Early Years

In 1970, when the Foundation was established, I moved all the
grants and contracts from three organizations (Ypsilanti Public
Schools, Eastern Michigan University, and the precursor High/
Scope Foundation) to fund the new institution. In a sense, the
decade of the 1960s, which preceded this move, was our start-up
time and the beginning of the development of our intellectual capital in terms of acquiring curriculum knowledge and prestige and
conducting research studies. However, there were no financial
resources to speak of other than the grants and contracts we
held at the time. While Superintendent Ray Barber was instru-

mental in requesting that I either leave the school system or work only on local public school projects, he was also instrumental in making possible my decision to establish an independent foundation. He not only signed off on the transfer of the contracts and grants committed to me through the schools but also extended the opportunity to keep such basic building blocks as chairs, desks, file cabinets, and other office equipment. Further, the central accounting office showed that the special services department owed a fairly large sum, for those days, of around $30,000 to central administration for various chargeable expenses. Barber cancelled that debt so I could start the new institution without any obligations except to the work at hand. In my last interview with him, he said, "Well, my thorn-in-the-side is leaving, but now who will I find to do the work?" Of the various superintendents under whom I worked during my 12-year tenure at the Ypsilanti Public Schools, Barber at least understood my programs and what I was attempting to accomplish. I almost felt like I was betraying him by leaving him alone to wrestle with the complex and endless problems of the public schools.

Establishing Rules for Accounting

In setting up the new institution I had several rules for its financial operation. In the Ypsilanti Public Schools, the chief financial officer had life-and-death control over all purchasing decisions and other expenditures for such things as field trips, special equipment, and so on. A crusty, experienced officer, Don Porter, ruled with an iron hand. He always facilitated my work, perhaps because I was always bringing him money, but he was the bane of all the principals. When I hired our young accountant/bookkeeper Len Federer in 1970 (Len remained with High/Scope in that position until he retired in 2001), I had two instructions for him. First, he was to keep us honest by monitoring all the detailed grant and contract provisions to keep us in compliance. Second, he was to sign all purchase orders if the proper procedures had been followed and there was money in the program

⌒

account: "It is not your decision whether or not the department needs the request, that is the province of the department director," I said.

Taking Risks for Financial Survival

The first year of Foundation operation was a financial nightmare. The just-appointed director of administration had a Ph.D., which I soon learned meant that he talked like a textbook but didn't offer any practical solutions to the real problems we were facing. He left at the end of that year, and Len Federer took full responsibility in 1971 for all of the finances, including budget construction, collection for services, working with outside auditors, and reporting to the board of directors. Collecting on contract services that High/Scope staff provided to various school districts did lend some levity to the process. In

"The first year of Foundation operation was a financial nightmare."

mid-October 1971, we received payment in full from a school district in Wyoming for a summer workshop our staff had conducted. The only address on the envelope was "Ypsilanti High Rise Group, Ypsilanti, Michigan." The post office decided that was us (it was) and delivered it. Our bank decided the name was close enough, and cashed the check. We made the monthly payroll once again.

Indeed, making the monthly payroll is an indication of a sound institution. In the early days, living up to this mark was more difficult to manage than I had imagined. Being new and not holding any investment capital, the Foundation had few reserves available to cover late-arriving checks or prepayments for needed services. In 1972, this was especially difficult. I worked out a solution with Chuck Wallgren, the new director of operations, that involved using the High/Scope Camp property owned by Phyllis and me as security for a temporary loan. I would go into our local Clinton Bank and meet with Dan Boutell, the executive vice-president and co-owner of the bank. (Yes, back in those days small towns had locally owned banks and the staff knew

187

all the customers. You could even call the bank and talk to the president without landing in voice-mail-jail.) I would say to Boutell that the Foundation (which held its accounts at his bank) would not be able to meet payroll this month because the various checks we were expecting had failed to arrive. Boutell would have the loan papers drawn up with the camp acreage as collateral, and I would sign for the loan. Miraculously, the late checks always arrived and the bank loan would be repaid within a week or two. Then a month or two later, the process would be repeated. Phyllis worried about the sudden loss of the Camp if some Foundation-related check finally did fail to arrive. Federer and Wallgren assured me that such a scenario could never happen, so I kept signing the loan papers as needed. Eventually, Foundation finances improved and some reserves were developed. Most interesting is that the last two times I took out the loan, Boutell made the loan with a simple handshake, no papers.

Experiencing Financial Audits

One of the prime issues in accounting is to keep the records straight to provide expenditure information to project directors. The flip side of this is to keep the records straight for outside auditors who either represent specific projects, agencies, or governmental groups, or are independent auditors the Foundation hires to review the books each year and report to the board of directors on the actual financial health of the institution. High/Scope has been fortunate to have an external local auditor who understands the work of the Foundation and yet, in the best tradition of the profession, holds our feet to the fire on even the smallest detail. Neil Loney and his staff have been most helpful in protecting the Foundation, first from itself by making very sure that we followed the rules, and second by enabling us to be prepared for agency-initiated audits. Two special audits come to mind.

Chuck Wallgren always had a way with handling money and resolving financial concerns. Usually, his input took the form of thoughtful development of an argument as to which direction to go on purchases, or which contractor to employ, or how to

~

negotiate with federal general accounting officers. Nevertheless, he had a complicated practical-joker side to him as well. The Foundation had obtained a large, multiyear grant award from the Lilly Endowment for conducting preschool training, one of our earliest projects. All of us were proud of our high-quality work. So when the auditor from Lilly called and said he wanted to inspect our books, he was more than welcome. He indicated to Wallgren he planned to visit in the early afternoon on a Friday in the spring. He commented that he hoped he could finish the audit in about an hour because we were a big institution and, from what he could see from our reports, kept proper accounts. After the audit review, he said, he would be heading to northern Michigan for the weekend to open his family's summer cottage and would appreciate an early start. Chuck assured him we would open all our records for him. He could certainly plan on an early start on his journey. Ah, but this is what actually happened:

> *The appointed Friday afternoon rolled around.*
>
> *The auditor arrived; parked in a guest slot; entered the building.*
>
> *Chuck gave him coffee; talked in detail about fishing and deer hunting.*
>
> *The auditor got restless as the time passed; looked at his watch.*
>
> *Chuck escorted him to Len's office off the mailroom in the basement; one high window.*
>
> *The auditor looked uncomfortable in the cluttered room, perched on a wooden teacher's chair.*
>
> *Chuck asked Len for all the grant records.*
>
> *The auditor looked relieved; focused his attention.*
>
> *Len picked up a shoebox stuffed with scraps of receipts, some loose change.*
>
> *The auditor looked both shocked and bewildered.*
>
> *Len shook the box and mentioned that it sounded as if there were a little money left over.*
>
> *The auditor sputtered something about a lost weekend; incompetent nonprofits.*

~

Chuck, feigning innocence, left him to hang and twist in the wind.

The auditor sat there, looking stupefied.

Chuck finally relented and gave him the complete computer printouts.

Everyone laughed—especially Chuck and Len.

The auditor was on his way to northern Michigan within the allotted hour.

Chuck and Len looked smug for the rest of the day.

Another audit, however, tested both the patience of the staff and the system of bookkeeping we had established. One morning on a brisk September day, I was working in the small solarium conference room in Hutchinson House, our headquarters in Ypsilanti. I noticed a black car drive in and park in the visitors' slot near the entrance. Two men in black suits, long coats, and briefcases alighted from the car. (Obviously not our usual visitors to see the preschool demonstration class.) A few minutes later, my secretary asked if I could step out and greet two unannounced auditors from United States Agency for International Development (USAID). With a little concern, I greeted the two and asked what we could do for them. After showing me their official badges, their next response was to read me my Miranda rights and ask me to direct them to our accounting department! They were there to audit our books. Soundly intimidated, I asked what area they wanted to look at and what year. "All areas, all years," was the very formal reply. I escorted them to the Accounting Department and asked that all assistance be rendered during their (unspecified length) visit. It seemed to me that the whole Foundation hushed as the word spread through the halls.

The USAID auditors had two fundamental questions: First, was the money being spent according to the terms of our USAID contract? Thus, they were looking at all of the international grant records. Second, was their money being spent with the same rules as applied to all the other foundation and government grants and contracts? This meant did we use the same policies for overhead rates, per diem reimbursement to staff, staff personnel policies, bidding procedures for materials, and so forth. To verify this policy, they planned to audit all of our books for all projects and all staff.

The initial weeks were glum. The auditors were hostile and assumed we were hiding things. They kept pushing the bookkeeping department and Len Federer, our accountant, for more specific detail as backup information. At the end of about three weeks the two auditors came to my office to ask me to explain myself. They had found that one staff member who worked on the AID grant only 25 percent of the time was being paid 100 percent of her salary. I said, "Yes, that was true." (She had a 25 percent appointment, and we always paid 100 percent of what was due, for whatever time we contracted.) Almost crestfallen, they asked about a similar salary arrangement for another staff member in another department. Same answer. Even people working 25 percent time want all of their salary that is due. I had a hard time understanding what the problem was.

After an extensive audit by one auditor for 12 weeks and two other auditors for a total of five weeks, the closeout meeting was a little disappointing:

"Why did you come to High/Scope and spend so much time on a relatively minor grant?" I asked.

"Oh," said they, "we were looking through agency records and noticed that High/Scope had not had an agency audit, so we came."

"What did you actually find that you can share with us?"

"Well, you wrongfully charged $10 in one USAID expense category. It belonged to another grant. Also, you charged your general fund $1,200 in travel expenses that should have been charged to the USAID grant."

"Do you have any recommendations?"

"Yes," said they, "you must keep daily and hourly time sheets on each individual to allocate costs more clearly. Yes, you must do so even for the professionals who are not paid on an hourly rate. Yes, you must do so even if they are working only on one grant or contract."

～

"Did you enjoy your long stay in the Ypsilanti–Ann Arbor area?" we asked, trying still to be polite.

"Yes," they said, "we stayed at the Holiday Inn on Carpenter Road, Ann Arbor, on the west side of the street. You see," they explained, "the per diem there is twice what we would be able to collect if we stayed near Ypsilanti on the east side of the road."

"All audits are welcome and necessary to keep organizations and staff conscious of the need for maintaining accurate records and proper procedures to protect both the work and the institution."

And then these protectors of our nation's integrity went out to their black car—in their black suits and long black coats, carrying their black briefcases—and left.

In actual fact, all such audits are welcome and necessary to keep organizations and staff conscious of the need for maintaining accurate records and proper procedures to protect both the work and the institution. This particular federal audit, however, had an element of intimidation that was either the natural working style of the individuals conducting it or some sort of planned but unsuccessful exposé, and I resented this.

Responding to Financial Challenges

Over the years, the Foundation has created a footprint of growth in response to the financial challenges. During our first fiscal year, ending June 30, 1971, the Foundation had a gross income of $826,000 from all sources. The primary income was derived from federal grants and a few awards from foundations. (The list in the appendices on p. 301 is a partial historic record of selected projects with their funding source indicated.) By 1981, the income of the Foundation from operations had risen by more than 300 percent to $2,574,000. During the next decade, the Foundation survived the impact of changes in grant giving during the Reagan Administration in the early part of the decade, and by 1991 operating income rose by more than 100 percent to $5,400,000. By 2001, the last year of my tenure, the operating income was $8,627,000, a 60 percent increase. But such numbers do not tell all of the story; indeed, they tell very little other than that from 1970 on we were successful in focusing on our work and gaining the support necessary to accomplish our training, research, and service goals.

However, we faced a major dilemma produced by rapidly rising prices and great inflation through the end of the 1990s: Even with rising income, the expense of staff and other costs associated with accomplishing our work increased in tandem. (See the sidebar on pp. 194–197 for a history of High/Scope facilities acquisitions.)

"Over the years, the Foundation has created a footprint of growth in response to the financial challenges."

In fiscal year 1971, the Foundation had 59 staff, about the same number as had moved with me in July 1970 from the Ypsilanti Public Schools and Eastern Michigan University to High/Scope. In 1981, full-time staff numbered 71, reflecting a fairly gradual growth. However, from 1982 to 1985, the Foundation had a reduction in income as long-term grants ended and no replacement funds were located to maintain staff. By 1985, at the bottom of the income loss, the number of staff members had dropped to 31. Since that time, the number of staff at the Foundation has gradually increased. Obviously, the increasing budget of the Foundation translated into higher salaries for staff, in keeping with inflation and payments for higher costs of doing business. The overall growth in the Foundation has been aided by the addition of numerous High/Scope–trained educational field consultants who help staff deliver high-quality training programs to teachers and administrators around the country and in other nations.

However, the funding the Foundation receives has changed dramatically over the years. In 1971, government contracts such as National Follow Through and Planned Variation Head Start provided most of our support. We no longer operated our demonstration preschool with state monies, but used resources from tuition and Foundation teacher-training projects. Our demonstration elementary school used curriculum develop-

High/Scope's Facilities:
Controlling Costs, Building Equity

Over the years, the Foundation has been housed in a number of buildings—initially rental buildings and then buildings we purchased to control costs and to build equity. In 1970, High/Scope rented the Greek Revival-style Breakey house on North Huron Street in Ypsilanti, where we had our offices when we were part of the Ypsilanti Public Schools. With its four massive Greek columns (common to this type of house) and formal rooms on the first floor, the Breakey house gave us a good feeling of solid permanence. Such a feeling was something staff of a brand-new organization needed, both for ourselves and for our visitors. All the rooms were converted to offices except for the formal living room, which served as our conference room. Even the low-ceilinged ballroom on the second floor was carefully divided into offices. Within the year, we also rented a Tudor-styled house located two buildings away to provide more space as we added more staff and projects.

In 1975, Mrs. Oscar Hobbs, owner of the Breakey House, requested a substantial increase in rents. Chuck Wallgren and I felt it was time to purchase our own building so we could better plan for the future, control costs, and permit participation in the appreciation of land values. We considered purchasing several historic houses directly across the street from the Breakey house. While old and requiring extensive repair, the historic houses were well constructed, the community would appreciate their restoration, and they looked out on Riverside Park and the Huron River. Unexpectedly, early one morning in late spring, Wallgren reported he had heard unofficially that a large historic landmark house on North River Street was for sale. Not yet on the market, a price had been set for it and the owner was anxious to sell without using a real estate agency.

Wallgren made an appointment to see the owner early one morning. I knew the house from the outside because I had driven by it for years. A large Queen Anne style building, it was set on three acres covering the River Street end of the block. It was a large, 40-room, four-story mansion that was built in 1902 by Shelly Byron Hutchinson, the man who founded S&H Green Stamps in the late 1800s. After his initial success in the trading stamp business, Hutchinson returned to Ypsilanti and built his mansion across the street from the small house that was his birthplace. His new home had grand views of the Huron River, the trains that went from Detroit to points west, and the Ypsilanti Normal College on the hill across the water. He used imported lumber and craftsmen and placed Tiffany-style stained glass windows throughout the house. Hutchinson was a building pioneer because he installed an indoor swimming pool, and he also built a ballroom with an orchestra gallery on the third floor. The Hutchinson House was converted to an apartment building in the 1940s, so the pool was covered and the ballroom was divided into rooms, with a false ceiling installed to permit more rooms on the fourth floor.

With the purchase of Hutchinson House, we remodeled to take advantage of a building large enough to hold all of the staff. For

A view of High/Scope's headquarters—the historic Hutchinson House in Ypsilanti, Michigan.

several places where the doorways were sealed or fireplaces covered for the apartment conversion, we were fortunate enough to find the complex moldings and fittings stored in the large attic. Thus, the building returned to a single-purpose structure. Unfortunately, we did not uncover the intact swimming pool nor restore the ballroom. Perhaps those steps will be taken in the future.

Since moving to the Hutchinson House, we have purchased seven residential houses adjacent to or near the property, each on deep lots, thus adding three and a third more acres to the High/ Scope headquarters and providing offices and house rental units. In 1976, one of these acquisitions (that had housed a large beauty salon and an attached three-car garage) was renovated to house some staff offices and our preschool demonstration school. The salon was modernized and became a conference training space. The extra-large three-car garage kept up our tradition of using found space to house our demonstration preschool center. Our central philosophy is that visitors need to see space that is like theirs with children similar to those they teach; not something so special they feel that the program works well because of an outstanding facility or unique children.

In the early days, finding space to operate our demonstration school was a little complicated. Leaving the one-room schoolhouses that had served as our classroom space for the High/Scope Preschool

High/Scope's Demonstration Preschool at High/Scope's headquarters in Ypsilanti, Michigan.

Curriculum Comparison Project and belonged to the public schools, we rented space in a local church—the First Baptist Church of Ypsilanti—for the 1970–1971 school year. The next year, we moved the school into rental space at the local Free Methodist Church. During that year, we decided to purchase an old Nash car dealership on East Cross Street in Ypsilanti that was two blocks away from our main buildings so that we could renovate it to house our demonstration classrooms. With the help of the W. T. Grant Foundation, the Nash dealership building was purchased and remodeled during the summer of 1972. This building provided space for us to continue our demonstration preschool and to expand the elementary classroom to include more grades. In 1976, the preschool was moved once again to the just-purchased Hutchinson House property, the elementary classroom was discontinued, and in 1978, High/Scope Press began its fulfillment operation in the renovated Nash dealership building. In 1990, the Nash dealership, then the High/Scope Press ware-

The unused Nash automobile dealership (top) that High/Scope purchased and extensively remodeled for one of our first staff training and child development centers. Later, this building housed the High/Scope Press warehouse until the building was sold in 1990. The second photo shows the exterior after extensive renovation.

house/fulfillment building, along with the neighboring house we used for Press staff offices, was sold to an Eastern Michigan University campus bookstore owner, Ned Shure. We used the income from that sale to purchase a 10,000 square foot warehouse and shipping facility, also in Ypsilanti. This move gave us a better facility for the growing High/Scope Press operations. Then, in 2002, that building was purchased by the City of Ypsilanti at four times the original cost to make space for a large-scale urban residential and services development.

In the fall of 2001, Phyllis and I donated the 70-acre High/Scope Retreat and Meeting Center (RMC), formerly known as High/Scope Camp, to the Foundation. While it will take several years to complete the process, the RMC gives High/Scope staff a unique place to schedule seminars, conferences, training, and our youth service programs. In the summer of 2001, the Foundation purchased an adjoining 20-acre farm, which makes the RMC a large, rectangular 90-acre track, thus protecting the RMC from unwanted commercial/residential development.

So, as of 2002, the Foundation owns the Hutchinson House and seven office/school/residential structures on six and a third acres in Ypsilanti. It also owns 90 acres with seven major buildings at the High/Scope Retreat and Meeting Center in Clinton, Michigan, about 25 miles to the southwest in open rolling fields and woods country. This real estate is held without debt and serves not only to house the staff but also as a basic asset for the institution.

ment money from National Follow Through. The parent-infant work with Carnegie Corporation funding was underway, and we were continuing the longitudinal follow-up of several early childhood projects.

With this funding as a framework, we began looking for other means of both being of service and supporting our curriculum development and research agenda. Two new directions were implemented. First, we began to look for other foundations and agencies that might be interested in our projects. (For example, that's when the Lilly Endowment began to fund High/Scope projects.) We strengthened our work with international agencies and governments. We began working with government bureaus beyond the Office of Child Development. Second, Dennis Deloria, then head of research for the Foundation, suggested we bid on various requests for proposals (RFPs) that the government was issuing. He had met many staff in both the academic and corporate worlds who made a business of responding to government-driven research and evaluation efforts. Why couldn't we? The concern was that outside research would distract us from fulfilling our own mission. The staff felt this problem could be contained and our work even enhanced by the larger staff such outside work would entail. Thus, in the late 1970s, Foundation growth was powered by continuing our systematic development of our long-term studies and by successfully bidding on a number of major government contracts. We kept the strands of our parent-infant work going with difficulty as elaborated elsewhere; we continued our longitudinal studies with funding from both the government and private foundations; and we relied on Follow Through to support our demonstration elementary school and curriculum services.

But the financial handwriting was on the wall for all our program areas. Follow Through was beginning to show signs of disintegration as politics played a greater and greater part in the

"From 1970 on we were successful in focusing on our work and gaining the support necessary to accomplish our training, research, and service goals."

program. The initial evaluation-oriented leadership under Robert Egbert ended, and new staff who were full-time civil servants took over under a politically appointed director. The Ypsilanti-Carnegie Infant Education Project encountered difficulty in funding for expansion, because of our own research results. Planned Variation Head Start was over. Our success at bidding for outside government contracts declined after our initial spring-like blooming in this area. Then another administration took office and major changes in social policies were introduced. We were called to Washington to testify before Senate committees on the findings from our long-term research in a successful effort to protect Head Start from cuts. However, even the growth in that program slowed down. Thus, the early 1980s saw a marked slowdown in our economic development and forecast a dangerous future. Indeed, a major Foundation reorganization was proposed by Chuck Wallgren to meet these challenges.

Wallgren came into my office one day in the spring of 1984 and, before he sat down, he closed the door, a sure sign of difficult business ahead. He laid out the prospects for income and expenditures for the next several years based on a realistic view (Wallgren's) as compared to an optimistic one (Weikart's). Pointing out that we had accumulated $200,000 in deficit spending over the past three years, he extended the current trends into the next three. Without question, the Foundation would be bankrupt without some action. "What do you propose?" I asked. Then he gave me the good news. We could survive by intensive focus on fundraising, by writing grants, and by expanding current effective lines of work. Then he gave me the bad news. We would have to lay off a significant number of staff. We would, in short, have to change our way of doing business. While this conversation went on for several weeks, the outcome was obvious. I would have to accept the message and design a solution. The Foundation's work and service were too important to lose, in my opinion, just because the decisions were going to be difficult for the institution and traumatic for the individuals affected.

Modifying Our Business Practices

Changing the way we were doing business meant that we
had to stop relying so much on grant or contract submissions
where a single grantor's decision determined our fate. The alternative was to develop strategies that provided multiple decision
points involving a wide range of individuals. One obvious area to
expand was High/Scope Press. To reach our market of individual
decision makers, we would have to advertise more widely. One
of our media technicians at the Foundation ran an electronics
supply house out of a rented storage facility in Ypsilanti. He recommended doing what he did: Print a tabloid-sized newspaper
on a web press such as supermarkets do. He did that and mass-
mailed it using a variety of purchased
mailing lists. He took orders by mail
and phone, then passed them on to
the manufactures who drop-shipped
the item directly to the consumer.
We took his advice and created *High/
Scope ReSource,* a free news magazine

*"Changing the way we were
doing business meant that we
had to stop relying so much on
grant or contract submissions
where a single grantor's decision determined our fate."*

for educators, tabloid-sized, printed on newsprint, and containing
both general articles about our work and a catalog of our training events and publications. This mailing allowed thousands of
individuals to learn about our work and to make their own
decisions about purchasing High/Scope products and services.
It met our objective of having multiple decision makers determine our fate. From 1984 to 1986, press sales increased from
$250,000 to $541,000, a huge endorsement of the approach.
Over the years, we have continued this strategy, and in 2001 circulated *High/ Scope ReSource* to more than 225,000 individuals.
That year, Press sales reached their highest level ever. But more
than advertising to increase program interest and income was
needed. Wallgren proposed that we eliminate our entire media
and graphic design staff, keeping only the editorial and marketing
staff; we would hire freelance designers and photographers as
needed. There was no alternative to this decision, but how do

you tell eight talented and dedicated people who are doing a wonderful job that it's all over? You wear a suit and tie to make the meeting formal, and you do the best you can to explain and support. In fact, many of these staff continued to work with us on a freelance basis and developed independent, successful graphic design businesses.

Developing Large-Scale Training— Trainer-of-Trainers Services

The other part of the strategy to reach many individual decision makers was to focus our training efforts on delivering workshops to groups requesting our services. In the early 1980s, four of us went to California to present a three-day workshop on the High/Scope Curriculum to the Los Angeles County Head Start Agency. It was exciting. We had not really done this before at this level of effort. Yes, there was a developing field training program in New Jersey for special education teachers, and we did extensive training in Follow Through, but a whole countywide Head Start agency, one of the largest in the country, was a special challenge. The curriculum presentations went well. Still in the throes of excitement, the leadership of the agency invited us to a late lunch at the end of the Saturday afternoon workshops. The nearby restaurant was nearly empty and half the lights were turned off in the far end of the room. As we gathered in what seemed like a setting for a secret cabal, we were asked to schedule a repeat visit for the next summer. We were all pleased by the endorsement, but I began to wonder what such an invitation meant aside from the obvious. If High/Scope was to have a national impact, it seemed as if some other training model was necessary. We could easily fulfill this particular request, but suppose there were to be hundreds more (as we hoped)? From this slender thread and our New Jersey experiences, we created the Training of Trainers model. High/Scope would train leaders in early childhood education who were working at agencies or at colleges and universities. These trainers would train teachers, providing them with classroom supervision to enable the development of appropriate High/Scope practices. This approach would make the validated High/Scope Curriculum widely available. Two large-scale training efforts illustrate this effort and are described next.

In the late 1980s, I was working with Shelby Miller, who was the Ford Foundation Early Childhood project officer at that time. She had maintained an interest in High/Scope research over the years and had even worked with us on a parent-infant project. I was in New York on one of my regular "visit foundations" tours. Over lunch, I explained our ongoing efforts to disseminate the High/Scope approach through the trainer-of-trainers community-building efforts. She was intrigued and asked that I submit a broader proposal that would permit more day care program staff to be involved. From this meeting, we put together a national effort that used Ford funds of over $1 million as matching money and raised about $7 million to provide training in many locales ranging from New York City to Miami to Los Angeles. Key to our success was that Clennie Murphy, acting director of National Head Start, encouraged local agencies to participate and use funds from the regional offices to cover enrollment fees. Private foundations, state departments of education, and individual donors all participated in funding the final program. Of course the secret was our modular approach to funding. While Miller at Ford and Murphy at National Head Start were core, all the other donors were local, so money could be raised one project at a time. Most required Ford funds and two to three other funders in addition to modest contributions from participating agencies. With multiple funders, timing of project initiation and expenditures was always difficult because coordination of the different groups was difficult.

This approach was repeated later for the State of Georgia—with a twist. Georgia was the first state to offer public preschool education for all children residing in the state. The legislature established an agency to administer the program and it was fully funded by state resources. That agency was headed by two High/Scope–endorsed trainers who were well aware of the need for high quality in whatever program the state sponsored. The state was committed to using any form of early education, profit or nonprofit, to accomplish the goal. High/Scope was invited to bid on the training task. However, it was evident that while cost was an issue, the main problem most bidders faced was both offering a validated curriculum approach and having a sufficiently large group of endorsed trainers who could uniformly accomplish the task. We got the contract. At one point, High/Scope was offering 42 four-week training programs in various locations around the state and reaching over 1,600 teachers. We were able to complete the program using 14 High/Scope endorsed trainers, including Rachael Underwood from the U.K. Institute. I will say that the mix of British and Georgian accents took some getting used to, but training was fine from the outset.

> *"Since 1985, the Foundation has focused on offering training and accompanying materials published by High/Scope Press to individuals and a wide range of agencies."*

Since 1985, the Foundation has focused on this approach of offering training and accompanying materials published by High/Scope Press to individuals and a wide range of agencies. By 2001, a considerable portion of the total Foundation income was derived from these two sources. This approach also allowed us to meet the needs of many individuals and to enable them to apply the validated High/Scope approach in broadly varied national and international settings. Of course, we keep submitting grant applications and maintaining involvement with various federal agency programs, but this second approach allows us to have more control over our fate, giving us an opportunity to continue the institutional focus on our mission and vision for children, youth, and families.

9

Development of
High/Scope Press

High/Scope Press was established as part of the strategy to rely less on individual decision makers in foundations and more on multiple decision makers in agencies and classrooms. If we could publish high-quality materials, both print and electronic, I believed the Press would produce a steady income flow for the Foundation to help us meet our training, research, and direct service goals. There were five objectives behind this decision:

1. If we managed the process successfully, it would make High/Scope curriculum materials and research readily available to the public relatively quickly. (Journal and book publishers have extended publication timelines and all works wait their turn, sometimes for years.)

2. If we controlled the production end of things, we could insure quality in both editing and design. Selection and quality of pictures, size of print, and page layouts are important decisions for the readability of any text.

3. If we owned the publication rights to our materials, we could make the work of the Foundation available and keep items in print over an extended period of time, allowing us to make decisions based on the professional needs of the field rather than solely on a market-driven basis. In addition, with the copyrights to our intellectual

capital in hand, we could negotiate directly with potential publishers on foreign language translations of our works.

4. If we set the prices, High/Scope materials, especially textbooks, could be reasonably priced for students and early childhood practitioners.

5. If we made a net profit from sales, the income could be used to finance the needs of projects and services that High/Scope provides rather than make profits for an outside publishing house.

All these objectives were achieved—with some unforeseen benefits and some problems.

First, are High/Scope materials and research more quickly available to the public? While the answer to this question is affirmative, it is given with some reservation. While the Foundation has writer/editors on staff and employs others from time to time for special assignments, moving through the volume of work takes time. The reality of the actual time it takes was a surprise to me. One major area of publishing that the Press does shorten is production time. Because we contract out much of actual production, including design and printing, we can draw on a wide range of high-quality contractors to facilitate a publication's release. Thus, when a monograph or set of materials is ready for actual publication, design and printing can proceed without delay. By using High/Scope Press, we can skip the year or two "pipeline" that most publication programs must maintain to operate efficiently.

"I believed the Press would produce a steady income flow for the Foundation to help us meet our training, research, and direct service goals."

Second, does production control insure quality? Our experience in this area suggests that it certainly does. Type size, use of color, selection and positioning of photos, page margins, binding, paper weight, and general text layout are all key factors. I will have to admit that we often disregarded careful cost-control to obtain the production quality we wanted in a product, and sometimes we had to adapt to new technologies, but in general I believe we produced a better product through our own press operation. For example, in 1981 we contracted with Grant McIntyre, a British publisher, to release a five-volume series on British education for children under five. The publisher agreed to permit us to photograph their books for our reprinting. This meant enormous savings because we did not have to re-type all the manuscripts, copyedit for errors, and go through all the related steps to insure we had it right. But we did do several other things in the production process. We made a new cover design in four colors. (After checking with the British Embassy in Washington, D.C., for proper protocol, we chose to use the British flag in various forms.) We chose a book size that permitted wider margins and larger print size for easier reading, and a better binding to increase durability. Grant McIntyre did not varnish their book covers, because, as the publisher said, "Adds ha' penny to the cost of each book." However, working with a publisher driven to control even the half penny was a good lesson for Press staff. Cost control is always difficult when other considerations enter the picture.

Third, does owning the copyrights make a difference? One of the goals of the Press is to maintain control of High/Scope's intellectual capital by owning the materials that document our programs, research, and services. Thus, we can publish and reprint as required to meet our institutional responsibilities. For example, *Longitudinal Results of the Ypsilanti Perry Preschool Project* was first published in 1970 in a typed, paperbound edition. This monograph was a great success at the time in making widely available to the public the first information on High/Scope's Perry Preschool Project. Then in 1993, the monograph was reissued, content unchanged (as much as I would have liked to bring the language used up to date), to give it the look established for the High/Scope monograph series. Slow-selling books such as this one are maintained in small quantities for students and researchers who require original information on the study.

"One of the goals of the Press is to maintain control of High/Scope's intellectual capital."

207

Copyright ownership has also helped in publishing our curriculum and research findings in other languages. (A list of publication translations as of 2001 is included in the appendices on p. 309.) A High/Scope staff member maintains contact with publishers in various countries to respond to their inquiries and to bring new publications to their attention for possible translation. Royalties from these transactions support High/Scope services, and access to the information enables persons in other countries to use our work in their development of programs for children.

Fourth, are we able to price products reasonably for the consumer, especially college students and early childhood practitioners? Trying to keep prices low has produced some difficult challenges for us because the cost of printing and production changes all the time. In textbooks and research monographs, High/Scope Press seems to consistently price products below similar commercial publications. This policy makes it possible for books like the 1978 edition of *Young Children in Action* (our first preschool manual) and the 1995 and 2002 editions of *Educating Young Children* to sell thousands of copies a year to colleges and universities, libraries, and early childhood education staff and caregivers. As more programs adopt our approach and more colleges and community colleges base their early childhood courses on High/Scope's approach, this number will rise. On the whole, High/Scope Press prices remain below or at the general market level, and the publications facilitate the work of the institution.

Finally, are there net profits from the Press that can be used for High/Scope projects and services? Clearly the answer is yes. While most income goes to support the activities of the Press—editing, production, marketing and order fulfillment, and inventory storage—sufficient amounts remain to support preparation of new training materials, information for parents, development of assessment instruments, and publication of general information for the public (through the preparation and circulation of *High/Scope ReSource* and our yearly product catalog). We could certainly release our research and curriculum information through other sources, but such an approach would both constrict the information available and reduce High/Scope services. In general, the original intention of the Press has been realized.

Unanticipated Benefits

In addition to the expected benefits, there have also been useful, unanticipated benefits in establishing the Press operation. One of the most important came from using in-house writer-editors to staff the Press. Over time, these writer-editors have gained a breadth of understanding about the Foundation and our work. In particular, Lynn Taylor, Press director, and Nancy Brickman, senior writer-editor, have added stability to the curriculum writings, especially those produced by new staff. Their years of wrestling with the intellectual issues that drive the curriculum and their personal family experiences of enrolling their own children in the High/Scope demonstration classrooms enable them to speak firsthand about the impact of the approach. They and their staff are involved in the planning, writing, and design of materials, quality control of all publications, helping staff consider historic usage of words and concepts, organizing and editing specific books and training videos for staff review, and developing and maintaining the Foundation Web site and online store. I did not at first recognize how valuable the in-house writer-editors would be for the overall work of the Foundation, but now their service is recognized as of enormous importance.

"I did not at first recognize how valuable the in-house writer-editors would be for the overall work of the Foundation, but now their service is recognized as of enormous importance."

Probably one of the most serious problems in maintaining an in-house Press is the concern for assuring scientific accuracy in our research publications. Are we just publishing reports, monographs, and other results on our research project findings to avoid the need for peer review and jury selection of important reports? The responsibility of publishing reports such as those on the High/Scope Perry Preschool Study or the High/Scope

Curriculum Comparison Study is, indeed, great. With these issues in mind, a policy of review and release of research findings
was established, covering the initiation of a project through the
public information and dissemination stage. This system was created to help avoid any possible conflicts of interest in the publication of research and yet move our information as rapidly as possible into the public information stream.

1. All research projects use advisory committees to help
   guide the design, operation, and analysis of the study.
   This step encourages us to anticipate problems and to
   avoid them if possible.

2. Before any major research report is published, we invite
   well-known experts in the field to evaluate what we have
   accomplished and write a critique of the report. Sometimes this step leads to further analysis, although by this
   stage the research is usually beyond major technical criti-
   cisms. The reports of the outside experts are published in
   the monograph with only copy editing. This step allows
   the reader to see evaluative comments immediately and
   not have to wait for other sources.

3. With the technical or scientific portion published, the
   third step is to issue a news release to generate publicity
   about the study and provide the public with a brief summary of the work. This step allows education reporters,
   such as those from *Education Week* or the *New York
   Times*, to have quick and timely access to the information
   for their stories, including critical comments and the brief
   summaries.

4. At the same time as a news release is being prepared, the
   fourth step begins. An article is prepared and submitted
   to a scientific journal to describe the study and its findings. This step is always difficult. How can a 250-page
   report be reduced to the 30 or fewer pages allowed in
   a journal?

5. Because of the publication lag after an article is accepted for inclusion in a scientific journal (often more than a year), the remaining activities usually overlap. For example, a short article is prepared for the more general education publications such as *Educational Leadership* or *Phi Delta Kappa* that reach a wide public school audience. A longer version of the article is presented in *High/Scope ReSource,* which is distributed free of charge to about 225,000 individuals connected in some way with High/Scope.

Sometimes High/Scope staff will be invited to a congressional hearing to discuss the relevance of a project to a current legislative concern. In the 1980s, Shirley Sagawa of Senator Edward Kennedy's staff worked with us on a number of presentations related to Head Start. As a consequence, testimony at the state level, presentations to a conference of governors, chief state school officials, and others occurred. In my opinion, this process is exhaustive and exhausting, but it does get the information out to both the policymakers and to the field. With newspaper articles and talk radio, the general public also gains some information. Important to note is that the original, complete report with its commentaries is always available at every stage.

"We have proceeded, I believe, in a solid, professional manner to make information available and insure that it is scientifically accurate."

We have proceeded, I believe, in a solid, professional manner to make information available and insure that it is scientifically accurate, thus accomplishing a major goal of the Foundation. Sometimes these procedures work better than one might think. In the late 1980s, I traveled to Newark, New Jersey, to give a speech on early childhood education, and the head of the New Jersey State Senate opened the meeting. He was a short, robust man from the docks, a former stevedore—high energy, pronounced views on what works. During his short speech, he presented, very accurately, the data from the High/Scope Perry Preschool Study. I was amazed. Where did he learn all this? How did he come to make these outcomes the centerpiece of legislation he was proposing? Apparently, sometimes interesting and important data do circulate, if only they can be made available.

High/Scope Press Operations

When the Press was initially established, the products were so few that we stored them in a small office building (an old house), which was part of our demonstration school complex. In 1975, when we closed the school and moved the preschool demonstration program to the grounds of the historic Hutchinson House, which now serves as our headquarters, the Press had grown sufficiently so that we used the old school as a warehouse for our products. The four large, garage-door service entrances allowed for sheltered deliveries and good ventilation in the spring and summer. The old preschool area, which had been a Nash automobile dealer's showroom, had plenty of office space. In back, the single large room, which had been the dealer's vehicle maintenance area, offered ample storage and a shipping area for both Press products and other training-related materials.

During this early period of development, a number of problems surfaced that bordered on the unbelievable. We did not have a defined system of advertising our products, so flyers and other direct mailing efforts were used. When orders were received, they went to one individual who prepared the packages and mailed them to the organizations or individuals placing the order. Things seemed to be going smoothly, with orders being filled and customers happy. Then we received an irate phone call from overseas: "Where are my books? I sent the money six months ago!" We looked into it and discovered that the order clerk had placed all the overseas orders and checks in the back of her desk drawer, ignoring them because she didn't know how to mail overseas. Incidents such as this made us realize how amateur we really were, and if we wanted to succeed as a serious publisher, we would have to avoid such problems. Our reputation was built on the quality of our work, but with the Press, it would also be built on the quality of our service.

Unexpected events also happened relative to housing Press operations. In 1990, Ned Shure, owner of Ned's college bookstores, walked into the warehouse one day and asked to buy the facility, including the office space in the house we owned next door. His Eastern Michigan University campus bookstores needed convenient storage and our buildings would meet their needs. But, should we sell? Don Moore, a member of the High/Scope Board of Directors, long-time friend, and participant in High/Scope's work, offered to sell us a warehouse he owned with 10,000 square feet of space that was located only a few blocks away. He was liquidating a long-time family business that sold high-end sailboat parts to the trade. He offered a price well below the appraisal for a facility designed for storage and shipping. After due board consideration, the offer was accepted and the Press fulfillment operations moved to the building on Water Street in Ypsilanti along the Huron River in a light industrial area. This facility served us well until 2002 when it was purchased by the City of Ypsilanti for a major residential and shopping development project. Our $130,000 investment in an old car dealership evolved into sufficient value to more than cover the cost of a real warehouse. While Ypsilanti paid enough for the Press building to cover the costs of purchasing another warehouse, the decision was made to contract out the fulfillment operations to a specialty firm. This process indicates again how important initial grants (which enabled us to purchase the original old car dealership in the early 1970s to use as our demonstration school) are for the long-term success of a nonprofit corporation. (For more information on the Foundations's buildings, see the sidebar on pp. 194–197.)

> *"Our reputation was built on the quality of our work, but with the Press, it would also be built on the quality of our service."*

Publicizing Our Work, Enhancing Our Image, Selling Our Products

Letting the field know what the Press had available was another major challenge. Direct mailings seemed to be effective but costly. Flyers passed out at training workshops were also some-what effective but were limited to a small audience. As I men-tioned earlier, on the advice of a staff member, Ken Asher, we created *High/Scope ReSource,* both as a professional news mag-azine and as a vehicle for offering a com-plete product catalog to the public. *Re-Source* has always been distributed at no charge. As of 2002 the paper is still free and is published three times per year. Dif-ferent departments within the Foundation are responsible for writing articles that re-flect their work and issues they are addressing. While we now employ a wide range of other marketing approaches to publicize our research and program findings, such as conference exhibits, magazine advertising, direct mailings, workshop handouts, and specific news releases for new products, the basic method of dissemination remains *High/Scope ReSource.*

> *"While we now employ a wide range of other marketing approaches, the basic method of dissemination remains High/Scope ReSource."*

Another dissemination mechanism was the development of a High/Scope preschool curriculum newsletter, *Extensions.* This eight-page document offers a focus on a single curriculum topic and relates to teacher training issues. It is released six times a year as a benefit to our High/Scope membership association. For many years, it was offered on a subscription basis. The idea is to provide curriculum information to the classroom teacher and to provide plenty of practical examples as well as training suggestions for High/Scope endorsed trainers. While the sub-scription side of things was a problem due to our inability to master the necessary marketing techniques, the newsletter itself has developed a solid reputation. Building on a suggestion from Frank Blackwell, our British consultant, to make the material more widely available, the writer-editors assemble and re-edit the newsletter articles about every five years and publish them in a series of focused High/Scope curriculum textbooks called *Supporting Young Learners.* These books have been very popular because all the articles are short, concise, easy to understand, and relate to topics of interest to teachers and parents. Thus, they make easy reading for students, teachers, caregivers, and parents. The three books published so far represent 20 years of High/Scope thinking about practical curriculum matters, and more editions will be published.

From gross sales of $750 in 1971, our first year of operation as an independent institution, sales increased to $12,000 in 1977. At the time, we were simply providing materials as an informal service. In the spring of 1978, the High/Scope Board of Directors endorsed the concept of an official High/Scope Press as a publishing arm of the Foundation. With the publication of several monographs in a new research series, such as the second major report on the High/Scope Perry Preschool Study, and a new curriculum textbook, *Young Children in Action,* the gross sales in that year reached $53,000, followed by $92,000 the next year. By 1985, the year of major staff layoffs because of major grants ending and the change in the political scene after the presidential election, sales topped $421,000. They went over the $1 million mark in the early 1990s and over $2 million in 1994. After dropping in volume after several large training projects phased out, reducing the need for Press materials, the sales jumped again to $2,422,000 in 2001, the last year of my tenure. The sales increase reflected the release of the new High/Scope curriculum textbook, *Educating Young Children* and several newly standardized and validated child assessment instruments such as the Preschool Child Observation Record.

> *"The Press has been and remains a major force in stabilizing the work of the Foundation, and it has successfully presented important information to the education field and reached its financial goals."*

Of course, there is a big gap between gross income and net income, but the Press covers all its own costs, including the cost of the writer-editors, and usually contributes to service activities of the Foundation such as the demonstration preschool and the adolescent Institute for IDEAS residential program. If income exceeds current needs, it is set aside to be available for later use. On the whole, the Press has been and remains a major

~

force in stabilizing the work of the Foundation, and it has suc-cessfully presented important information to the education field and reached its financial goals. It now provides about one third of the Foundation's gross income.

In the 1980s, we saw what a sudden change in the political winds can do to government funding streams and how various shifts in foundation funding priorities can thwart us in meeting our goals and objectives. High/ Scope Press has more than fulfilled its promise of helping us become more financially self-sufficient. Most important, it has provided high-quality books, training guides, assessment materials, recordings, videos, and other materials to assist classroom teachers and inform the public. I believe it has a great future in enabling the Foundation to reach its goals of service to children and families.

10

Governance:
The High/Scope
Board of Directors

No one creates an organization without some intention, a clear purpose. Perhaps it is a business objective to be achieved, a service to be provided. In any case, some event triggers the action. For me, the initiation of the High/ Scope Educational Research Foundation came about because of a decision I made that was precipitated by the Ypsilanti superintendent of schools. I enjoyed working in the public schools and I very much wanted to continue. Having such a base gave me a sense of mission and pride. I belonged to a tradition. I wanted to demonstrate that the public school staff—with concrete knowledge of the problems in education and with access to the children involved—could make a significant contribution. However, as the Ypsilanti school superintendent began to recognize the extent of the work undertaken by my special services department in providing consulting services to other school districts and related research projects, he began to ask questions. We were located in a large house that was on the historic building list in Ypsilanti and thus had identifiable rental expenses. The number of staff involved in both the service components and research projects exceeded staff of the high school, the largest unit in the district. Our out-of-state travel budget was greater than all the rest of the system combined. We were able to obtain independent financing through the Washtenaw County Intermediate School District, the State Department of Education, federal programs, and private foundations. Thus, while we provided extensive classroom services and paid overhead to the district from all the outside grants, the actual fact was that our funds and, indirectly, our supervision came from outside organizations.

In the spring of 1968, I hesitated to take any more funding from outside sources, fearing I would "rock the boat" even more. Yet a number of exciting opportunities were at hand. The Ypsilanti-Carnegie Infant Education Project funding was accepted, under protest, by the superintendent. *"I enjoyed working in* To avoid school system issues, I accepted the *the public schools and* large-scale National Follow Through Project *I very much wanted* through Eastern Michigan University. There *to continue."* were plans afoot by the Head Start Agency in Washington to fund a curriculum comparison study with Follow Through sponsors, and I wanted to participate. Clearly, there was a problem, and I knew I needed to reconcile the various issues.

Establishing an Independent, Nonprofit Foundation

In early winter of 1967, I was working at High/Scope Camp, coordinating the facility services for a weekend rental group of 30 persons involved in a passion of the times, sensitivity training. On Saturday night, after a long day, I was wrapping up the work in the kitchen. One of the participants, Bill Dannemiller, an Ypsilanti attorney, wandered in looking for a cup of coffee. We began talking about the youth program the camp operated in the summer, how it was funded, who attended, how we recruited staff and campers, and so forth. He was fascinated. I think the contrast between his meeting discussions about interpersonal relationships and the description of the actual delivery of camp services intrigued him. After about an hour's discussion, Dannemiller finally asked how all these things were administered—in short, who owned the programs. There I stumbled, because the conflict with the schools was obvious, and the administrative organization was a mess. Dannemiller then talked about independent nonprofit organizations, and he asked if I had thought of such a solution. I hadn't. Indeed, we were just starting to work with the Carnegie Corporation of New York, and it did not even have the word "foundation" in its name. Speak of ignorance. He encouraged me to think about it and then to call him. He offered to prepare the necessary papers and file them on a *pro bono* basis. Needless to say, I was speechless; excited by the opportunity, challenged by the vision. After talking with Phyllis and thinking about the implications, I called Dannemiller and accepted his offer. Thus, a limited version of the High/Scope Educational Research Foundation actually began in the fall of 1968. The first High/Scope Board of Directors included Bill Dannemiller, Phyllis Weikart, and me. Our first contract was the National Planned Variation Head Start Project. Staff were hired. One new foundation was launched.

This slight change in contract arrangements, however, only served to complicate my general situation even more. The relationship with the Ypsilanti Public Schools came to a head in the fall of 1969. Placing National Follow Through at the university and Planned Variation Head Start with the new High/Scope Foundation did little to change the basic issue: My staff provided service to projects and schools outside the boundary of the Ypsilanti Schools. The specific event that precipitated the creation of the second version of the High/Scope Foundation occurred in November 1969. The new school superintendent, Ray Barber, who had replaced Paul

> *"The conflict with the schools was obvious, and the administrative organization was a mess."*

Emerich in 1968, was sympathetic toward my work. Nevertheless, one day he called me in for a meeting. He said I could continue working for the public schools if I wished. However, to do so I had to drop all the outside research and consulting work. I was stunned. Although I had guessed it was coming, I was personally distraught because I knew the necessity and quality of the work. Trying to find some perspective on the issues, I asked a group of outside advisors who were friends and whom I trusted to help me review my options:

1. Stay with the public schools and drop all outside contracts and grants.

2. Accept the invitation to move all operations to the local university.

3. Create an independent agency if the schools would let me move accounts, contracts, grants, and my staff—if *they* were willing to move. (Not an easy option for staff with retirement plans, guaranteed employment, and good salary schedules if they stayed with the schools; uncertainty on all counts if they went with the new independent agency.)

The group of advisors included Bill Dannemiller, attorney, Ann Arbor; Philips Foster, professor of economics, University of Maryland; Jim Gosselink, professor of botany, University of Louisiana; Joe Molder, headmaster, Westover School for Girls in Middlebury, Connecticut; and John Porter, Michigan Department of Education. After extensive discussions with school system representatives and staff from Eastern Michigan University, the advisors recommended that I continue on the path of establishing an independent, nonprofit foundation. Bill Dannemiller offered to assist by recruiting an attorney who specialized in nonprofit organizations to review and then resubmit our articles of incorporation and the bylaws. Again, the work was accomplished on a *pro bono* basis. On July 1, 1970, a fully formed High/Scope Educational Research Foundation was officially established with headquarters in Ypsilanti, Michigan. All of my staff transferred to the new organization. ("Why not?" they said. "You've always raised the money

"After extensive discussions with school system representatives and staff from Eastern Michigan University, the advisors recommended that I continue on the path of establishing an independent, nonprofit foundation."

∼

Original board members attending a meeting in 1972 at High/Scope Camp: John Porter on left, Bill Dannemiller, Jim Gosselink, Phyllis Weikart, Joe Molder, Philips Foster, and the author.

that paid our salaries, and besides, the work is interesting.") The superintendent went out of his way to facilitate the transfer of staff and equipment, writing off the paper debts of the department to the general fund and overlooking ownership of some office and research equipment. The new High/Scope Foundation stayed in the rented house, so there was little upheaval for staff. All the grantor and contractor organizations accepted the change and reassigned the work to the newly formed High/Scope Foundation. The five outside advisors I had brought together to assist me in evaluating my options agreed to support their recommendation by forming the first High/Scope Board of Directors for the re-registered nonprofit 501(c)3 organization. They added both Phyllis and me to the board, resulting in a seven-person membership. (As I explained in a previous chapter, the name "High/Scope" was drawn from the adolescent summer camp program for talented teenagers from the United States and abroad that my wife and I had operated since 1963.) All formal aspects of the High/Scope Educational Research Foundation were now in place.

During the early years (up to 1985), the High/Scope Board of Directors' membership remained constant. Their primary function was to advise me on plans for development and to monitor the finances of the Foundation. They acted as a conciliatory body on such key issues as salary settlements with staff and reviewing staff benefits. One early question was who would pay for health insurance. Foster, the economist on the board, asked why the Foundation paid 100 percent of that cost. The board adopted his recommendation that the staff should share in the cost by paying 10 percent of the total. Of course, at that time a generous family benefit policy was $32 a month, so the staff contribution was about $3.20 per month. (The future of skyrocketing health care costs was yet to unfold.) The two-day meetings were held three times a year over vacation periods so they would not interfere with the regular work schedule of the members: New Year's weekend, Memorial Day weekend, and Labor Day weekend. Board members were encouraged to bring their families, at their own expense, to the New Year's meeting as it was usually held at High/Scope Camp so costs could be kept low. At times, meetings were held in more exotic places. One of these meetings almost cost me my life and that of one of my daughters and two members of another board member's family. Here's what happened.

The board found a good arrangement at a small hotel, Zazil Ha, on Isla Mujeres just off the Cancun, Mexico, coast for the 1972 New Year's meeting. The official meetings were held in the mornings and evenings, leaving the afternoons for families to explore the island, swim in the ocean, and play games on the beach. One afternoon, the kids tired of the small waves on our shallow beach and wandered over to a windward beach around the point of the island where the wind kicked up much larger surf. Cathy Weikart and Shanti Foster decided to go in to play. They were swiftly drawn out in a strong undertow. Deni Foster, Phil's wife, went in to help. Not thinking (after all my Red Cross training), I simply went in as well to help. I quickly reached the group and started to tread water dropping my feet down into the undertow. The next thing I knew I was pulled under and tossed up to the surface some 15 yards further out from the kids and Deni.

Furious at my carelessness and clearly entering physical shock from both the situation and being under the water so long, I looked to the beach to wave good-bye to my wife, sure that I would not survive this experience. Remembering her life-saving training, she was frantically pointing up the beach. Finally, her warning dawned on me: You do not fight an undertow; I should travel with the water up the beach and allow the natural swirl of the current to work with me. Scared I had lost the kids because I could not see them, I turned on my back and tried to relax in the buoyant salt water as much as possi-

"During the early years (up to 1985), the High/Scope Board of Directors' membership remained constant."

ble with the wind and waves washing over me. After what seemed to be a very long time, I felt a touch of sand under my dragging feet. Unable to stand, I struggled up to the point where my head was out of the water and lay there, unable to make any more effort. Shortly after, my mother (who was with us on the trip) arrived and lifted my head up out of the sand. Then, after what seemed like a long time, two men arrived with a stretcher to take me to the beach first aid station where I was given some shots and treated for shock. To my great surprise and relief, my roommate was Deni Foster, undergoing the same treatment. She told me the kids were safe. After I had become trapped, a board member ran to a nearby hotel to ask for aid. The staff said they could do nothing, but two American tourists rushed out to help with an innertube and small, raftlike boat. They reached Shanti and Cathy in time. Then they returned for Deni. After a few hours all of us were united and deeply grateful for the foresight and bravery of the two young men who helped us. Kindly, no one mentioned our own stupidity!

⁓

The next day we all walked back to the beach, feeling a strong need to view the scene. As we stood there, we realized it was actually a small cove. The water was naturally forced to the center where it pulled back to the sea, precisely where the kids had gone in to play. An obvious place for a major undertow. Facing us in the center at the high water mark was a bright red-painted sign on a stout, newly installed post: *Peligro*. Thankfully, not all board meetings were as eventful as this one.

Changing to Reflect High/Scope's Growing Needs

As the institution matured, the board began to change to reflect the growing needs. In 1985, Phyllis resigned from the board in recognition of her increased training responsibilities in movement and music around the country. In 1986, James Gosselink resigned because his federal Sea Grant program on the Louisiana coast expanded. With these changes, in 1987 the board took on new members and enlarged its membership from 7 to 13. The board began to shift its focus from an advisory role to a Foundation goals and policy review role. The idea of terms limits and rotating membership on a planned basis came up for discussion. Also, the board felt achieving a wider ethnic representation and adding more women would assist the Foundation in meeting its goals and responsibilities.

With the inevitable recognition that the passage of time requires, my eventual retirement and Foundation transition in leadership became an important issue for the board to consider. The board needed to be ready for this eventuality by having experienced leadership and a systematic process to guarantee continuity for the Foundation. Thus, in 1995, board membership was increased to 16 members. Each appointment, two per year, was for a four-year term, renewable by election of the board for another four years of service. At the end of this

"In 1986, the board began to shift its focus from an advisory role to a Foundation goals and policy review role."

time, members were required to leave the board, although they could be reappointed after a year. This plan would make for an orderly progression of board members, with two coming on the board and two leaving each year. It would allow for the accumulation of experience, mentoring of new members into assuming board responsibilities, and, most important, it would provide for new blood to meet new needs. The original board members were grandfathered in so that they could continue to serve, especially to provide a historic overview and maintain institutional coherence. At this writing Joe Molder and I are the only two of the original seven members still serving.

As the board expanded, meetings on holiday weekends with families were discontinued. The board now meets three times a year from Friday morning to Saturday evening. As I write this, the board is organized into standing committees:

1. An Executive Committee to act between board meetings if necessary but such action is subject to ratification by the full group

2. A Membership Committee to review all the legal functions of the institution

3. An Institutional Planning and Policy Committee to focus on strategic planning and fundraising

4. A Program Committee to review the progress of the program divisions

Special committees such as the Endowment Income Disbursement Committee, and Finance Committee meet outside the regular yearly meeting schedule either in person or by telecommunication links. Additional committees are appointed by the board as necessary. Several outside committees with at least one board member and knowledgeable community members are also used routinely. These committees report periodically to the board on their activity. For example, the High/Scope Trust Advisory Committee reviews and monitors the investments of the Foundation both of High/Scope's own endowment funds and the various charitable trusts established by donors to benefit the institution after their death. Some High/Scope departments also have advisory committees. For example, the Adolescent Department has an Institute for IDEAS Program Advisory Committee look specifically at our service to adolescents. The Movement and Music Education Department benefits from a Regional Advisory Committee composed of endorsed trainers. Finally, the High/Scope Retreat and Meeting Center has a Facility Advisory Committee to help guide the development of that service and property.

These board adjustments and expansions were made in recognition of the fact that I would not always head the Foundation and that the board needed to assume the traditional role of boards with responsibility to fully set policy and monitor finances. Thus, the board was focused on assuring a smooth transition in Foundation leadership whenever it became necessary. The path to this logical and obvious transition was not a smooth one, however. It is easy to put off the future. In 1987, my retirement and the resultant leadership change seemed to be issues for the future, very distant for both me and the board. I was a young 56 years of age and the future was just that—very distant.

All this avoidance and detachment came to a sudden halt in 1989. That summer I was diagnosed with non-Hodgkins lymphoma, an ethmoid tumor located in the sinuses. Cancer. The fall of 1989 through to September 1990 was a period of uncertainty for both me and the Foundation. With chemotherapy treatments every three weeks, I was of little use to anyone, although I tried to be available as much as was possible. I was usually in the office two or three hours a day but not every day. I was able to take a few trips out of state, particularly to complete my responsibilities for the National Commission on Children. Aside from my personal terrors, the board was desperate to make a transition plan should I not survive the treatments. It was a time of confusion, and some ill-considered steps were proposed. Understandably, my attendance at board meetings pro-

First Lady Barbara Bush welcomes the author into the White House living quarters. In 1991, the National Commission on Children members were thanked for the submission of their report on their work at a reception held by Mrs. Bush.

voked an even greater urgency in board decision making and gave substance to their fears, because I looked awful. They were aghast when, in the middle of the September 1989 meeting, I slipped out to go the hospital emergency room to be treated for a possible heart complication. (I thought I had concealed it pretty well by going on the lunch hour.)

With treatment, I survived, as many cancer patients do. However, at times during the year of chemotherapy it hardly seemed worth the effort. Nonetheless, I came to a board meeting in September 1990 with the chemotherapy complete and CT scans indicating the tumor vanquished. The board now was clearly committed to developing a realistic transition plan and to setting a date for that to occur. The threat of sudden loss of leadership the board members experienced during my illness put the issue on the front burner. For High/Scope Foundation to continue its growth and service, the board had to assume leadership in arranging for this inevitable transition. Several things hap-

High/Scope Board of Directors on a 1997 site visit to a Bureau of Indian Affairs training program operated by High/Scope in Cañoncito, New Mexico. Chuck Wallgren on left, Donal Moore, Matt Hennessee, Bernice Brown, John Barr, Harriet Egertson, Roger Neugebauer, the author, Marilyn Thomas, Joe Molder, Lord Amir Bhatia, Bill Dannemiller.

pened. The board began the search for new members to bring it to a full operating strength by 1995 of 16 members in the rotation cycle. A 13-month plan for locating and installing my successor was developed by the board with staff assistance. My date for retirement was officially set for December 1996 when I would turn 65.

The health scare was over, however, and when I turned 65 and offered to resign my post as president of the Foundation and chairman of the board, the members asked me to stay on. They felt, as founder, I should continue to lead the Foundation for a while longer. Upon reflection, I think the board was still not ready to assume their own Foundation leadership role. I was happy to continue, though, as long as the decision was evaluated each year in September to give the board the 13 months they required to hire my successor.

In 1999, we reached an agreement that I would retire on January 1, 2001, marking my official Foundation tenure of 30 years. This decision was final for new health reasons. In December 1998, I was diagnosed as having chronic lymphocytic leukemia, a treatable but incurable cancer of the blood. The board was prepared this time, and with precision implemented a smooth, well-planned transition strategy. I retired to the role of president emeritus and orchid grower (a small but successful collection that seems to thrive on neglect and summer rains), and continued to battle CLL, as it is called, giving a dread disease an unearned sense of familiarity.

"In 1999, we reached an agreement that I would retire on January 1, 2001, marking my official Foundation tenure of 30 years."

With the transition complete, Joe Molder was elected chairman of the board. In the meetings since the transfer, the board role has been transformed again. The board is now focused on establishing policy and goals for the institution. There is a stronger sense of responsibility for oversight of the office of the president. And there is a commitment to a close monitoring of finances. With this renewed sense of responsibility, the board remains deeply committed to the work of the institution.

Lessons Learned

Over the years, I have learned many lessons about nonprofit boards of directors, at least from the High/Scope experience. My first and most important observation is that they are vital to the health of the institution. The High/Scope Board of Directors—in its various compositions—has been essential to our success. The members initially assumed the role of friendly, committed, and reflective advisors. They looked at plans, discussed curriculum issues, and reported on what they heard in the field about High/Scope. They even pitched in when they thought it would help. Philips Foster, for example, as an economics professor, saw me struggling to accomplish a benefit-cost study of the High/Scope Perry Preschool Project with little insight into what the economics world needed to know. So he and one of his graduate students undertook our first real benefit-cost study of the project and broke new ground in the understanding of human resource development. Robert Egbert, a professor of education, used one of his sabbaticals from the University of Nebraska to spend six months teaching in our demonstration laboratory school, providing us with invaluable insights. This depth of commitment was appreciated by all Foundation staff. One of the board's central roles in the early phase of its development was to act as an arbitrator between staff and administrators over compensation issues. Setting staff salary and benefits is a highly emotional issue, often (I think) bordering on the irrational. The board acted as an effective arbitrator between staff and management in this area by usually allocating a little more money for staff salaries and benefits than the administration felt could be afforded. But they also made tough decisions when necessary. (No salary or benefits settlement was universally applied; each staff member was reviewed and received the increase based solely on performance.)

"The High/Scope Board of Directors—in its various compositions—has been essential to our success."

My second observation relates to the next period of board development—selecting new board members. As a national organization, our board members live and work in many areas of the country. Not only is extensive meeting time involved in board membership, there is also extensive travel time. The High/Scope Board of Directors is a working board. Committee structure, financial oversight, fund development, policies, goals, objectives, and many other issues are considered by the board. Thus, new members need to recognize and accept this level of action. Attendance at meetings is 90 percent or better. Indeed, if a member misses three meetings in a row for any reason, they no longer serve on the board. What we have found is that a successful board member needs some link to High/Scope and not just to the field of education. Some board members became acquainted with us through the grant application and project monitoring process; others, through observing High/Scope curriculum training and the impact it has on staff and children. Some have worked with us as attorneys on special projects and have become committed to our mission. Several have worked at High/Scope or at the adolescent camp program and know the opportunities provided by the Foundation from the inside. In short, a successful board member needs to be linked to High/Scope through a personal experience or some other relationship. When we have tried to involve individuals who are actually working in the field but not tied to High/Scope in any way, we have found that they often have difficulty supporting our work with their time and advice. They may find the board role to be in conflict with their central work obligations, their attendance drops off, and their participation becomes sporadic and not in the Foundation's best interests. We have also discovered that we need a core group of members who live nearby (in southeastern Michigan). A number of committees require face-to-face meetings, and a board member needs to serve on each of the advisory committees as well as the Trust. Finances take more than a few hours at each board meeting. Thus, we have invited local individuals to become members of the board (these persons are well known to board members although they may not know much about High/Scope). Most of these individuals have served the Foundation, its work, and its staff very well.

My third observation is that board members want to have real decision-making responsibility and not just act automatically to approve administrative actions and decisions. One member stated during his interview for a board appointment that he had once served on a national board where all decisions were made by the staff. The board's role was to enjoy the luxurious surroundings and the great food and vote "aye" when asked. He wanted no part of that, so his question was, "Could the High/Scope Board of Directors make real decisions?" Needless to say, he is happy to serve on our board and has more than enough real decisions to make. This role is of greater importance now that the leadership has changed. The board must assert its required role: (1) hiring a president (which they have done), (2) setting and monitoring institutional policy and objectives, and (3) closely supervising financial affairs.

The Foundation has been unusually fortunate in the quality of its board. A list of the individuals who have served on the High/Scope Board of Directors since the institution began in 1970 up until 2002 is presented in the appendices on pp. 311. While not a fundraising or donor group, the board has presided over the successful development of an important and unique educational institution. Board members have encouraged innovation and have tolerated occasional commitments of Foundation resources that offered no financial reward at all, only educational outcomes. (For example, the extraordinary expenditure on the IEA Preschool Project of over $2 million of institutional assets over the 15 years of the project.) They go into the next generation of High/Scope development strongly committed to its mission and vision and able to provide the necessary leadership. It was a good time for me to retire!

11

Development—A
Personal Perspective

I have often been questioned about the mix of opportunities
and forces that enabled me to develop High/Scope and its
projects. What led me to establish the High/Scope adolescent
camp? Why did I initiate the High/Scope Perry Preschool
Study? What personal qualities and experiences led me to
found an independent, not-for-profit institution?

It is difficult to answer these questions effectively, as I
have learned in struggling to do so in this account. Why does
anybody do what they do? Clearly, a number of unique and special factors were at work or there would be many other High/
Scopes with extensive longitudinal projects. But they don't seem
to exist. Robert Egbert, former dean of Teachers College, University of Nebraska, and former member of the High/Scope
Board, once commented that individuals with theories are fairly
common, as are people who operate programs. What is unique
about High/Scope, Egbert believed, is that it combines both a
consistent theory and a consistent practice within an institution
dedicated to strengthening the field of education. Looking back
over 40 years to understand why all these events occurred
brings forth a series of reflections—some deeply personal, some
professional, some situational, and all only a part of the whole
picture, because I will never know precisely what drove me to
take this direction. However, here are some reflections.

~

General Opportunities Provided a Base

It was the result of my family upbringing

My parents were community social workers. My father ran settlement houses in Youngstown, Ohio, until his death in 1947 at
age 45 when I was 15 years old. My mother left social work at
that time and switched to elementary school teaching, which
gave her the regular schedule necessary for
raising four youngsters as a single parent.

*"What is unique
about High/Scope is
that it combines both
a consistent theory
and a consistent
practice within an
institution dedicated
to strengthening the
field of education."*

Service to others was a hallmark of the family.
Throughout my childhood, all kinds of people
visited our home—from newly arrived immi-
grants struggling to adjust to life in a new
country to professionals discussing issues
facing the community. I remember sitting for
hours at the dining table or in the living room
listening to the adults discuss these issues.

These experiences gave me an enduring respect for individuals,
regardless of race, creed, or ethnicity, because of all those who
came to our house and talked about important events and challenges. It also brought home the complexity that surrounds any
problem, and the realization that there are usually no simple solutions. The discussions also underscored the need for goodwill if
sensible outcomes are to be reached, and the need for individuals
to take action. Problems don't solve themselves; someone must
act. A problem is always complex; expect that and move toward
a plan to solve it.

It was the result of my education

While attending elementary school and high school in Youngstown, Ohio, I had the opportunity to associate with others from
many different ethnic and racial backgrounds. I can't say I was
aware of the cultural differences in elementary school, but I certainly was in high school. The tensions and issues I experienced as
a teenager in such an environmental mix in the late 1940s reinforced my enduring sense of hope for the future. World War II

234

was over; great changes were predicted. (For a male adolescent, the most important news was that cars were being produced again!) College was very important for all the acknowledged reasons that still hold true today: new ideas, exacting academic standards, new friends, challenging freedoms, and the responsibility to blend all these into serious thinking and learning. Using money earned from years delivering newspapers, part-time work, and student loans, I enrolled at Oberlin College. No better place could have been found for me. The first college in the United States to admit students irrespective of color (in 1835), and the first (in 1841) to grant undergraduate degrees to women, Oberlin has a proud heritage of a commitment to learning and to application of that knowledge in socially responsible ways. This tradition blended well with my family's focus on the individual's obligation to understand what is going on around you in the world at large, in order to act responsibly. The college was also intellectually demanding and forced me to develop many new interests and abilities.

It was the result of my experience in the U.S. Marine Corps at the end of the Korean War (1953–1955)

All the lofty goals of my liberal arts education were knocked about by the practical demands of learning to be a Marine Corps machine gun platoon leader. It was a startling experience to grasp the full meaning of the military's revision of "Thou shalt not kill" from my boyhood Methodist Church teaching to "Thou shalt not commit murder." It was also important to my personal development and future work performance to realize that explanations of why something failed to happen or was late were actually excuses. Explanations and excuses were not acceptable in the Marine Corps, the only thing that mattered was getting the job done as directed. During my two years serving as a lieutenant, the military life shaped me into an adult with strong views: Be in charge of yourself; set goals that must be reached; provide leadership; take responsibility; make no excuses. While treasuring the central influences of my

"A problem is always complex; expect that and move toward a plan to solve it."

childhood and family, my adult experiences in the military threw my life into sharp relief. After leaving the military, I figured if I could meet those demands, adjust, and survive, then I could meet the demands of any civilian supervisor as a young professional. In fact, it turned out that such demands were nothing compared to those of my battalion commander!

It was the result of the times

When Rosa Parks sat at the front of the bus in Montgomery, Alabama, it marked the beginning of the end of segregation in the United States. Parks liberated many of the rest of us to ask why things were as they were locally. Why did people of color have to live south of Michigan Avenue in Ypsilanti? Why did educational practices exist that generated such different achievement outcomes in different schools? Why accept persistent differences caused by conditions and events when they could be changed—or at least influenced? In such a bubbling cauldron of intense social questioning, it was easy to create innovative educational approaches and to believe that those new approaches would produce different and better outcomes. Not only was I responding to the excitement of the times but so were my staff. They expected me to organize an effective plan of action and were willing to lend their support. We all wanted to accomplish something; to make a difference.

"We all wanted to accomplish something; to make a difference."

It was the result of attending graduate school at the University of Michigan

Advanced academic study gave me the opportunity to maximize my engagement with new ideas, to "think big," to imagine various futures. Thus, when several members of the ad hoc advisory committee for what became the High/Scope Perry Preschool Study expressed the belief that disadvantaged children of preschool age would be harmed by my proposed preschool program, it was a natural step for me to convert that opinion into an hypothesis and to structure the service program as a research project. The university lectures on research design, statistics, and especially sample selection provided me with standards. No one mentioned that our design for a random sample study was rarely implemented because field studies present too many difficulties and force too many compromises. Some common folk wisdom applies here: *When you are given lemons, make lemonade.* But, of course, you have to know how. Graduate school helped me learn how.

The author and his wife, Phyllis, celebrate his doctorate in education and psychology at the University of Michigan, Ann Arbor, 1966.

It was the result of holding a job with genuine service responsibility

As director of special services, I was responsible for the identification and education of all disabled children within the system. When I assumed the position, there were almost no services for this group in Washtenaw County, other than a small program offered by Eastern Michigan's laboratory schools. I had the opportunity to create the entire program using state and county special education funding under local district administration. The school system management staff were competent in performing their jobs within traditional expectations. With the exception of the three reform-minded principals I mentioned in Chapter 2, they believed they were doing all they could, indeed, all that was required. The advantage to me was that they were not concerned with what I did as the special services department director as long as I established programs for the children they couldn't manage in regular classrooms. The central administration was not concerned with what I did either, as long as the direct expenses were covered by county, state, or other sources. So, while there was little support for inventive solutions or new initiatives in the schools, so too was there little professional constraint. My responsibility was clear. Though this freedom to act began to erode as the programs expanded, the groundwork was laid.

~

It was the result of a change in state regulations

The state opened up the opportunity for counties to establish intermediate school districts funded by county millage to finance expansion of special services to disabled youth, aged 3 to 25. Because of the availability of these funds, I was hired as a part-time psychological examiner in the fall of 1957 to help identify elementary children for two new classes for the mentally disabled. I simply stayed on when the immediate work was done, even though I was not officially asked to do so, and I moved into the full-time director's position when the post was created in 1958. Funds could be obtained for all special education programs by simply filling out the state forms and meeting diagnostic standards. With few current programs in operation and extraordinary pressure for countywide programs in most disability categories, the only limit was creating effective ideas. With hard work, these ideas could be implemented.

General Support From Family and Staff Provided a Base

Beyond taking advantage of the general opportunities my life presented, what were some of the more personal support factors that influenced me to start the High/Scope Camp and, later, the Foundation and its decades of interrelated studies?

The support of my immediate family was invaluable

Over the years, I have been unusually fortunate to have strong family support for all my undertakings. I don't think I could have accomplished even a fraction of my work without it. While my wife, Phyllis, was an active professional in movement and music training, she took the major responsibility of caring for our four daughters. When she was away, especially over weekends at meetings, playing field hockey, or providing training in movement and dance, I became "Mr. Mom." My four

"Support for my endeavors was truly a family affair."

Weikart family picture taken at the author's retirement dinner, December 2000. From the left: Dale and Cynthia W. Embry, Jennifer W. and Vince Danko, Phyllis Weikart and the author, Gretchen Weikart, Catherine W. and Mark Yeckel.

girls—Cindy, Cathy, Jenny, and Gretchen—accepted this change in routine, and even ate most of the meals I prepared with little comment or complaint. A major exception was when I served pancakes one Saturday evening with bananas and various vegetables mixed in. I thought it was a clever way to use leftovers and give the girls a new experience. They won't let me forget that trial, even in my dotage. We did have some wonderful trips as "Mr. Mom" and his four girls. In Mexico City, where I went to give a lecture while Phyllis was presiding at the National Field Hockey Association annual meeting, the Mexican hotel staff took the girls under their wing, calling them *las plomitas* (little doves), and they floated as a covey about the hotel.

In addition to providing me with continual support and counsel, Phyllis had a very active professional life outside of the home. She served as president of the National Field Hockey Association for five years and led the association to acceptance as an Olympic sport. She has developed the Education Through

Movement program as a department of the High/Scope Foundation and has published many books and training materials, including a series of 15 CDs of traditional folk dance music. Though she is retired from the University of Michigan's Department of Kinesiology, she has developed and supports a nationwide group of endorsed High/Scope movement trainers.

Support for my endeavors was truly a family affair. Making the High/Scope Camp function required that everyone pitch in to the extent of their abilities. Phyllis codirected the program until the Foundation took it over in 1980. From a very young age, our four daughters helped with weekend rental groups by serving tables and doing dishes. As they got older, they also ran the Ford 501 tractor to mow the lawns and playing fields. My mother, Catherine Weikart, also played an essential supportive role, especially during the summer camp program. She assumed primary care for our young daughters starting the first year of the program, 1963, while Phyllis and I fulfilled our professional responsibilities. After her retirement from the Youngstown Public Schools in 1968, she built a new home on the campgrounds and assisted as long as she was able with general camp operations, especially working with weekend groups. Until her death in 1994, she maintained a lively interest in the youth attending camp, providing late evening star nights, helping young people learn about birds and identify rocks, and observing most evening events. Without this extensive family support, much of what I was able to do for both the camp program and the Foundation would not have been possible.

Staff support was also essential

In terms of support, there have been many staff members over the years, some for short periods and many for many years, who have been instrumental in helping the organization function. To be sure, all staff did their official jobs, but I am grateful to all the individuals who threw their whole soul into the development of the camp and/or the Foundation. Among so many, there are four I would like to mention especially. Charles and Mary

Early years: The author with Phyllis Weikart (left) and Mary and Charles Hohmann, High/Scope Camp, Clinton, Michigan

Hohmann started their careers at the camp—Charles, in 1963, Mary, in 1966. Later, they guided the camp for a number of years and worked exhaustively on the High/Scope educational approach. Charles Wallgren, chief operating officer of the Foundation from 1972 to 2001, provided wisdom, technical support, outstanding problem solving, and occasional lessons in business ethics. Clay Shouse, director of Educational Services and now High/Scope's vice president, began work at the Foundation as a demonstration teacher in our training center in 1972, also supervising its remodeling. He has guided the growth of our training and services effectively since

> *"I have been fortunate to have the help of so many talented individuals. Little of what I have accomplished over the years would have happened without their active and positive support."*

the mid-1980s. I have been fortunate to have the help of so many talented individuals. Little of what I have accomplished over the years would have happened without their active and positive support.

My Personality Provided a Base

Of course, various facets of my personality were at play to drive this type of program and service development. And, of course, I actually have little idea as to what they are. Building on what friends have said, however, and what I think may be true, I will attempt some partial guesses.

I have always had a need to do something, be of service, to help others, to share what is important to me

I also like to provide opportunities for others. They could be staff who are starting out in their careers at the Foundation and who could benefit from challenging field assignments or from representing the Foundation at meetings or who need a forum that considers their ideas without criticism because of their status. High/Scope Camp became a laboratory for youth to explore ideas in a situation that set aside the reality of the family and pop culture so they could experiment with ideas and relationships free from fear of failure or censure. Then, too, I like to embrace big ideas that may offer a dramatic shift in the manner in which things are done. The findings of the preschool studies have enabled policymakers to wrestle with the challenges and recognize the potential for a major change in American education. I am grateful for the opportunity to be of genuine help to disadvantaged youth because programs we have developed create long-lasting change. This sense of service is very important to me.

I have a strong work commitment

I don't mind working until the job is complete—whatever it takes to do so. When directly operating the camp program, for example, I was involved seven days a week, all the time. Out of season, I, and usually my family members, worked at the facility almost every weekend. My motto: *When there is no money to pay others to do the work, you have to find ways to do it yourself.* While I occasionally felt extended to the limit, I genuinely enjoyed the challenges and looked forward to accomplishing the tasks. In my youth, I was always a hard worker, volunteering extra time beyond the normal requirements, carrying three paper routes totaling 270 subscribers each day throughout high school, and establishing a youth partnership to distribute furniture polish made by a local furniture refinisher. I had to assume many responsibilities early in my life as the oldest boy in the family after my father's early death in 1947. Thus, the work at the camp and the work at the Foundation, both requiring my extensive attention and labor, were always seen as an opportunity and not a burden.

I take an interest in many things, thus satisfying my intellectual curiosity

Though not much more than an average student at Oberlin College, I relished opportunities for discussions on serious topics. I was most interested in learning skills and gathering information that I could use in my work with youth. Thus, I took summer courses in camping taught by Maine Guides, in swimming and canoeing taught by the Red Cross, and in folk dance taught by Michael Herman and his wife, Mary Ann. At Oberlin, I took a course in music composition for liberal arts majors (those not enrolled in the Oberlin Conservatory of Music) after I had finished a course on music appreciation. A high point of college was the night my composition for cello and voice was played at Chapel. At the University of Michigan, I took a combined program in education and psychology, opening the door to broader theories and eventually forming the base for the High/Scope Perry Preschool Study. This general element of intellectual curiosity also led to the development of a camp program focused on the arts and sciences rather than the more traditional recreation orientation. I believe my intellectual curiosity has led to my commitment to traditional folk culture, love of classical music, adoption of the underlying theories for my work, and my constant need to question what I can do to be of use and make the world better.

"At the University of Michigan, I took a combined program in education and psychology, opening the door to broader theories and eventually forming the base for the High/ Scope Perry Preschool Study."

I enjoyed working for others but much prefer to set my own goals

It was difficult working for others who wanted to control my work. Perhaps it was a matter of maturity, but I much preferred the freedom of working for myself and with a staff I could count on rather than trying to guess what others wanted me to do. So I always preferred to operate on my own in the world of work. I had no problem in working for a supervisor who held the leash lightly, tossing out ideas and reacting to mine. When I worked for Weldon Hester, Rochester (New York) director of camping, he would say, "Here is the problem, give me your ideas, and work it out." In the public schools, I worked well with superintendents who allowed me to move ahead with special services programs under a general charge to solve educational problems. But I was well aware that I wanted to develop programs based on my own analysis of the situation. I think I was seen as a very good administrator, effectively creating and executing good solutions to problems. However, as Ray Barber, Ypsilanti superintendent of schools, said, I was "a thorn in his side." The intellectual challenges I tackled and my increasingly strong desire to work on my own certainly played a part in the establishment of the High/ Scope summer program for talented teenagers in 1963 and the High/Scope Educational Research Foundation in 1970.

I have a propensity to see opportunity in most situations

I think persons who exhibit this trait have an even temperament: Bad news or serious difficulty cannot overwhelm; good news cannot reduce alertness. I have a touch of "Pollyanna" in my

244

background and adopt a positive outlook on most things. In the Marine Corps, for example, the physical and social aspects were very new for me. I treated the demands as a challenge, relishing my ability to overcome the motto: *There is a right way, a wrong way, and the Marine Corps way.* Later, in examining research outcomes from various projects, I found that when our working hypotheses seemed to be in error, my response was to find what little was helpful in the data and assist the staff to build on that information. Can we find a way around the impasse? In short, always start from the known facts,

"Do not let an issue prevent you from acting; seize the opportunity to act."

seek solutions that will fulfill goals, and deal as necessary with the problems of permission from higher authorities, explanations to staff, or information to participants. Overall, do not let an issue prevent you from acting; seize the opportunity to act.

Personal and Professional Impact

Longitudinal studies have personal impact

How an individual responds to work requirements actually determines the outcomes of that work. These demands must be seen as positive or at least bearable because they so dominate the life of the individual. Undertaking decades-long longitudinal research studies requires an extensive commitment on the part of the principal investigator. It is not just a time commitment but also a recognition that one's professional life will be shaped by the study. I have worked with children of all age levels; indeed, given a choice, I would choose adolescents, but other issues and opportunities conspired to create the High/Scope Perry Preschool Study. The study, once formulated and launched, meant I had to turn down other professional job opportunities—not always an easy decision. In my case, the study sample was geographically based, and I felt I needed to work for the public schools or at least somewhere nearby while conducting the follow-up phase of the study. (Obviously, the decision also determined where my wife and I raised our family.) Given the extraordinary permission, coordination, and financing issues, a researcher based outside of the schools would have found it difficult if not impossible to operate the study. The other side of the coin is that one's employer must accept the value of the work and permit it to go forward. I was fortunate that the local school district officials and most of the building principals recognized the work's value to the children and families in the community as well as to the public interest. Indeed, they seldom questioned the service. Though most of my colleagues were uninterested in helping, they also did not hinder.

"I was fortunate that the local school district officials and most of the building principals recognized the work's value to the children and families in the community as well as to the public interest."

The theory selected to guide the work is another keystone

The theoretical position chosen to define any research project represents a major professional decision and commitment that must stand up over time. Select a weak or marginal theoretical position and eventually you will fail. Select a theory that is not compatible with your world view and you will encounter a series of real problems. I do not believe in moving from theory to theory or fad to fad as seems to be so common in education. When that happens, a long-term research study becomes irrelevant. One of the major functions of the principal investigator is to act as the "lion at the gate," and to provide protection to the project's integrity—its design, its staff, its sample. It seems as if "the newest" answer lasts about 20 years. Either a study must be completed within that time frame or one must be ready to defend the right to stay with the "old." For example, I've been asked, "Why do you not use Vygotsky's theory instead of Piaget's as a curriculum framework? His concept of a zone-of-proximal-development seems to describe your teacher-child interaction recommendations so much better." The questioner, however, has overlooked the historical record: Piaget's theories became generally accessible to the American audience in 1961 after J. McVicker Hunt and others wrote about his theories and research. Vygotsky's theories didn't appear in American research publications until the 1980s. Clearly, useful longitudinal research information results from a well-designed and well-executed study based on sound theory and practice. If well-constructed, a study will stand on its own merits over time, as has the High/Scope Perry Preschool Study.

On the whole, then, I did what I did as the result of my background, opportunities, and personal abilities. I do not really know why I have been so fortunate to be able to accomplish what I have done. I do know, however, that my entire working life is the product of many influences, especially being part of a family and a group of colleagues who could and would tolerate and support change.

> *"If well-constructed, a study will stand on its own merits over time, as has the High/Scope Perry Preschool Study."*

12

High/Scope
Foundation: From the
Past to the Future

Based on High/Scope research since 1962, what unique ideas does the Foundation have to offer? At one level, I can make many small observations. At a more theoretical level, I can say that we have validated a central core of ideas that are essential for truly effective education. Following are samples of the many small observations:

- Teachers prefer to have information that can be used directly in the classroom; hold the theory.
- Young children and adolescents have difficulty maintaining steady beat in movement and finding musical pitch—both are important skills that indicate an internal discipline to attend to an external stimulus.
- Staff are usually very good at the central task of their job, but rarely work well on alternative assignments.
- If the general opinion of the public or the academic discipline does not look with favor on what you are proposing, it takes an unusual foundation project officer to accept your idea.
- Persistence is key to fundraising, and such work is no place for those who lack confidence in themselves or their mission.
- Children around the world are essentially the same, no matter how they look, speak, or dress.

- Adolescents will engage in academic programs if their interests and needs are respected.

The purpose here, however, is to outline the major findings of our work—the ideas we feel we have either confirmed or at least on which we have shed some light; to present the elements essential for educational reform that define high-quality educational programs for all age groups; and to identify specific areas for High/Scope's future work.

Findings From High/Scope Research— A Brief Review

The High/Scope Foundation was established to develop effective educational answers to the learning problems faced by children in schools. The central programmatic thrust of the Foundation is to deliver a well-developed, documented, and validated curricula to parent-infant education programs, to early childhood programs such as Head Start, to elementary programs in public schools, and to adolescent programs in nonformal residential and after-school settings and alternative schools. These initiatives require two supporting activities from the Foundation: *careful research* to describe and validate the ideas, and *careful documentation* to train teachers and teacher trainers in the application of what we develop. While the general direction of the work and the specific sequences of projects are often determined by the opportunities available for funding created by the changing fashions in foundations and Washington, the organization's focus remains clear: Develop a theory-based curriculum approach; document that curriculum; validate that approach through longitudinal studies of performance outcomes; create effective dissemination strategies; and implement the program by providing effective staff training at the local level. Now, after over 40 years of development (10 years in the public

"The High/Scope Foundation was established to develop effective educational answers to the learning problems faced by children in schools."

schools and 30 years at High/ Scope Foundation), what are the results of our efforts to date?

High-Quality Education Makes a Difference

We are not just victims of our genes or of our circumstances. We can act and achieve a difference. While we can do little to alter inherited traits, we can learn to be effective members of a community; to be objective evaluators of problems to be solved; to be respectful judges of others and their differences; and to be active individuals engaged in learning and applying knowledge as a tool for serving family and community. How are these objectives reached? In my experience, they are achieved little by little through an accumulation of high-quality experiences drawn from validated approaches—a rigorous standard few educational programs meet. Here's what we know.

> *"We are not just victims of our genes or of our circumstances. We can act and achieve a difference."*

High-quality early childhood education improves lives

Perhaps the most important finding from the 40 years of work is that high-quality, center-based early childhood education experienced at ages 3 to 5 produces major long-term improvement in the lives of poor children. "High quality" is used in this context to mean the successful application of the five principles that undergird the High/Scope approach to education. (These principles are presented later in this chapter.) High/Scope's definition of high quality is much more specific than the usual use of the term to mean teachers with college degrees and certification, good salaries, and an appropriate teacher-child ratio. These are important elements for teacher welfare, but have only a modest general relationship to high-quality classroom practices and outcomes.

The research that supports this viewpoint on high quality is based on the longitudinal High/Scope Perry Preschool Study. When compared to a randomly assigned no-program group, the children who received the High/Scope Perry Preschool services had a higher rate of academic success during school years, graduated on time from high school at a higher rate, and reported less delinquency as adolescents. During adult years, they were more often married, had fewer children out of wedlock, held better paying jobs, used social welfare services less frequently, more often owned their own homes, were arrested less often, and had lower rates of illegal drug use. These indicators suggest a better quality of family life, more responsible contributions to the community, and better economic health. It is important to note that these indicators are "real world," reflecting the hard judgments that employers make on a daily basis and the relentless screening of public behavior community police are entrusted to carry out. These High/Scope Perry Preschool Study findings are significant for the individual, the family, and the community at large. If fully applied nationally, providing high-quality early childhood education at ages 3 to 5 could change for the better the face of America.

High-quality early childhood education is a good public investment

A corollary finding is that the public pays less to support early childhood education programs for disadvantaged children than it pays in costs that result from failing to provide such programs.

When an economic benefit-cost study was undertaken of the High/Scope Perry Preschool Study participants at age 27, we found that for every $1.00 the taxpayer spent on the program group, the taxpayer also spent $7.16 on the no-program group. This finding is the result of a careful analysis of all the program costs adjusted for inflation, such as the extra years in preschool of the program group, the expense of special education schooling for the no-program group, and all of the social welfare, crime, labor costs, and income tax payments into adulthood of both groups. This benefit-cost study is a major contribution because it was one of the first to present such complete data on children as a human resource, and it opened a portal to the business community and public policy planners. While these groups enjoy appeals to the heart, appeals based on economic facts receive a better hearing.

~

Conclusion

High/Scope data show that early childhood education can change the life pattern of participating children into adulthood, and further, that early childhood programs are very cost effective as social investments. The benefit-cost outcomes influence both hard-headed businessmen and policymakers. These findings are important because the public did not know these facts before the outcomes of the High/Scope Perry Preschool Study were made available.

The High/Scope Curriculum Approach Is Highly Effective

While I began the High/Scope Perry Preschool Study with the admonishment from professionals that the project experience would harm the children, the long-term data vigorously support quite the contrary conclusion. The program was of great benefit to the participants, their families, and the community. However, the question remained, How does the High/Scope Curriculum compare to other early childhood approaches? Is it enough to offer any early education program based on any theory, or do only specific curricula with particular characteristics, such as those of the High/Scope approach, obtain significant long-term, positive results?

Different curriculum approaches produce different outcomes

The High/Scope Preschool Curriculum Comparison Study was established to explore the idea that different theoretical approaches to early education might have different outcomes. The study randomly assigned groups of disadvantaged children to one of three methods:

- The Direct Instruction method developed by Engelmann in the mid-1960s was selected to represent a centrally derived curriculum based on behaviorist theory. This approach to education was popular because it was a no-

253

nonsense, teacher-directed, clearly academic approach thought to prepare preschool children for school.

- The traditional nursery school curriculum was selected to represent the approach to early education evolved over the last 100 years out of various child-centered, European-based theories. This approach to education was popular because it drew on traditional child development theory, especially that regarding children's social and emotional development.

- The High/Scope Piagetian-based curriculum approach was selected as a clear third alternative. This approach to education was of interest because it facilitated engagement by the child in educational activities, greatly reduced discipline problems, and had positive effects that both teachers and parents could see.

All outcomes from the study follow the same systematic pattern through the last data collection point at age 23. While the High/Scope approach has somewhat better results than the traditional nursery school method, both produce outcomes that are clearly superior to the Direct Instruction approach we studied.

These results are more than a little surprising. In spite of the two years of academic drill and practice, at no point throughout the follow-up school years did the children in the Direct Instruction group achieve at a significantly better level than the children from the other two groups. Further, 49 percent of them were labeled and educated by the schools as learning disabled or emotionally impaired compared to only 6 percent in either of the other two groups. Further, the Direct Instruction participants recorded twice as many lifetime arrests as the High/Scope group. Finally, when compared to the High/Scope group, they were far more likely to report that individuals in the community, such as landlords, police, shopkeepers, and family members, harassed them and gave them a "hard time." Interesting findings, especially relevant now when there seems to be a move to more direct instruction for youngsters of preschool age.

～

What makes the High/Scope early education approach so effective?

The High/Scope approach is unique in the opportunity it presents for the child to use *intentional learning* and *extensive language* to pursue deeply personal interests in partnership with a teacher who supports the learning process to take full advantage of the child's interests and abilities. This summary is a fairly radical statement, because it points to specific experiential elements as essential to successful education. It casts the teacher in a sophisticated role of mentor and conversationalist rather than lecturer and tester. The High/Scope educational approach focuses on two key elements that are necessary for any high-quality early childhood method: fostering *child initiative* through the daily plan-do-review process and *child accountability* through teacher support for child language to describe, explain, and discuss personal learning experiences.

Conclusion

The High/Scope Preschool Curriculum Comparison Study highlights the methods and classroom processes that are effective in meeting the definition of a high-quality program. When we began our preschool work in the 1960s, the question was whether or not such a program would harm children. It does not, and in fact, when properly implemented, provides a great advantage. Now the task is to incorporate these effective programs elements in all programs.

Service Programs for Infants and Toddlers Have Yet to Be Proven Effective

In 1967, I began a carefully designed program to bring essential educational and support services to infants and toddlers (newborn to age 3) and their mothers who were from disadvantaged backgrounds. I knew that we were having initial success with the High/Scope preschool programs, so I thought perhaps by starting even earlier we could prevent the lag easily measurable

255

at age 3 in many poor children with limited opportunities. Knowledge that we would be unsuccessful in our efforts was much work and years away.

High/Scope parent-infant education offers confusing outcomes

The High/Scope program in infant education began in 1968 as a research project with funding from the Carnegie Corporation of New York. As with other High/Scope research projects, careful attention was paid to random assignment of samples. At the conclusion of the project, after 16 months of service, we found that the program group significantly out-performed the no-program group on major measures such as intelligence and verbal development. Mothers showed a pattern of more frequent mother-child interaction and a more positive maternal teaching style. However, upon follow-up a year after the completion of the service, our enthusiasm was considerably dampened. Upon retest, all significant differences had disappeared. The gains of the program could still be seen, but they were no longer significant. A second follow-up, four years later at the end of second grade (age 7) found the same lack of significant program impact beyond what the no-program children had gained without participation in the service. Program children still had better vocabulary development and their mothers, a more positive teaching style, but these differences did not reach statistical significance levels. We continued with the work, but the focus shifted to helping agencies use nonprofessionals in their parent support efforts.

Conclusion

While home teaching with parents as a means of influencing child development is an outstanding idea based on the reality of the parent's extensive contact with the child, High/Scope's Carnegie Infant Education Project did not deliver on its promise. Indeed, as similar projects have operated throughout the country, very paral-

lel findings of no impact or modest outcomes are being reported. To be effective, this type of program will need to be redeveloped. The policy finding is that investment in other periods of children's development may be a more effective use of resources than investment in parent-infant education. Because the need for such progress is still apparent, however, experimental program development should continue.

Adolescence Is an Opportune Time for Effective Intervention

Since 1963, the High/Scope Institute for IDEAS and its predecessor residential camp programs have enrolled 14- to 17-year-old talented adolescents from all sectors of society for an arts and science program delivered along the same principles as the early education efforts.

Residential program offers special opportunities

During the time when youth are establishing an independent identity with regard to their families, when relationships with peers are of major importance for understanding one's self, and when the future looks both enticing and scary, having an opportunity to spend significant time away from home, family, and friends can be a major force for life changes. The High/Scope IDEAS model creates such an environment. It is residential, and it gives maturing teenagers time to think, discuss, and reason. At the Institute, the daily routine is organized into blocks of time when staff build on youth interests, choices, and decisions in developing program experiences. Youth leadership is emphasized, and extensive time is provided for group self-governance. Rather than a traditional camp sports and crafts orientation, the program focuses on arts and science topics. It adds program events that require use of intellectual skills and problem-solving abilities in a social context. The program enrolls a diverse group of teenagers to enrich the experience for all and to enable friendships across national, language, and racial lines.

Longitudinal study discovers long-term impact

As in other areas of High/Scope work, a longitudinal study was undertaken to examine the long-term outcomes from this intensive adolescent experience. The findings, five years after the experience, indicate that adolescence is indeed a time of great change, and, like early childhood, may be a window of opportunity to introduce services and experiences. With support from the Ford and Mott Foundations, a five-year longitudinal study was undertaken with youth who participated compared to youth who were selected but for some neutral reason could not attend (received a last-minute injury, death in the family, summer job offer, mother went to work so had to babysit younger siblings, and so on). From a telephone survey conducted by contracted interviewers not connected to the program, several important outcomes were discovered. First, the youth who attended the four-week residential program returned to high school with a renewed interest in education. Second, they attended college at a significantly higher rate (75 percent) than did the contrast group (55 percent). Indeed, those who were considered to be low achievers by the schools prior to attending the residential program more than doubled their college attendance rates (65 percent versus 29 percent). Third, youth from the program were more successful at staying in college even if they had major problems: lost their job at the college; got pregnant; or had difficulty with course work. The methods of engaging adolescents have their roots in the same theoretical thinking that undergirds the High/Scope early childhood program. The question is, How can these effective methods be used in academic programs, after-school activities, and other opportunities for youth?

"The methods of engaging adolescents have their roots in the same theoretical thinking that undergirds the High/Scope early childhood program."

Conclusion

Adolescence marks another time when intervention can be highly effective. The validated High/Scope program was based on engage-

ment of youth in planned, intentional learning during which they made extensive use of language to explain their work and discuss issues. The policy finding is that there are opportunities to assist youth as well as young children and High/Scope's specific approach works in this regard.

Elementary School Reform Shows Promise

A series of studies in elementary school, especially at the K–3 level, indicate that the High/Scope educational approach can be used as a vehicle to create better classroom settings and more successful experiences for children than traditional approaches. Children in High/Scope classrooms achieve academically at a higher rate than children in those classrooms not participating. This observation is true of schools with children from disadvantaged backgrounds as well as children with greater opportunities. In these studies, both the academic development and the social maturation of the students are seen as important. Teachers report around a 50 percent reduction in discipline referrals to the building principal during the first year they applied the High/ Scope approach. When children can plan what they are going to accomplish around a given topic, and when they are actively engaged in the work they and their teacher have planned, why interrupt it with inappropriate behavior? They don't!

Conclusion

Changing classroom educational practices in schools is exceedingly difficult. Teachers want to know specifically what they should do: "Tell me the activities on a day-by-day basis." Teachers want to maintain firm control of the classroom: "I don't see how I can share control with the children. What if their behavior gets out of hand?" Inservice training is needed to enable teachers to learn how to work together with students in a shared-control educational setting. All this requires time, resources, and the goodwill of all concerned to be successful and effective.

Elements of High-Quality Curricula and School Reform

Politicians want schools to be accountable; parents want schools to be effective; teachers want students to be cooperative; and administrators want test scores to rise to show they have things under control. Yet, these objectives are often in conflict, and the individual who is last in line is the child. School time is central to a child's life; indeed, it almost *is* the child's life. Some of a child's most important waking hours are spent in a classroom with peers and with a nonfamily adult in charge. If the setting is well organized and child friendly, the child is typically responsive and generally happy. If the setting is disorganized or overly structured, and the child feels threatened either psychologically or physically, stress produces all manner of negative outcomes that can damage the child, the family, and the community. School is for all children, but only the best and brightest succeed and are rewarded for their participation. We are at loss as to what to do with the many, especially from disadvantaged homes, who do not or cannot prosper. Imagine the impact on a child who somehow fails to measure up in the eyes of the teacher—day after day after day.

"Imagine the impact on a child who somehow fails to measure up in the eyes of the teacher—day after day after day."

Successful school reform must be built on a base that recognizes that *all* children will succeed to the extent they are enabled to initiate, direct, and control their own learning and have the support and attention of adults and peers when discussing their studies and extending their experiences. Successful school reform will change utterly the relationship of the teacher, the learner, and the parents because of the recognition of a new definition of high quality in education. Making these advantages available for all children would represent a major shift in classroom organization and teaching, in teacher preparation and supervision, in pupil behavior, in pupil assessment, and in relations with parents.

As an adult, the successful scientist, artisan, business executive, chef, or plumber applies a framework of thought and behavior that enables effective problem solving, extended learning, and personal contributions. Strangely, there is little disagreement on the adult traits that seem necessary for success in any field:

- Initiative
- Problem-solving ability
- Planning ability
- Capacity to work with and to have respect for others
- Extended language use
- Attaining standard academic goals in reading, math, writing, science, and so on

What our current educational system seems to do is select out only a few of these important values and traits for attention and disregards the others, focusing the child's education on only a limited number of specific traits of the truly successful adult. What is not recognized is that in high-quality education *all* these values and traits must be engaged concurrently, appropriate to age-level capacity.

It is *age-level capacity* that confuses the issue. Young children and youth obviously are not able to be contract plumbers or laboratory scientists. It is a difficult challenge to define adult traits in terms of the human scale (development) of the child. Our responsibility is to identify the major educational goals that are possible at each age level and to construct high-quality educational programs that incorporate these goals. The purpose is to provide programs that allow a child to live life as a child *not* as a miniature adult.

For High/Scope, we have identified the following five guiding principles of a high-quality program that can be applied at all age levels, always remembering that adaptations will be necessary to allow for the physical and cognitive developmental level of the children and youth involved. The many High/Scope books and publications give in-depth examples of these principles.

Education is most effective when learners plan activities, carry them out, and reflect on their experiences with the support of adults and peers

Fundamentally, this core principle asks that the basic scientific method of thinking, hypothesis generation, experimentation, and integration of knowledge, undergird all educational activities. Of course, this approach completely alters the way adults present information and forces traditional teaching into an alternative channel. The main purpose of high-quality education is to insure that children and youth have the opportunity to learn to fully function in the manner of a successful community of adults. The principle also emphasizes that high-quality education involves children in fruitful experiences with knowledgeable and active teachers and with a community of peers where the child feels both psychologically and physically safe.

The learner develops awareness and understanding through active involvement with people, materials, events, and ideas

Many basic abilities are granted to us at birth, the product of generations of human evolution: the ability to make sounds, various reflexes such as sucking, interest in the human face. Also, some basic physical requirements insure an infant's survival: proper temperature, human contact, nourishment. Beyond these psychologically primary and biologically expectant conditions, all else is learned from active involvement with what the environment provides. The words of a lecture, the pictures in a book, the story on TV or a video game, or definitions from the dictionary may appear to be educational, but they preclude much of the three-dimensional experience that creates the meaning necessary for learning. The participant's self-planned and active involvement offers the most effective method for fully capturing complex learning at any age.

"The purpose is to provide programs that allow a child to live life as a child, not as a miniature adult."

A variety of developmentally related active learning experiences contributes to the individual's intellectual, social, emotional, and physical development

A monochrome educational experience offered in a setting of quiet isolation is not effective education, no matter how disciplined or apparently academically correct it appears. The four walls of the classroom, the ritual of the daily school schedule, the pages of a workbook, and the routine of TV at home can be detrimental to complex development. Active participation in a multihued program with a wide range of direct experiences supports the development of all aspects of the personality. The teacher is a key player in presenting new opportunities and providing support for extending children's skills to more complex levels. This active teacher role is especially apparent in areas that don't lend themselves to direct physical experimentation. Organizing field trips, introducing musical instruments, developing steady beat and physical movement, adding complex art equipment to encourage in-depth exploration, and supporting and extending the child's attempts at sophisticated language usage and reasoning are some of the many teacher responsibilities necessary to insure a wide range of learning experiences. High-quality programs do not "instruct" in all areas, but establish a supportive context that enriches children's necessary development in all areas of learning.

Consistent support and respect for personal decision making strengthens the individual's personal effectiveness and social responsibility

The first three principles focus on the essential operational aspects of high-quality educational programs. This fourth principle relates to how the teacher conducts the program, and it is perhaps the most difficult to embrace. Teachers usually focus their program content on what they think administrators and parents expect. Typically, they are very resistant to any process that might loosen their classroom control, even when they realize that this resistance often subjects many children and youth to very limited learning opportunities and to personal stress that can lead to discipline problems. Yet, changing teacher-child relationships is at the heart of high-quality education. The High/Scope plan-do-review process opens the door to a different teacher-child relationship because it enables the child, with teacher support, to connect to learning in a direct, hands-on way. Teachers initiate conversations with students where the mutual goal is understanding the work the student is undertaking. Such conversations fail when they involve test-type questions for the student to answer. Such conversations succeed when teachers respond with complex language that introduces new words and new ideas to children and that is an expression of genuine interest in specific aspects of the children's work. Teachers also ask children for solutions to daily operational and social problems that are natural to the classroom, avoiding the imposition of adult views. High-quality education requires this kind of deep involvement by the teacher in observing, interacting with, and supporting the child. This involvement enables the teacher to naturally introduce new learning opportunities as the child progresses. This respectful and supportive role by a powerful adult greatly strengthens the child's sense of personal effectiveness and the development of social responsibility.

"The High/Scope plan-do-review process opens the door to a different teacher-child relationship because it enables the child, with teacher support, to connect to learning in a direct, hands-on way."

Scientific research produces knowledge, which contributes to the development of effective educational and social policies and programs

Many educational practice and education reform proposals are based on someone's beliefs and personal philosophies. While these are a rich source for inspiration and hypotheses, valid scientific research knowledge is required for high-quality educational reform. Does the belief translate successfully into practice? A number of educational programs are in use today that when scientifically evaluated, are shown not to be effective. Many more are offered only after a limited evaluation and without the necessary information on the program's overall impact on the children. The question is not only whether a child knows something (the alphabet, for example) but also what were the conditions under which it was learned. Effective research, although tedious at times and difficult to pursue, is a cornerstone of high-quality education.

Conclusion

What is high-quality education? We know there is no simple answer or it would already be accomplished. We have demonstrated that for a young child to reach a consistent level of success in later teenage and adult life, only high-quality approaches such as defined by the five High/Scope guiding principles will produce the long-range outcomes desired. In its most general form, high-quality education is defined by the extent to which children are actively engaged in a rich learning environment with genuine opportunities for self-determined work and for in-depth conversations with adults and peers. Such an approach reflects the environment and daily processes used by successful adults and adapted to the developmental levels and needs of children and youth.

High/Scope for the Future

High/Scope has successfully traversed four decades of educational innovation. We have developed a curriculum approach that integrates aspects of traditional learning with active student engagement through use of the scientific method (plan-do-review). We have defined the role of the teacher as an educational leader who carefully observes children, identifies and supports their interests and abilities, converses with them often and in depth, and takes advantage of opportunities to increase the complexity of their experiences through the careful introduction of content. We have validated our approach through longitudinal research studies. Make no mistake, this High/Scope method demands great energy on the

"We have validated our approach through longitudinal research studies."

part of the students—they must take initiative and think. It demands great change on the part of the teachers—they must share control of the classroom and curriculum with students and spend much more time observing students and engaging in conversations with them about their work intentions and outcomes. It demands initiative from administrators—they must establish a total school environment that focuses on a breadth of accomplishments far beyond the typical school goals of keeping children controlled and quiet. When these demands are met, however, students are prepared to become thoughtful, active, and successful adults who are a credit to themselves, their families, their communities, and the nation.

The major task of assuring the Foundation's success in the future is to capitalize on the work of the past. Even after decades, the work of the High/Scope Foundation in research, curriculum development, and training is only beginning. The work at the parent-infant level is back at the starting gate, although we have years of direct program experience and research to draw on. Turning the knowledge we have gained about high-quality early childhood education programs into widespread implementation remains a massive task. Then, too, the challenge we face at the elementary and secondary levels is enormous.

"The major task of assuring the Foundation's success in the future is to capitalize on the work of the past."

Content areas such as art, music, movement, reading, and mathematics are under development and being integrated into the High/Scope approach, but we are a long way from fully implementing their power. School reform is not a simple task.

For High/Scope, the past is clearly a prologue to the future. There is enormous opportunity for the services that High/Scope can render as a curriculum, training, and research force in education reform. What are the new core components that have grown out of our classroom experience and research to date that were not obvious in the theories or practices that we employed? Can we gain new insights into the ever-evolving world of educational theory and practice that will improve the life chances of children and their families? Following are some of my specific thoughts and ideas for future directions in teacher training and Foundation services.

Teacher Training

Language

The need for further development of High/Scope training programs for teachers at all levels is a given fact; we must keep the materials and research moving along and fresh. We can't rest on old, distinguished laurels; they dry and crumble. The research, both our own and others, suggests one powerful explanation as to why the High/Scope approach is so vigorous and robust. That factor is the way in which the High/Scope Curriculum fosters the widespread use of language at all levels of education and training. *Language* as a tool of thinking: Make a plan, carry on a conversation while you work, explain what you have done. *Conversation* as a way for children to interact with adults and peers, discuss ideas, and impart views, not as a microtest of teacher-directed assignments.

> *"Turning the knowledge we have gained about high-quality early childhood education programs into widespread implementation remains a massive task."*

Even the High/Scope conflict resolution approach is wrapped around the idea that the best solution to problems comes from the child's thinking, discussion, and verbal commitments—not from an adult's analysis and prescription. Teachers encourage children to explain things in their own words, and they listen carefully to understand the child's thinking and the logic of the discussion.

Future task—language

One task for the future is to develop language strategies for parents and teachers to use in conversations with students of all ages. Considerable related research is already at hand. While more information is necessary, the major task is to develop the classroom (and home) applications that will be effective.

Using technology wisely

One of the great strengths of the High/Scope approach has been its avoidance of passing fads in education and adherence to the disciplined application of basic theory molded by practical ex-

"High/Scope values the development of a team approach to education."

perience. However, with the advent of the internet we have access to new ways of providing information and offering additional opportunities for learning (computer learning can be nonlinear, it can be controlled by the recipient as to pace, additional information can be searched at any time, and so forth). This technology, however, must be carefully developed so that both parents and teachers can have internet access to and training in the High/ Scope educational approach for all ages. Tough questions need to be asked: Can High/Scope training and support be delivered effectively over the internet, or are face-to-face training situations required for best results? Do some components of training—such as the various assessment instruments—lend themselves to internet training? Recently, Foundation staff began to experiment with such an idea both for providing online teacher training and parent information. The personal skill development that occurs in High/Scope's training—whether it is learning to manage conflict resolution in the classroom or helping students gain competence with steady beat in movement learning experiences—makes me cautious in viewing internet training. Information dissemination seems a natural for the internet, but developing new practices and skills involves much more than just assimilating facts and principles. High/ Scope values the development of a team approach to education. Will using internet training increase an individual's isolation? But if the internet is used wisely and well in combination with more personalized training in the educational approach, there could be an enormous benefit to children and their families. Internet training will be of value only if we can bring about broader, less expensive training while maintaining the quality of the application and making use of an individual's relationships with coworkers and agency trainers. Even with the uncertainty, such a venture into the future is well worth the risk, if well conceived and well received.

Future task—technology

The internet offers a major opportunity and a major challenge. High/Scope needs to develop projects and research to both explore and exploit the improvement of service delivery and the possible means of maintaining the quality of High/Scope programs that technology offers.

Affective climate

Classrooms, day care centers, nursery schools, residential programs, training sessions for adults, parent meetings—indeed, all learning and social interaction settings—must be based on positive and affirming interactions. At the Institute for IDEAS, staff insure that teenagers are given a chance to try new skills with staff support and to fail such trials without negative criticism. Preschool staff use encouragement based on the child's specific performance rather than general praise (which is not based on components of the task) or negative comments. Instead of focusing on a child's self-esteem, which rests only on a good opinion of self—no competence necessary—children are encouraged to be confident in what they can do. Teachers focus on assets that the learn-

"Teachers focus on assets that the learner has rather than deficits that must be corrected."

er has rather than deficits that must be corrected. Parents discover what children can do and enjoy the sharing of success that occurs when their child applies that ability to related tasks.

Future High/Scope research and curriculum efforts, as they develop, will need to pay careful attention to insuring that programs are operated under an umbrella of positive interactions and feedback. Positive mother-teaching style, when combined with rich language use, results in better-measured intelligence in children improved and general academic performance. When children enter school after having only experienced negative language used with negative affect, a powerful curriculum model is necessary to produce adequate and positive change. With this information as a foundation, and drawing from our successful curriculum development efforts, High/Scope has a chance of greatly improving both the social and the academic success of America's students.

Future task—climate

Based on actual performance, High/Scope needs to develop systems to explore this critical issue and promote teacher training to support developing and sustaining positive relationships in the classroom and in the home.

High/Scope Services

Maintaining training quality

An important challenge for the future is to develop effective means to insure delivery of a high quality of service by High/Scope certified trainers in the field. Of course, we already publish training materials, offer conferences both nationally and regionally, and establish ongoing opportunities for trainers' personal development. For example, mentoring certified trainers to enable them to offer new course content is a well-established program. Courses and new materials for movement, music, folk dance, art, conflict resolution, reading, math, and program and child assessment are all available. But can we maintain the high quality of staff training and classroom performance over time?

"Many program innovations fail because they cannot maintain quality in field applications."

People leave the profession, retire, raise families, get promoted, are attracted to alternative beliefs, and in many ways reflect the changing demands and opportunities of our world. Many program innovations fail because they cannot maintain quality in field applications. High/Scope staff must pursue this issue very carefully and develop a range of methods to solve any problems identified.

While newsletters, distribution of new materials, regional conferences, and similar means of dissemination are currently used, the Foundation needs to explore new avenues of communication. One avenue might be to assist local groups of certified trainers to establish High/Scope "educator associations" drawn from the national High/Scope membership association. These groups would register with the Foundation, be made up of clusters of teachers and trainers committed to high-quality programs that they, themselves, deliver, and make a commitment to improving the field through engagement in public policy efforts. Without a doubt, such associations would be difficult to establish and keep operating, but through sharing our experiences and activities, we would greatly improve program quality at each level of education for which we provide service.

Another avenue might be to encourage innovation and documentation by individuals implementing the High/Scope approach in the field. Their work can be shared so others can benefit from their day-to-day experiences. For example, a High/Scope trainer in a very rural area of Wyoming developed a number of training sessions around specific curriculum issues, from "Who Is Piaget?" to "How to Develop an Appropriate Message Board." Each session has all the necessary materials assembled into a box. After the general training, teachers working in teams study the issues at their own pace by checking out the relevant box as they come to that topic. Another High/Scope trainer, Joyce Vermeer, has also developed a series of boxed training materials on the topics of active learning and conflict resolution for her staff and others. These have been published by High/Scope Press.

Using technology, a demonstration High/Scope classroom might be the base for a real-time video-streaming effort on the internet or through a consortium of local-access television stations. Perhaps each Friday morning a highly experienced High/Scope consultant could provide commentary on the actual classroom activities while teachers in remote locations view the scenes with their usual trainer. (This procedure has worked well for large groups visiting the High/Scope Demonstration Preschool.) Large-scale video-streaming would reduce costs and develop a common understanding of classroom process and application.

Future task—training quality

While a wide range of approaches will be necessary, High/Scope needs to develop effective member organizations and means for supporting trainers and teachers in the field in order to maintain high-quality service delivery.

Future leaders

High/Scope has a special obligation to future leaders in the field of education. The Foundation developed by trial and error in a field with little communication or support. A series of national institutes for emerging leaders in all the various fields within our focus (research, curriculum, and staff training) would make a significant contribution to the field. High/Scope can build on its innate respect for the human spirit to provide an extraordinary service to children and families by using our skill, knowledge, and opportunity in this manner.

There are many famous institutes. Aspen Institute provides seminars and discussion opportunities for the rich, famous, and powerful. Wingspread offers meeting space for distinguished groups to discuss issues of special interest. However, in most cases, it is the powerful who attend these events. What I propose is that High/Scope national institutes focus on reaching those young professional leaders who in the future will make the world a better place through service to children, youth, and families. Without new visions and opportunities to develop realistic new ideas, education will remain as it is. Just as I required a stimulus (a supportive group with whom to exchange ideas) and an opportunity to invent, so do others. Effective institutes could help provide these necessary ingredients.

Future task—leaders

New leadership and new ideas are essential for educational improvement. A High/Scope national institute for emerging leaders in education could be a catalyst to help promote new solutions for perplexing problems. It will take effort, will, and imagination to enable such an institute to fulfill its potential, but the return to children and families would be well worth the price.

Final Thoughts

In this chapter I have celebrated the success of our pattern of long-term research on program delivery to find valid approaches to education and teacher training. I have outlined the working components of the High/Scope definition of high-quality education. And, finally, I have suggested a few specific areas for High/Scope to focus on in the future. What else is needed? I would say that we continue to need breakthrough ideas: Ideas that put a new slant on an old problem, or suggest a new process or procedure. Establishing preschools for disadvantaged children was one idea; using parents to teach parents was another, at least for education. Sometimes a breakthrough idea is old cloth sewn into a new shirt; sometimes a breakthrough idea is made from a brand-new fabric. Can I identify any new breakthrough ideas out of these 40 years of personal and institutional experience? One perhaps: *The recognition that any successful curriculum is built around active, intentional learning.* The application of that single principle would completely alter the way children are educated and tested. It would support the idea that the personal, civic, and economic behavior of adults is the direct outcome of the way in which they learned as children. It would mean educating the whole child in a challenging, rigorous, and affirming way.

> *"Sometimes a breakthrough idea is old cloth sewn into a new shirt; sometimes a breakthrough idea is made from a brand-new fabric."*

∽

When young researchers and curriculum developers in the future meet to discuss what they will undertake in education, they will have a different task than the one I had in 1960. I had to explore the issue of whether or not early childhood education was good for children. High/Scope and others following that same question have found the answer: *yes*. During this process, I also found that certain procedures were better than others to use with all children and youth. Indeed, the findings are so strong that if alternative educational methods are employed, they must be assessed under strict research conditions or they may be unethical. Thus, the young leaders of the future start at a much more advanced point than I did. There is solid information upon which to build. And I wish them well.

Appendices

Preschool Research and Curriculum Development—References

High/Scope Curriculum Approach

1. The gradual growth of the High/Scope approach to early childhood education is documented in a series of curriculum publications and videos. A booklet of about 50 pages was the first effort to record information about the curriculum. It was written in response to a need for a description during the High/Scope Curriculum Comparison Project. Each of the subsequent curriculum manuals has been popular in college classes, as research references, and as handbooks for practitioners. The second book presented our thinking at the end of almost a decade of work with the curriculum. It was published by ERIC and the National Association for the Education of Young Children. It had two sections. The first presented the general approach, and the second gave a series of small-group activities that the teachers provided as well as general commentary on the activities of the day. While we hoped to show the range of useful activities that could be developed as an illustration of what is possible, the section became lesson plans for teachers. That use, of course, greatly compromised the value of the curriculum approach for meeting the needs of individual children. It also brought to our attention the need for greater care in explaining the approach.

   1 a. McClelland, D. (1970, out of print). *The Cognitive Curriculum* (Photocopy). Ypsilanti, MI: High/Scope Educational Research Foundation.

   1 b. Weikart, D. P., Rodgers, L., Alcock, C., & McClelland, D. (1971, out of print). *The Cognitively Oriented Curriculum*. Washington, DC: National Association for Young Children.

2. The following curriculum textbook was the first complete statement of the approach. Using many actual classroom examples, the book illustrated both the general theory as well as the practical application. The book also provided many suggestions to teachers after each content discussion. The goal was to engage teachers in thinking about the approach and their role in helping children gain the intellectual and conversational skills involved. The book was organized to present the content of the curriculum around the High/Scope's key experiences in child development.

   2 a. Hohmann, M., Banet, B., & Weikart, D. P. (1979, out of print). *Young children in action*. Ypsilanti, MI: High/Scope Press.

This textbook was accompanied by a teacher study guide. The exercises in the study guide encouraged reflection and application through a careful series of questions, exercises, and discussions. Its purpose was to facilitate the transfer of curriculum concepts into daily practice. It was especially useful with college classes and beginning teachers. Many trainers found the exercises important in their development of teachers they were training.

2 b. Hohmann, M. (1984, out of print). *A study guide for* young children in action. Ypsilanti, MI: High/Scope Press.

3. The next textbook in the curriculum series updated the curriculum, reflecting our increased understanding of the needs of both preschoolers and teachers. For the first time, it included a section on social and emotional growth, something I resisted for years because of the preschool teacher's historic penchant for giving primary focus to that area. However, within the broad content focus of this book, it seemed appropriate to include this important area. (This 1995 edition is still available in other languages: Arabic, Chinese, Dutch, Finnish, French, Portuguese, Norwegian, Slovenian, Spanish, and Turkish.)

3 a. Hohmann, M., & Weikart, D. P. (1995, out of print). *Educating young children—Active learning practices for preschool and child care programs.* Ypsilanti, MI: High/Scope Press.

3 b. Hohmann, M., & Weikart, D. P. (2002). *Educating young children—Active learning practices for preschool and child care programs* (2nd ed). Ypsilanti, MI: High/Scope Press.

The student workbook was also updated.

3 c. Hohmann, M. (2002). *A study guide to* educating young children: *Exercises for adult learners* (2nd ed). Ypsilanti, MI: High/Scope Press.

Curriculum Support Materials

1. The Foundation publishes an eight-page newsletter six times a year for its membership organization, each issue highlighting a single curriculum concept. It includes information for High/Scope trainers on ways to enrich their training and responds to typical questions from teachers in the field.

Brickman, N. A. (Ed.). *Extensions—Newsletter of the High/Scope Curriculum.* (Volume issued as six parts per year; authors vary by issue). High/Scope Press: Ypsilanti, MI.

2. About every five years these *Extensions* articles are re-edited, updated, and compiled into book format to be used as textbooks and as general teacher information resources. These books are often

used in beginning courses because each chapter is organized around specific curriculum concepts. These materials make the High/Scope approach accessible and understandable for all educators, college students, and researchers.

2 a.   Brickman, N. A., & Taylor, L. (Eds.). (1991). *Supporting young learners 1: Ideas for preschool and day care providers.* Ypsilanti, MI: High/Scope Press.

2 b.   Brickman, N. A. (Ed.). (1996). *Supporting young learners 2: Ideas for child care providers and teachers.* Ypsilanti, MI: High/Scope Press.

2 c.   Brickman, N. A. (Ed.). (2001). *Supporting young learners 3: Ideas for child care providers and teachers.* Ypsilanti, MI: High/Scope Press.

3.   Because of teacher requests to help them think through the possibilities that the approach offers to children, a series of teacher idea books and other publications have been written by High/Scope staff and trainers and published by High/Scope Press. These publications and videos offer a rich range of activities organized the way teachers might develop similar ones in the classroom. (A complete list and descriptions of these early childhood materials are available on the High/Scope Web site: *www.highscope.org.*) The hope is to enable teachers to see how they might use both their child observation information and children's interests to support an expanded curriculum.

3 a.   Graves, M. (1989). *Daily planning around the key experiences: The teacher's idea book 1.* Ypsilanti, MI: High/Scope Press.

3 b.   Graves, M . (1996). *Planning around children's interests: The teacher's idea book 2.* Ypsilanti, MI: High/Scope Press.

3 c.   Graves, M.. (1997). *100 small-group experiences: The teacher's idea book 3.* Ypsilanti, MI: High/Scope Press.

3 d.   Graves, M. (2000). *The essential parent workshop resource: The teacher's idea book 4.* Ypsilanti, MI: High/Scope Press.

3 e.   Vogel, N. (2001). *Making the most of plan-do-review: The teacher's idea book 5.* Ypsilanti, MI: High/Scope Press.

3 f.   Evans, B. (2002). *"You can't come to my birthday party!" Conflict resolution with young children.* Ypsilanti, MI: High/Scope Press.

3g.   Hohmann, M. (2002). *Fee, fie, phonemic awareness—130 prereading activities for preschoolers.* Ypsilanti, MI: High/Scope Press.

3h. DeBruin-Parecki, A., & Hohmann, M. (2003). *Letter links: Alphabet learning with children's names.* Ypsilanti, MI: High/Scope Press.

3i. High/Scope Foundation. (1999). *Creative representation—High/Scope preschool key experiences* (booklet and video). Ypsilanti, MI: High/Scope Press.

3j. High/Scope Foundation. (2000). *Language and literacy—High/Scope preschool key experiences* (booklet and video). Ypsilanti, MI: High/Scope Press.

3k. High/Scope Foundation. (2002). *Initiative and social relations—High/Scope preschool key experiences* (booklet and video). Ypsilanti, MI: High/Scope Press.

3l. High/Scope Foundation. (2003). *Classification, seriation, and number (Early math)—High/Scope preschool key experiences* (booklet and video). Ypsilanti, MI: High/Scope Press.

3m. Epstein, A. S. (2002). *Helping your preschool child become a reader—Ideas for parents.* Ypsilanti, MI: High/Scope Press.

3n Ranweiler, L. W. (2004). *Preschool readers and writers.* Ypsilanti, MI: High/Scope Press.

4. Movement, music, and art are important content areas for all ages, including the young child. High/Scope has produced, under the direction of Phyllis Weikart, a set of 15 CDs presenting folk music selected from around the world. She and colleagues have also prepared books that support teachers as they apply these areas in the classroom. Since movement and music do not "naturally" develop without outside support, these materials are of special importance to teachers. Working with consultant Eli Trimis, University of Thessaloniki, in Greece, High/Scope staffer Ann Epstein organized information useful to teachers in supporting children's development in art. The book also shows how to help children become consumers of art as well as observers and describers.

4 a. Weikart, P. S. (creative director). (1983; redigitized 2003). *Rhythmically moving* series 1–9 (music recordings, CD format). *Changing directions* series 1–6 (music recordings, CD format). Ypsilanti, MI: High/Scope Press.

4 b. Weikart, P. S. (1997). *Movement plus rhymes, songs, & singing games* (2nd ed, CD included). Ypsilanti, MI: High/Scope Press.

4 c. Weikart, P. S. (2000). *Round the circle: key experiences in movement for young children* (2nd ed). Ypsilanti, MI: High/Scope Press.

4 d. Epstein A. & Trimis, E. (2002). *Supporting young artists: The development of the visual arts in young children*. Ypsilanti, MI: High/Scope Press.

4e. Weikart, P. S. (2002). *Movement in steady beat: Activities for children ages 3 to 7* (2nd ed). Ypsilanti, MI: High/Scope Press.

4f. Weikart, P. S. (2003). *85 engaging movement activities— Learning on the move, grades, K–6* (CD included). Ypsilanti, MI: High/Scope Press.

4g. Weikart, P. S. (2004). *75 ensemble warm-ups—Learning on the move, grades 4–12* (CD included). Ypsilanti, MI: High/Scope Press.

Evaluation

5. An instrument is available to monitor the growth of children in the program and another instrument has been developed to assess program quality. Rather than a checklist of events, these instruments each offer five-point scales with 1,3, and 5 anchor points. The observer or teacher ties specific behavior to these anchor points. This approach provides much more information about the child or the program than is typically offered by checklists. Each decision is based on an observable event and so avoids summary judgments. Others can review the information to see the basis of the judgment.

5 a. High/Scope Educational Research Foundation. (2003). *Preschool Child Observation Record* (2nd ed.). Ypsilanti, MI: High/Scope Press.

5 b. High/Scope Educational Research Foundation. (2003). *High/Scope Program Quality Assessment* (2nd ed., Preschool Version). Ypsilanti, MI: High/Scope Press.

Research Reports on the High/Scope Perry Preschool Study

6. Over the years of the High/Scope Perry Preschool Study, periodic monographs have been published. Later volumes reflect the comments and questions raised in the earlier work. The latest monograph contains the most complete information, but each monograph describes the status of the project at that point in time. The study has been unique in using a cost-benefit analysis of the data. As the study has gained international recognition, staff have worked to assist in the use of the information for educational and general public policy purposes.

6 a. Weikart, D. P. (1967). Results of preschool intervention programs. *Journal of Special Education, 1*(2), 163–181.

6 b. Weikart, D. P. (Ed.). (1967). *Preschool intervention: A prelimi-nary report of the Perry Preschool Project*. Ann Arbor, MI: Campus Publishers.

6 c. Weikart, D. P., Deloria, S., Lawser, S., & Wiegerink, R. (1970). *Longitudinal results of the Ypsilanti Perry Preschool Project* (Monographs of the High/Scope Educational Research Foundation, No. 1). Ypsilanti, MI: High/Scope Press.

6 d. Weikart, D. P., Bond, J. T., & McNeill, J. (1978). *The Ypsilanti Perry Preschool Project: Preschool years and longitudinal results through fourth grade* (Monographs of the High/Scope Educa-tional Research Foundation, No. 3). Ypsilanti, MI: High/Scope Press.

6 e. Weber C., Foster, P., & Weikart, D. P. (1978). *An economic analysis of the Ypsilanti Perry Preschool Project* (Monographs of the High/Scope Educational Research Foundation, No 5). Ypsilanti, MI: High/Scope Press.

6 f. Schweinhart. L. J., & Weikart, D. P. (1980). *Young children grow up: The effects of the Perry Preschool Program on youths through age 15* (Monographs of the High/Scope Educational Research Foundation, No 7). Ypsilanti, MI: High/Scope Press.

6 g. Berrueta-Clement, J., Schweinhart, L. J., Barnett, W. S., Epstein, A. S., & Weikart, D. P. (1984). *Changed lives: The effects of the Perry Preschool Program on youths through age 19* (Monographs of the High/Scope Educational Research Foun-dation, No. 8). Ypsilanti, MI: High/Scope Press.

6 h. Schweinhart, L. J., Barnes, H., & Weikart, D. P. (1993). *Sig-nificant benefits: The High/Scope Perry Preschool Study through age 27* (Monographs of the High/Scope Educational Research Foundation, No. 10). Ypsilanti, MI: High/Scope Press.

6 i. Barnett, W. S. (1996). *Lives in the balance: Age 27 benefit-cost analysis of the High/Scope Perry Preschool Program* (Mono-graphs of the High/Scope Educational Research Foundation, No. 11). Ypsilanti, MI: High/Scope Press.

International Public Policy

7. As early childhood education programs have become more wide-spread in response to the growing numbers of women entering the paid workforce in many countries, the need has increased for infor-mation for planning and to inform overall public policy. At the re-quest of UNESCO, the following 93-page document was prepared

~

for the International Institute for Educational Planning. They published it under their monograph series, *Fundamentals of Education Planning*.

Weikart, D. P. (2000). *Early childhood education: Need and opportunity.* UNESCO: International Institute for Educational Planning, Fundamentals of Educational Planning, No. 65.

Summary Statements

8. Over the years, a number of brief summary statements about the curriculum and the research have been published in a range of volumes for different audiences. A partial list is given below.

8 a. Weikart, D. P. (1983). A longitudinal view of a preschool research effort. In M. Perlmutter (Ed.), *Development of policy concerning children with special needs: The Minnesota Symposia on Child Psychology: Vol. 16* (pp. 175–196). Hillsdale, NJ: Lawrence Erlbaum Associates.

8 b. Weikart, D. P. (1989). Early childhood education and primary prevention. In R. E. Hess, & J. Delong (Eds.), *The National Mental Health Association: Eighty years of involvement in the field of prevention* (pp. 285–306). NY: Haworth Press.

8 c. Weikart, D. P. (1989). *Quality preschool programs: A long-term social investment, Occasional Paper Number Five* (Ford Foundation Project on Social Welfare and the American Future). NY: Ford Foundation.

8 d. Weikart, D. P. (1990). A perspective on High/Scope's early education research. In A. S. Honig (Ed.), *Optimizing early child care and education* (pp. 29–40). NY: Gordon and Breach Science Publishers.

8 e. Weikart, D. P., & Schweinhart, L. J. (2000). The High/Scope Curriculum for early childhood care and education. In J. L. Roopnarine, & J. E. Johnson (Eds.), *Approaches to early childhood education* (3ʳᵈ ed.). Upper Saddle River, NJ: Prentice Hall.

High/Scope Press publishes an annual catalog with currently available publications and these are also listed on our Web Site: *www.highscope.org/welcome.asp*.

Differential Curriculum Outcomes: Preschool Curriculum Comparison Study— References

Information on the Curriculum Comparison Study has appeared in a number of edited books and as both journal articles and High/Scope monographs. The essential ones are listed in order of publication. The description of curricula are in their respective publications. (See the High/Scope Perry Preschool Study reference list, p. 281, for the High/Scope references.)

1. **Initial Report.** An initial report prepared while the study was still under way; includes a description of the work and some first impressions.

   1 a. Weikart, D. P. (1970). A comparative study of three preschool curricula. In J. Frost (Ed.), *Disadvantaged child* (2nd ed.). NY: Houghton Mifflin.

2. **Symposium Paper.** Presented at the Hyman Blumberg Symposium on Research in Early Childhood Education, Johns Hopkins University, this paper discusses early information from the study. It gives special focus on the role of the teachers and their attitudes toward working in a curriculum comparison study where all aspects that are possible to control *are* controlled, such as funding for each child, space in classrooms, home visits, administrative procedures. With only the curriculum approach being different, the teachers felt special pressure and commitment to their programs. The article is especially interesting because it was prepared at a time when very little long-term data were available, so I did a lot of introspection and speculation.

   2 a. Weikart, D. P. (1972). Relationship of curriculum, teaching, and learning in preschool education. In J. C. Stanley (Ed.), *Preschool programs for the disadvantaged* (pp. 22–66). Baltimore, MD: Johns Hopkins Press.

3. **Age-10 Report.** The report on the Curriculum Comparison Study presented findings through grade 4. The surprising finding: "Of the three major preschool models compared, … all were effective and none was more so than another." We fully expected to find achievement test differences in favor of the DISTAR group, and general cognitive development differences highlighting the High/Scope Curriculum approach. We were not prepared to find such initial equivalence. We concluded that preschool education can produce positive long-term impact on children, that any model effectively delivered can produce this impact, and that classroom observations document

that different models produce significantly different experiences in the learning process for children. The striking differences in personal behavior, school performance, and general social success were not yet evident.

3 a. Weikart, D. P., Epstein, A. S., Schweinhart, L. J., & Bond, J. T. (1978). *The Ypsilanti Preschool Curriculum Demonstration Project: Preschool years and longitudinal results* (Monographs of the High/Scope Educational Research Foundation, No. 4). Ypsilanti, MI: High/Scope Press.

4. **Age-15 Report.** The youngsters in the Curriculum Comparison Study were located, interviewed, and tested when they turned age 15. Because of the lack of significant differential results at fourth grade, this phase of the study was seen as especially critical. What we found was that the earlier equivalence in academic performance and cognitive ability remained the same. No essential differences were found in school performance. However, large social and behavioral differences were discovered. The group of children who attended the DISTAR program reported many more incidences of juvenile delinquency than did the youth in the other two groups. The schools diagnosed 49 percent of the group as needing special services for emotional problems. These findings and other related problems suggested that the Direct Instruction program failed to build essential mental and social skills that are required for adolescent and probably adult thinking and problem solving. Since such instruction appears not to have any advantage during school years, this study gives little support for the use of such programs, no matter how attractive they look in terms of "teaching the basics."

4 a. Schweinhart, L. J., Weikart, D. P., & Larner, M. B. (1986). Consequences of three preschool curriculum models through age 15. *Early Childhood Research Quarterly, 1,* 15–45.

5. **Age-23 Report.** As might be expected, advocates for and owners and publishers of direct instruction programs were very critical of our age-15 findings, and several articles were written to rebut the findings. Typically, these articles presented reasons why our design was flawed (e.g., differences in actual racial numbers in each group) and our test procedures inadequate (use of self-report for delinquency). However, these critics did not produce alternative preschool studies to buttress their beliefs. Indeed, several other longitudinal studies support the High/Scope findings (for example, the work of psychologist Maria Emilia Nabuco in Lisbon, Portugal). Important to these discussions, the age-23 study was a way to move from informal self-reports to actual records of state and local police. We also collected information on labor force participation,

family formation, and other indicators of success by young adults now out of high school. The data clearly continued to indicate that something was flawed in using direct instruction systems with young children. The young adults from the Direct Instruction preschool group continued to do more poorly than those in the other two groups. They also reported significantly more problems with others in their daily social interactions. The study also raised questions about the assumption that if parents are involved in their children's education the child will benefit, because all children in this study had the same number of home visits with extensive parent involvement. The overall results underlined the importance of curriculum approaches based on child-initiated learning for the long-term welfare of the child.

5 a.   Schweinhart, L. J., & Weikart, D. P. (1997). *Lasting differences: The High/Scope Preschool Curriculum Comparison Study through age 23* (Monographs of the High/Scope Educational Research Foundation, No. 12). Ypsilanti, MI : High/Scope Press.

6. **Head Start Comparison Study.** Twenty years after the end of the National Head Start Planned Variation Project, it seemed appropriate to look at the possible long-term impact of it on some participants. It was beyond my capacity to mount a national study, but with the help of Clennie Murphy, acting director of the Head Start Agency, we developed a project to look at the High/Scope programs in Ft. Walton Beach, Florida, and Greeley, Colorado. Our rationale was the large reported gains in Stanford-Binet Intelligence Test scores that the High/Scope participants recorded at the end of the Head Start experience. No other model sponsor had such findings. Sherri Oden of the High/Scope Foundation undertook to locate and examine over 600 of the original sample, including a post-hoc contrast group. The study was almost too complex. Even finding the records for the youngsters almost defeated us. In order to protect the participants, all records of the identity of children in the original study had been destroyed. However, by working with High/Scope records, retired teachers who still had class lists, and careful interviews with parents, the samples were satisfactorily reconstructed. Using two outside experts for data analysis and a review board of statistical experts headed by Sheldon White of Harvard University, some slim findings emerged. First, there was an impact on girls through improved education performance. Second, the impact on boys was a slight reduction in crime rates. Third, the High/Scope model curriculum could increase significantly the possibility of more positive outcomes. This complex study is one of the few longitudinal studies of Head Start.

∽

6 a. Oden, S., Schweinhart, L. J., & Weikart, D. P., with Marcus, S. M. & Xie, Y. (2000). *Into adulthood: A study of the effects of Head Start.* Ypsilanti, MI: High/Scope Press.

7. **Other Resources.** Discussions of issues resulting from the High/Scope Curriculum Comparison Study have appeared in many places. However, a presentation at the Hyman Blumberg Symposium is of special interest. It presents a review of the teaching staff and how they felt about the project and their role in it. It is also the first presentation of the quadrant I presented earlier that organizes early education theories in the literature. The second volume is a good representation of the way different editors have used the High/Scope information in college textbooks.

7 a. Weikart, D. P. (1972). Relationship of curriculum, teaching, and learning in preschool education. In J. C. Stanley (Ed.), *Preschool programs for the disadvantaged: Five experimental approaches to early childhood education.* Proceedings of the First Annual Hyman Blumberg Symposium on Research in Early Childhood Education. Baltimore, MD: Johns Hopkins University Press.

7 b. Weikart, D. P. (1995). Early childhood education. In J. H. Block, S. T. Everson, & T. R. Guskey (Eds.), *School improvement programs: A handbook for educational leaders.* NY: Scholastic, Inc.

Parent–Infant Education—References

1. **Ypsilanti-Carnegie Infant Education Project (1968–1971)**
   High/Scope's experience in the field of family support programs
   began in 1968–1971 with the High/Scope Ypsilanti-Carnegie Infant
   Education Project funded by the Carnegie Corporation of New
   York. This project trained professional staff to work as home visitors
   with low-income families with infants aged 3, 7, and 11 months at
   project entry. Its overall purpose was to help parents understand
   their child's development and provide support to the child. Meeting
   once a week for 16 months, the home visitor and parent used the
   baby's actions as the focal point for their interactions. Adults initiated activities with the child, responded to games and other activities
   initiated by the child, and discussed child development. Using a curriculum structured in part around Piagetian principles, home visitors
   and parents planned sessions together, each sharing their special
   knowledge in determining the goals and practices of effective child-
   drearing. Expert knowledge helped home visitors be responsive to
   and supportive of the individual needs of parents and children. Research findings from this project revealed that mothers who participated in the home visits showed more verbal interaction with their
   infants than mothers in the two comparison groups. The home-
   visited mothers' increased positive verbal interaction facilitated their
   children's cognitive development. They tended to have a more positive relationship with their children. The group differences were not
   maintained over time.

   1 a. Lambie, D., Bond, J., T., & Weikart, D. P. (1974). *Home teaching with mothers and infants: The Ypsilanti-Carnegie Infant Education Project—An experiment* (Monographs of the High/
   Scope Educational Research Foundation, No. 2). Ypsilanti,
   MI: High/Scope Press.

2. **High/Scope Infant Videotaping Project (1971–1973)** The
   second undertaking was the High/Scope Infant Videotaping Project, also supported by the Carnegie Corporation of New York.
   Project staff visited local homes to work with parents and infants,
   this time accompanied by a media crew who recorded the interactions and activities that developed during the home visiting sessions.
   The result was a library of 270 hours of videotapes documenting
   home visitors, parents, and young children engaging in informal interactions and discussions. High/Scope used the raw footage to
   produce a series of tapes on home visitor training, parental support
   of early learning, and early childhood development. The tapes enabled the Foundation to begin disseminating its work in the family
   support arena.

   ∽

3. **The Ypsilanti-Carnegie Infant Education Project, Longitudinal Follow-Up (1975–1976)** A longitudinal follow-up was conducted five years after the completion of the original work, towards the end of second grade. The purpose was to find out if the initial end-of-project advantages accruing to the treatment group had some possible long-term differences in language development, assessed general intelligence levels, or achievement patterns in the child. Also, we wished to find out if the initial significant changes in mother's verbal interaction and teaching style still were observable. Through home observation of verbal interaction and mother's teaching style and school test results for the children, we did find that verbal interaction patterns when the children were 2 years old (all children in both groups) were significantly related to school performance five years later. While not significant, the treatment group mothers used more positive teaching styles than the no-treatment mothers, creating a more positive relationship with their child in the home. However, there were no significant group differences paralleling the earlier findings a year after the end of the project.

3 a.   Epstein, A. S., & Weikart, D. P. (1979). *The Ypsilanti-Carnegie Infant Education Project: Longitudinal follow-up* (Monographs of the High/Scope Educational Research Foundation, No. 6). Ypsilanti, MI: High/Scope Press.

4. **Parent-to-Parent Home Visit Project (1975–1978)** In the next step, the project consolidated the earlier experiences and training materials into the High/Scope parent-to-parent model. Between 1975 and 1978, with funds from the Lilly Endowment and the National Institute for Mental Health, High/Scope refined and implemented the Parent-to-Parent Home Visit Project. The goals were to demonstrate the efficacy of using paraprofessionals to work with families and to document the training and delivery system for future dissemination. In the first part of the project, four women from the local Ypsilanti community, who had earlier been service recipients, were trained by Foundation staff to become home visitors themselves. The shift from using professionals to paraprofessionals as service providers reflected trends in the field at that time. The basic idea was that members of the community might be more effective than outside experts in establishing rapport and sharing child development information with families. In the second part of the project, we piloted the dissemination process for the first time by implementing the model in another community within the state. The parent-to-parent model now was firmly based on staffing the work with women from the community to be served.

4 a.   Reschly, B. (1979). *Supporting the changing family: A guide to the parent-to-parent model.* Ypsilanti, MI: High/Scope Press.

5. **Parent-to-Parent Dissemination Project: Community Implementation (1978–1981)** Based on a successful pilot project in one community, High/Scope was ready to test the dissemination process on a broader scale. From 1978 to 1981, with primary support from the Bernard van Leer Foundation, we disseminated the parent-to-parent model in seven communities throughout the United States. This project was a challenge because of the diversity of the populations served, the different views of service by host agencies, and the geographic spread of the program sites. Populations included adolescent parents, military families separated from traditional family support systems, parents of handicapped infants, economically stressed families, and families at risk of child abuse and neglect. Working in isolated rural areas as well as densely populated inner cities, we adapted the model to fit the service delivery system of public schools, community mental health agencies, the military chain of command, and the federally funded Head Start network. Home visiting constituted the core service in six of the seven programs; one program emphasized center-based activities with Head Start parents; and all brought families together for parent meetings and occasional field trips. The High/Scope project staff provided ongoing technical assistance to the local sponsoring agencies. This assistance included program development, staff training, evaluation, community advocacy, supplemental fundraising, and overall logistical support and problem solving.

5 a.   Epstein, A. S., Wacker, S. W., Reschly, B., & Evans, J. L. (1980). *Evaluation of the Parent-to-Parent Dissemination Project: Interim report of program implementation.* Ypsilanti, MI: High/Scope Press.

5 b.   Epstein, A. S., Halpern, R., Reschly, B., & Evans, J. L. (1981). *Innovation and institutionalization: Evaluation of phase 1 of the Parent-to-Parent Dissemination Project.* Ypsilanti, MI: High/ Scope Press.

5 c.   Evans, J. L., Epstein, A. S., Wacker, S. W., Parker-Crawford F., & de Pietro, L. (1984a). *Roots and wings: The High/Scope Parent-to-Parent Dissemination Project* (Vol. 1). Ypsilanti, MI: High/Scope Press.

5 d.   Evans, J. L., Epstein, A. S., Wacker, S. W., Parker-Crawford, F., & de Pietro, L. (1984b). *Roots and wings: The High/Scope Parent-to-Parent Dissemination Project* (Vol. 2). Ypsilanti, MI: High/Scope Press.

6. **Parent-to-Parent Dissemination Project: Regional Training and Dissemination Centers (1981–1984)** In 1981, the parent-to-parent model took another major step with the establishment of three Regional Training and Dissemination Centers (RTDCs). With a second grant from the Bernard van Leer Foundation, we contracted with two of the program sites to become RTDCs; High/Scope itself became the third RTDC. The idea behind this step was to prepare local staff to take over the role heretofore played by the Foundation as trainers and resources for service agencies beyond their own communities. Each RTDC was to provide technical assistance to agencies in its geographic area serving comparable populations who wished to establish their own family support programs.

6 a. Epstein, A. S., Larner, M., & Halpern, R. (1995). *A guide to developing community-based family support programs.* Ypsilanti, MI: High/Scope Press.

7. **Follow-Up of Parent-to-Parent Dissemination Program: Regional Training and Dissemination Centers (1999–2001)** During 1998, discussions were held with Ruth Cohen of the Bernard van Leer Foundation regarding their interest in conducting "tracker studies." Accordingly, the van Leer Foundation provided a small grant to track the High/Scope work they had originally funded. Essentially, the van Leer Foundation was interested in discovering if there were any long-term outcomes. High/Scope Project Director Jean Montie contacted the centers originally involved in the dissemination program and interviewed staff who could be located as well as High/Scope staff who were involved in the original project. In general, the findings were that the training program provided by High/Scope staff to the professionals at the centers had a significant impact on their subsequent service provision. Until the local or state funding policies changed, several of the centers maintained the pattern of parent-to-parent service for years after the end of the van Leer–funded project. It was surprising to find such an effect after 20 years! The follow-up did not track individual families and their children who participated in the original programs; such a research project was beyond the scope of this study. The final monograph in this series presents a summary of the work since 1967.

7 a. Epstein, A. S., Montie, J., & Weikart, D. P. (2002). *Supporting families with young children: The High/Scope Parent-to-Parent Dissemination Project* (Monographs of the High/Scope Educational Research Foundation, No. 13.) Ypsilanti, MI: High/Scope Press.

Curriculum

1. The first major curriculum guide that High/Scope staff produced after issuing the original monographs and program videotapes was a general overview of infant development from the parent and practitioner viewpoint. It had an accompanying activity guide.

    1 a. Evans, J., & Ilfield, E., (1982). *Good beginnings: Parenting in the early years.* Ypsilanti, MI: High/Scope Press.

    1 b. High/Scope Educational Research Foundation. (1982). *Activities for parent-child interaction.* Ypsilanti, MI: High/Scope Press.

2. The first major effort to integrate the High/Scope infant-toddler curriculum theory with daily practice was a joint effort of long-time High/Scope staff member Mary Hohmann and an infant-toddler day care center teacher, Jacalyn Post, of Ann Arbor, Michigan. The resulting textbook contains information on infant and toddler development, parent involvement, effective High/Scope practices, and numerous strategies for teachers and caregivers. All the examples in the book are actual ones from day care centers. While the book was being written, the High/Scope U.K. Institute in London developed a related training video and provided an edition for the United States.

    2 a. Post, J., & Hohmann, M., (2001). *Tender care and early learning: Supporting infants and toddlers in child care settings.* Ypsilanti, MI: High/Scope Press.

    2 b. High/Scope Institute U.K., (2000). *The High/Scope approach for under threes* (Video). Ypsilanti, MI: High/Scope Press.

3. As in the preschool programs, an observational assessment instrument is used to track infant-toddler development. As with the preschool model, items have five points anchored with examples at levels 1,3, and 5. This method allows the child's behavior to be documented and reduces the amount of inference that the observer must draw from the behavior. As with other levels of the curriculum, we have also developed a program quality assessment instrument, again based on a documented scale for each item. Like the others, the instrument has validity and reliability studies behind it.

    3 a. High/Scope Educational Research Foundation. (2000). *High/Scope Infant-Toddler Child Observation Record.* Ypsilanti, MI: High/Scope Press.

~

3 b.   High/Scope Educational Research Foundation. (2001).
High/Scope Program Quality Assessment for Infant and Toddlers.
Ypsilanti, MI: High/Scope Press.

Other High/Scope Family Support Projects

High/Scope implemented two other family support projects whose
practical aspects and research results validated the lessons learned from
the parent-to-parent studies and extended to the Foundation's ongoing
work with infants and toddlers into the 1990s.

4. **The Adolescent Parents and Infants Project (1977–1980)**
    This project was a research initiative funded by the U.S. Adminis-
    tration for Children, Youth, and Families. The findings demonstrated
    that adolescent parents expected "too little, too late" in terms of
    their infant's development and emphasized the need for programs to
    help young parents become better observers and supporters of their
    baby's growth. Moreover, family and community support was vital
    to encourage the young mother to continue her own development
    so she, in turn, could facilitate the development of her child.

    4 a.   Epstein, A. S. (1980). *Assessing the child development informa-
    tion needed by adolescent parents with very young children* (Final
    report for grant no. 90-C-1341 submitted to the U.S. Adminis-
    tration for Children, Youth, and Families). Ypsilanti, MI:
    High/Scope Educational Research Foundation.

5. **Child Survival/Fair Start Project (1982–1989)** High/Scope re-
    ceived funding from the Ford Foundation to evaluate its *Child Sur-
    vival/Fair Start Project.* The Ford Foundation effort had many simi-
    larities to the High/Scope Parent-to Parent Dissemination Project;
    both worked with low-income parents and infants in diverse agency
    settings and communities around the United States. High/Scope
    consolidated the lessons learned from these two multisite projects in
    A Guide to Developing Community-Based Family Support Programs, a
    book with guidelines for designing, implementing, and evaluating
    comprehensive child development programs for families with very
    young children. After successfully completing the project, we were
    disappointed when Ford Foundation awarded a long-term grant to
    Columbia University in New York City to serve as a resource cen-
    ter for information on early childhood infant development programs.
    The new center hired several veteran High/Scope staff to assist
    with the new operation.

5 a. Epstein, A. S., Larner, M., & Halpern, R. (1995). *A guide to developing community-based family support programs.* Ypsilanti, MI: High/Scope Press.

5 b. Larner, M., Halpern, R., & Harkavy, O. (1992). *Fair start for children: Lessons learned from seven demonstration projects.* New Haven, CT: Yale University Press.

Elementary Program—References

Curriculum

1. The High/Scope approach has always been an active learning program incorporating a daily plan-do-review sequence. By deciding on and stating an intention, a youngster makes a commitment to the learning process. Taking advantage of the growing intellectual abilities of this age group, teachers using the elementary approach partition the day and also offer workshop periods to focus children's attention on specific areas of learning such as math, science, social studies, and language and literacy. Students use curriculum materials and participate in interesting activities to accomplish their plans. The approach encourages children to engage in an active, hands-on experimentation with materials and supports the students' increasingly complex explanations of what they have learned, observed, and experienced. At the elementary level, the plan-do-review sequence enables students to actually begin to embrace the more mature form of the scientific method. The following books have been published by High/Scope Press for teachers who have adopted this view of elementary education.

1 a. Hohmann, C. (1996). *Foundations in elementary education: Overview.* Ypsilanti, MI: High/Scope Press.

1 b. Hohmann, C., & Buckleitner, W. (1992). *Learning environment: High/Scope K–3 Curriculum series.* Ypsilanti, MI: High/Scope Press.

1 c. Maehr, J. (1991). *Language & literacy: High/Scope K–3 Curriculum series.* Ypsilanti, MI: High/Scope Press.

1 d. Hohmann, C. (1991). *Mathematics: High/Scope K–3 Curriculum series.* Ypsilanti, MI: High/Scope Press.

1 e. Blackwell, F., & Hohmann. C. (1991). *Science: High/Scope K–3 Curriculum series.* Ypsilanti, MI: High/Scope Press.

1 f. Weikart, P. S., & Carlton, E. (1995). *Foundations in elementary education: Movement.* Ypsilanti, MI: High/Scope Press.

1 g. Carlton, E., & Weikart, P. S. (1994). *Foundations in elementary education: Music.* Ypsilanti, MI: High/Scope Press.

1 h. Weikart, P. S. (creative director). (1983; 2003). *Rhythmically moving* series 1–9 and *Changing directions* series 1–6 (music recordings, CD format). Ypsilanti, MI: High/Scope Press.

~

2. In addition to these basic textbooks outlining the High/Scope approach, a number of supporting materials are available, especially in language, math, and science.

   2 a. Morrison, K., & Dittrich, T., (2000). *Literature-based workshops for language arts: Ideas for active learning, grades K–2.* Ypsilanti, MI: High/Scope Press.

   2 b. Morrison, K., Dittrich T., & Claridge, J., (2002). *Literature-based workshops for mathematics: Ideas for active learning, grades K–2.* Ypsilanti, MI: High/Scope Press.

   2 c. Blackwell, F. (1996). *Life and environment.* Ypsilanti, MI: High/Scope Press.

   2 d. Blackwell, F. (1996). *Structure and form.* Ypsilanti, MI: High/Scope Press.

   2 e. Blackwell, F. (1996). *Energy and change.* Ypsilanti, MI: High/Scope Press.

Research

3. Unlike the work in the adolescent, preschool, and parent-infant areas, High/Scope research at the elementary school level has been constrained by our participation in the large-scale National Follow Through Project. In this undertaking, national samples were established and random assignment of groups was not possible. Indeed, school system sites selected model sponsors from those specified by the national program. Many school systems went into the program to obtain the extra funds to support their meager local budgets; they did not necessarily want real school reform. Thus, outside reviews of the basic National Follow Through research declared that the research design was so flawed little could be drawn from the multimillion dollar contractor efforts. However, when possible, High/Scope has conducted a number of small-scale projects on our model sponsor sites to determine possible outcomes of our approach. These are listed below.

   3 a. Weikart, D. P., Hohmann, C., & Rhine, W. (1981). High/Scope Cognitively Oriented Curriculum model. In W. Rhine (Ed.), *Making schools more effective: New directions from Follow Through* (pp. 201–247). New York, NY: Academic Press.

   3 b. Schweinhart, L. J., & Smith, C. (2001). Effects of recent High/Scope curriculum support on school achievement and reducing discipline referrals (Unpublished paper). Ypsilanti, MI: High/Scope Educational Research Foundation.

3 c. Schweinhart, L. J., & Wallgren, C. R. (1993). Effects of a Follow Through program on school achievement. *Journal of Research in Childhood Education, 8*(1), 43–56.

3 d. Smith, C. (2001, Fall/Winter). Revalidating the High/Scope elementary curriculum a decade later, Part I: Achievement tests. *High/Scope ReSource* (pp. 4–8). Ypsilanti, MI: High/Scope Press.

3 e. Smith, C. (2002, Spring). Revalidating the High/Scope elementary curriculum a decade later, Part II: Higher order thinking skills. *High/Scope ReSource* (pp. 4–7). Ypsilanti, MI: High/Scope Press.

History of High/Scope's Major Grants and Contracts

This is a history of grants and contracts obtained by or awarded to the High/Scope Foundation. Not all awards are listed and, where possible, the total amount of the award is given the year it was made. Thus, most of the larger ones are for three to five years' duration. Usually, unless there is some special significance of the project or the grantor agency, only the larger awards are listed. The annual audit reports of the Foundation give the exact dollar amounts and final totals. The administrative records and department reports from the early days are sometimes incomplete. However, this listing is given to provide an idea of who funded our work and the approximate amount of each bequest.

FY 1971

Office of Education (DHE): National Follow Through—curriculum reform in cooperation with local school districts. $545,853.

Office of Child Development (DHEW): Planned Variation Head Start—implementation and comparison of various curriculum models. $156,346.

Office of Child Development (DHEW): Parent-Child Development Center—planning grant. $31,720.

National Institute of Health: High/Scope–Carnegie Parent-Infant Education Project—close-out research grant. $29,500.

FY 1972

Office of Education (DHEW): National Follow Through—curriculum reform in cooperation with local school districts. $297,920.

Carnegie Corporation of New York: High/Scope Infant Education Project—videotapes of home teaching with parents to develop staff training videos. $289,890.

Birmingham Parent-Child Development Center: Program consulting. $30,575.

Ford Foundation, Bogota Office, Colombia: Harvard Infant Nutrition Project—consulting. $75,000.

FY 1973

Office of Education (DHEW): National Follow Through—curriculum reform in cooperation with local school districts. $597,860.

Office of Child Development (DHEW): Home Start—evaluation of national program of home teaching. $1,918,755.

Spencer Foundation, Chicago: Longitudinal evaluation of the High/Scope Perry Preschool Study. $292,000.

Grant Foundation, New York: Purchase and remodeling of the High/Scope Staff Training and Child Development Center (TDC). $60,000.

Bureau of the Education of the Handicapped (Office of Education, DHEW): High/Scope Preschool Demonstration Project. $65,000.

Ecumenical Institute, New York: Evaluate the Fifth City Preschool Center, Chicago, Illinois. $44,633.

Office of Child Development (DHEW): Child Development Associate Consortium—to develop instrument to assess child development. $40,250.

Education Commission of the States: Three prototype mother-infant education videos. $45,045.

Office of Child Development (DHEW): Audio-visual training materials. $25,000.

FY 1974

Office of Education (DHEW): National Follow Through—curriculum reform in cooperation with local public schools. $609,307.

Benton Harbor (Michigan) Public Schools: Consulting to demonstrate high-quality preschool programs. $22,500.

Del Rio Public Schools, Texas: Consulting to assist implementing bilingual and bicultural education. $50,000.

Office of Child Development (DHEW): Supplemental training workshops for Head Start personnel. $149,970.

Bureau of the Educationally Handicapped. (Office of Education, DHEW): Preparation of specialists and media-assisted training models. $742,560.

Carnegie Corporation of New York: Development of proposal concepts for new work in parent-infant education. $38,000.

FY 1975

Office of Education (DHEW): National Follow Through—curriculum reform in cooperation with local public schools. $578,478.

Lilly Endowment, Indianapolis, Indiana: Early Childhood Demonstration Program. $100,000.

Carnegie Corporation of New York: Follow-up of High/Scope Parent-Infant Education Program. $321,597.

Office of Child Development (DHEW): Project Developmental Continuity—a look at the relationship between early childhood Head Start and later schooling. $1,981,324.

UNICEF: Consulting in preschool education and teacher training, Peru. $11,025.

Robert Sterling Clark Foundation, New York: Travel costs related to Latin American proposals: $10,000.

FY 1976

Office of Education (DHEW): National Follow Through—curriculum reform in cooperation with local public schools. $484,163.

Appalachia Regional Commission: Consulting for video project on home teaching. $16,516.

Lilly Endowment, Indianapolis, Indiana: Parent-Infant Education Project. $200,000.

National Institute for Mental Health: Training professionals and paraprofessionals in parent-infant education. $150,000.

UNICEF, Venezuela Home Day Care—program consulting and research technical assistance. $50,000.

Venezuela, Ministry of Education: National Preschool Education Program—consulting. $15,000.

U.S. Agency for International Development: Puno, Peru—early childhood in rural development program. $26,000.

U.S. Agency for International Development: Chimbote, Peru—special education project. $15,250.

FY 1977

Office of Education (DHEW): National Follow Through—curriculum reform in cooperation with local school districts. $477,226.

Office of Child Development (DHEW): Develop, implement, evaluate bilingual/bicultural preschool education approach. $356,000.

Michigan State Department of Education: Develop professional staff development model. $90,000.

Inter-American Development Bank: Provide curriculum consulting to Catholic University of Santiago, Chile. $11,800.

Rosenberg Foundation, San Francisco, California: Curriculum training for the Tribal American Indian Council of Los Angeles. $15,000.

Harry E. Bagley Foundation, Detroit, Michigan: Purchase High/Scope Preschool Demonstration School facility. $100,000.

Carnegie Corporation of New York: Language development assessment. $97,330.

FY 1978

Office of Education (DHEW): National Follow Through—curriculum reform in cooperation with local school districts. $321,796.

Michigan Department of Education: Evaluation of Career Education Dissemination Project in Michigan. $148,100.

Cooperative Service Agency of Portage, Wisconsin: Survey of preschool programs in Latin America. $51,429.

Bureau of Education for the Handicapped (Office of Education, DHEW): First Chance—outreach for dissemination and training. $615,092.

Bureau of Education for the Handicapped (Office of Education, DHEW): Training for personnel in early childhood education. $78,827.

Benton Harbor (Michigan) Public Schools: Technical assistance and training. $10,283.

Leflore County (Mississippi) Public Schools: Follow Through Resource Center. $49,678.

Child Nutrition Corporation (CONPAN): Technical assistance. $4,318.

Administration for Children, Youth, and Families (DHEW): Assess child development information needed by adolescent parents. $118,463.

Organization of American States: Evaluation of the Inter-American Institute of the Child. $19,270.

FY 1979

Office of Education (DHEW): National Follow Through—curriculum reform in cooperation with local school districts. $442,560 and $108,215.

Carnegie Corporation of New York: Develop measures of writing ability. $200,000.

Bureau of Education for the Handicapped (DHEW): Study of the impact of new federal legislation on the handicapped. $329,861.

Bernard van Leer Foundation, The Hague, The Netherlands: Disseminate the High/Scope Parent-to-Parent Model. $337,000.

Richmond (Virginia) Public Schools: Training and technical assistance. $20,000.

FY 1980

Office of Education (DHEW): National Follow Through—curriculum reform in cooperation with local school districts. $444,860.

Carnegie Corporation of New York: Center for the Study of Public Policies for Young Children—Voices for Children Project. $443,483.

Bernard van Leer Foundation, The Hague, The Netherlands: Evaluation for the Parent-to-Parent Model. $120,000.

U.S. Agency for International Development: Technical assistance to private voluntary agencies regarding implementation of early childhood education. $35,000.

Agency for Children, Youth, and Families (DHEW): Basic Educational Skills Project—consulting with five school districts. $408,333.

Office of Education (DHEW): National Diffusion Network—disseminate information and materials regarding the High/Scope Curriculum. $39,994.

German Marshall Fund, Washington, DC: Training for German child care providers. $7,750.

FY 1981
Office of Education (DHEW): National Follow Through—curriculum reform in cooperation with local school districts. $216,717.

Cooperative Education and Training, Region 7: Operate four-week May–June camp program for talented northern Michigan rural youth. $103,511.

Office of Education (DHEW): National Diffusion Network—disseminate information and materials about the High/Scope Curriculum. $25,000.

Levi Strauss Foundation, San Francisco, California: Technical assistance to the County Council of Strathclyde (Glasgow, Scotland). $101,482.

FY 1982
Department of Education: National Follow Through—curriculum reform in cooperation with local school districts. $193,806.

U.S. Agency for International Development. Latin America Regional Program—work with private voluntary organizations (PVOs) to develop and disseminate strategies for working with children and families. $545,000.

U.S. Agency for International Development: St.Kitts/Nevis—expand current network of child care facilities. $1,200,000.

Cooperative Education and Training, Region 7: Operate four-week May–June camp program for talented northern Michigan rural youth. $151,137.

Local Training of Trainers projects: Los Angeles, California; Kansas City, Missouri; Dayton, Ohio; State of New Jersey. $262,592.

Bernard van Leer, The Hague, The Netherlands: Dissemination of the Parent-to-Parent Model. $397.478.

National Institute of Mental Health: Study of delinquency among High/Scope Perry Preschool samples. $90,640.

National Institute of Education: Study of mechanisms of continuity of education in the public schools. $102,046.

FY 1983
Department of Education: National Follow Through—curriculum reform in cooperation with local school districts. $102.998.

Bureau of the Education for the Handicapped (DOE): Long-term follow-up of High/Scope Perry Preschool Project children. $95,252.

Agency for Children, Youth, and Families (DHHS): Operational services for Basic Skills. $399,699.

Ford Foundation, New York: Child Survival/Fair Start—cross-site evaluation of parent-infant programs. $897,922.

Gulbenkian Foundation, Lisbon, Portugal: Training foundation curriculum developers. $6,000.

Cooperative Education and Training, Region 7: Operate a four-week May–June camp program for talented northern Michigan youth. $98,340.

Ford Foundation, New York, Agency for International Development and other international grantors: Consultative group for early childhood development in developing countries. $27,650.

FY 1984
Department of Education: National Follow Through—curriculum reform in cooperation with local school districts. $103,000.

Aga Khan Council, Aga Khan Foundation, New York: Support for three-week camp program for Ismaili youth. $38,360.

Cooperative Education and Training, Region 7: Operate a four-week, May–June camp program for talented northern Michigan youth. $70,027.

Carnegie Corporation of New York: Support various longitudinal studies and plan the International Evaluation of Educational Achievement (IEA) Preprimary Study. $193,328.

Jardine Matheson Corporation, Hong Kong: Prototype of early childhood software programs. $15,000.

Grant Foundation, New York: Consult on development of Grant's action research program. $110,850.

Gund Foundation, Cleveland, Ohio: Policy Center—Voices for Children expansion in the Cleveland area. $12,943.

Ford Foundation, New York, Agency for International Development and other international grantors: Consultative group on early child development in developing countries. $281,994.

FY 1985

Department of Education: National Follow Through—curriculum reform in cooperation with local school districts. $78,897.

Cooperative Education and Training, region 7: Operate a four-week May–June camp program for talented northern Michigan youth. $90,927

UNICEF: Conduct workshop on child development and prepare report. $18,098.

Ford Foundation, New York, Agency for International Development and other international grantors: Consultative Group on early child development in developing countries. $324,500.

FY 1986

Department of Education: National Follow Through—curriculum reform in cooperation with local school districts. $54,169.

Multifunders, with Ford Foundation as lead grantor, National Head Start, ACYF regional offices, local and regionally focused foundations: High/Scope Training of Trainers—develop local experts implementing the High/Scope Curriculum. $817,750.

Job Training and Partnership Act (JTPA), Region 7: Operate a four-week May–June camp program for talented northern Michigan youth. $92,000.

Skillman Foundation, Detroit: Research on impact of Institute of IDEAS experience on youth. $60,000.

Carnegie Corporation of New York: Planning activities on need of women in developing countries. $23,500.

Ford Foundation, New York, Agency for International Development, other international grantors: Consultative group for early child development in developing countries. $308,777.

Office of Human Development Services (DHHS): IEA Preprimary Project—initial im- . plementation of the project in the United States. $74,800.

Multifunders, with Ford Foundation as lead grantor, National Head Start, ACYF regional offices, local and regionally focused foundations: High/Scope Training of Trainers—develop local experts implementing the High/Scope Curriculum. $1,160,800.

Office of Children, Youth, and Families (DHHS): Longitudinal study of Planned Variation Head Start at two High/Scope sites—20 years after. $330,000.

FY 1987

Department of Education: National Follow Through—curriculum reform in cooperation with local school districts. $42,000.

Multifunders, with Ford Foundation as lead grantor, National Head Start, ACYF regional offices, local and regionally focused foundations: High/Scope Training of Trainers—develop local experts implementing the High/Scope Curriculum. $806,616.

Ford Foundation, New York, Agency for International Development, other international grantors: Consultative Group for early child development in developing countries. $176,465.

Job Training and Partnership Act (JTPA), Region 7: Operate a four-week May–June camp program for talented northern Michigan youth. $69,325.

FY 1988

Department of Education: National Follow Through—curriculum reform in cooperation with local school districts. $57,000

Multifunders, with Ford Foundation as lead grantor, National Head Start, ACYF regional offices, local and regionally focused foundations: High/Scope Training of Trainers—develop local experts implementing the High/Scope Curriculum. $1,134,479.

Ford Foundation, New York, Agency for International Development, other international grantors: Consultative Group for early child development in developing countries. $257,149.

FY 1989

Department of Education: National Follow Through—curriculum reform in cooperation with local school districts. $131,642.

Multifunders, with Ford Foundation as lead grantor, National Head Start, ACYF regional offices, local and regionally focused foundations: High/Scope Training of Trainers—develop local experts implementing the High/Scope Curriculum. $1,584,688.

Ford Foundation, New York, Agency for International Development, other international grantors: Consultative group for early child development in developing countries. $286,046.

United Nations Development Fund: Consulting and training—day care workers in Iraq. $28,000.

Carnegie Corporation of New York: Dissemination of research information on the High/Scope Perry Preschool Study. $120,000.

Ford Foundation, New York: Child Survival/Fair Start—cross-site evaluation of parent-infant programs. $430,000.

Mott Foundation, Flint, Michigan: Longitudinal follow-up on High/Scope Training of Trainers projects. $264,740.

FY 1990

Department of Education: National Follow Through—curriculum reform in cooperation with local school districts. $162,624.

Ford Foundation, New York, Agency for International Development, other international grantors: Consultative group for early child development in developing countries. $309,539.

Multifunders, with Ford Foundation as lead grantor, National Head Start, ACYF regional offices, local and regionally focused foundations: High/Scope Training of Trainers—develop local experts implementing the High/Scope Curriculum. $1,229,625.

FY 1991
Department of Education: National Follow Through—curriculum reform in cooperation with local school districts. $105,151.

Pew Charitable Trusts, Philadelphia; Prudential Foundation, Newark, New Jersey; Fairfax County (Virginia) Head Start; Phil Harden Foundation, Jackson, Mississippi: IEA Preprimary Study of early child development in 15 countries. $490,000.

Multifunders, with Ford Foundation as lead grantor, National Head Start, ACYF regional offices, local and regionally focused foundations: High/Scope Training of Trainers—develop local experts implementing the High/Scope Curriculum. $828,422.

Agency for Children, Youth, and Families (DHHS): Longitudinal follow-up of the High/Scope Perry Preschool Study. $142,929.

Mott Foundation, Flint, Michigan, and Ford Foundation, New York: Longitudinal study of adolescents who attended High/Scope Camp. $100,000.

FY 1992
Department of Education: National Follow Through—curriculum reform in cooperation with local school districts. $137,629.

Bureau of Indian Affairs (DOE): Training and support for early childhood projects on Indian reservations and in Indian schools. $224,080.

Ford Foundation, New York, Agency for International Development, other international grantors: Consultative group for early child development in developing countries. $311,932.

Multifunders, with Ford Foundation as lead grantor, National Head Start, ACYF regional offices, local and regionally focused foundations: High/Scope Training of Trainers—develop local experts implementing the High/Scope Curriculum. $1,035,207.

Ford Foundation, New York: Child Survival/Fair Start—cross-site evaluation of parent-infant programs. $46,679.

Mott Foundation, Flint, Michigan: Longitudinal follow-up of High/Scope Training of Trainers projects. $36,415.

Ford Foundation, New York: Longitudinal research on the High/Scope Perry Preschool Study. $72,520.

IBM Foundation and local agencies: Partnerships with local school districts to employ computers in classroom. $944,770.

Multifunders, with Ford Foundation as lead grantor, National Head Start, ACYF regional offices, local and regionally focused foundations: High/Scope Training of Trainers—develop local experts implementing the High/Scope Curriculum. $1,035,207.

FY 1993
Department of Education: National Follow Through—curriculum reform in cooperation with local school districts. $137,629.

U.S. Agency for International Development: IEA Preprimary Study of early child development in 15 countries. $100,000.

U.S. Agency for International Development, other international grantors: Consultative group for early child development in developing countries. $180,000. UNICEF. $35,000.

Department of Education: National Diffusion Network—consulting and training in the High/Scope Curriculum. $169,000.

Bureau of Indian Affairs (DOE): Training and support for early childhood projects on Indian reservations and in Indian schools. $191,000.

Mott Foundation, Flint, Michigan: Best early childhood training practices. $55,000.

Multifunders, with Ford Foundation as lead grantor, National Head Start, ACYF regional offices, local and regionally focused foundations: High/Scope Training of Trainers—develop local experts implementing the High/Scope Curriculum. $904,000.

Dewitt Wallace–Reader's Digest Fund: Dissemination, training, and internships in High/Scope adolescent programs. $412,000.

FY 1994
Multifunders with states of Georgia and California as major sources: High/Scope Training of Trainers—develop local experts; Lead Teacher Training—improve classroom practice. $1,649,022.

World Bank and other international grantors: Consultative group for early child development in developing countries. $105,000. Others. $226,800.

Mott Foundation, Flint, Michigan: Best early childhood training practices. $55,000.

Anonymous Foundation, New York: Follow-up at age 23 of High/Scope Curriculum Comparison Study, $75,000.

Gund Foundation, Cleveland, Ohio: Development of the High/Scope Child Observation Record (COR). $155,000.

State of Georgia: Evaluation of High/Scope training in Georgia. $121,427.

Smith Richardson Foundation, Westport, Connecticut: Longitudinal study of Planned Variation Head Start in two High/Scope sites—20 years after. $220,776.

Department of Education: National Diffusion Network—consulting and training in the High/Scope Curriculum. $483,601.

FY 1995
Department of Education: National Follow Through—curriculum reform in cooperation with local school districts. $137,629.

Ford Foundation, New York: Dissemination of results from the High/Scope Perry Preschool Study. $50,000.

Multifunders with states of Georgia and California as major sources: High/Scope Training of Trainers—develop local experts; Lead Teacher Training—improve classroom practice. $2,101,500.

Multiple funders: Institute for IDEAS—two four-week residential programs for adolescents. $164,400.

Dewitt Wallace-Reader's Digest Fund: Dissemination, training, and internships in High/Scope adolescent programs. $419,482.

FY 1996

State of Michigan, Kellogg Foundation, Battle Creek, Michigan: Michigan School Readiness Program—design and implementation of evaluation. $183,860

World Bank: Study of child development in 15 countries. $375,000.

Multifunders with state of Georgia as major source: High/Scope Training of Trainers—develop local experts; Lead Teacher Training—improve classroom practice. $2,495,920.

Aga Khan Foundation, Geneva, Switzerland, World Bank, UNICEF, and other international grantors: Consultative group for early child development in developing countries. $430,000.

IBM Foundation and local agencies: Partnerships with local school districts to employ computers in the classroom. $174,000.

Bureau of Indian Affairs (DOE): Training and support for early childhood projects on Indian reservations and in Indian schools. $182,408.

Multiple funders, including McGregor Fund, Detroit; Knight Foundation, Miami; and San Franciso Foundation: Institute for IDEAS—two four-week residential programs for adolescents. $165,000.

Community Foundation for Southeastern Michigan, Detroit: New Directions—create a network of organizations serving youth. $125,000.

Administration for Children, Youth, and Families (DHHS): Head Start Quality Research Center—examine important aspects of National Head Start to determine effectiveness of high-quality practices. $2,400,000.

FY 1997

Multiple funders, including Wilson Foundation, Detroit; Ratner Foundation, Detroit: Institute for IDEAS—two four-week residential programs for adolescents. $190,000.

Bureau of Indian Affairs (DOE): Training and support for early childhood projects on Indian reservations and in Indian schools. $387,020.

Multifunders with state of Georgia as major source: High/Scope Training of Trainers—develop local experts; Lead Teacher Training—improve classroom practice. $1,307,000.

Nord Family Fund, Lorraine, Ohio: Evaluation of various program strategies to facilitate access to postsecondary schooling. $26,708.

Packard Foundation, Los Altos, California, and Kauffman Foundation, Kansas City, Missouri: Recognition of high-quality early childhood programs with the cooperation of the National Association for the Education of Young Children. $113,280.

FY 1998

Multiple funders, including Knight Foundation, Miami; Gilmore Foundation, Kalamazoo, Michigan; and Detroit Edison Foundation: Institute for IDEAS—two four-week residential programs for adolescents and related community agency training. $310,000.

Multifunders from community and local area foundations: High/Scope Training of Trainers—develop local experts; Lead Teacher Training—improve classroom practice. $1,707,000

Bureau of Indian Affairs (DOE): Training and support for early childhood projects on Indian reservations and in Indian schools. $344,840.

State of Michigan, Kellogg Foundation, Battle Creek, Michigan: Michigan School Readiness Program—design and implementation of evaluation. $183,860

State of Michigan, Kellogg Foundation, Battle Creek, Michigan: Michigan School Readiness Program—design and implementation of evaluation. $300,000.

Bernard van Leer Foundation, The Hague, The Netherlands: Twenty-year follow-up on the impact of the Parent-to-Parent model training on staff and agencies. $39,800.

FY 1999

Multiple funders, including Knight Foundation, Miami; Gilmore Foundation, Kalamazoo, Michigan; Community Foundation for Southeastern Michigan; Kalamazoo Community Foundation; and Detroit Edison Foundation: Institute for IDEAS—two four-week residential programs for adolescents and related community agency training. $310,000.

State of Ohio: Education Through Movement program—teacher training for southwestern Ohio. $145,000.

Multifunders from community and local area foundations: High/Scope Training of Trainers—develop local experts; Lead Teacher Training—improve classroom practice. $1,825,000.

Multiple local funders: Elementary-level teacher training. $145,000.

Bureau of Indian Affairs (DOE): Training and support for early childhood projects on Indian reservations and in Indian schools. $344,840.

McCormick Tribune Foundation, Chicago: Longitudinal follow-up at age 40 of the High/Scope Perry Preschool Study. $435,000.

State of Michigan, Kellogg Foundation, Battle Creek, Michigan: Michigan School Readiness Program—design and implementation of evaluation. $300,000.

Packard Foundation, Los Altos, California, and Kauffman Foundation, Kansas City, Missouri: Recognition of high-quality early childhood programs with the cooperation of the National Association for the Education of Young Children. $79,370.

FY 2000

Multiple funders, including Knight Foundation, Miami; Gilmore Foundation, Kalamazoo, Michigan; Kalamazoo Community Foundation; and Detroit Edison Foundation: Institute for IDEAS—two four-week residential programs for adolescents and related community agency training. $295,000.

McGregor Fund, Detroit: Education Through Movement Program—teacher training in the Detroit area. $57,400.

State of Tennessee: Education Through Movement—teacher training in Springfield. $55,000.

Multifunders from community and local area foundations: High/Scope Training of Trainers—develop local experts; Lead Teacher Training—improve classroom practice. $1,200,000.

Multiple local funders: Elementary-level teacher training. $225,000.

Bureau of Indian Affairs (DOE): Training and support for early childhood projects on Indian reservations and in Indian schools. $115,000.

FY 2001

Skillman Foundation, Detroit, and Knight Foundation, Miami: Youth agencies in Detroit to receive staff training and assistance in program evaluation. $200,000.

Gilmore Foundation, Kalamazoo, Michigan, and Kalamazoo Community Foundation: Training of youth-serving agency staff. $75,000.

Multifunders from community and local area foundations: High/Scope Training of Trainers—develop local experts; Lead Teacher Training—improve classroom practice. $1,207,000.

Multiple funders, including the Ratner Foundation, Detroit; DeRoy Testamentary Fund, Detroit; Bank One, Ann Arbor; and Comerica, Ann Arbor: Institute for IDEAS—two four-week residential programs for adolescents and related community agency training: $150,000.

Mott Foundation, Flint, Michigan: Training of adults who serve on American Indian reservations. $500,000.

Multiple local funders: Elementary-level teacher training. $303,740.

State of Michigan, Kellogg Foundation, Battle Creek, Michigan: Michigan School Readiness Program—design and implementation of evaluation. $699,000.

Albertson Foundation, Boise, Idaho: Evaluation of National Association for the Education of Young Children program certification in Utah. $54,000.

Foreign Translations and Publications

Translated Titles	Language	Translated Titles	Language
Active Learning— An Introduction	Dutch	Young Children in Action	Portugese
		Educating Young Children	Portugese
Outdoor Learning	Dutch	Supporting Young Learners	Portugese
Adult-Child Interaction	Dutch	Educating Young Children	French
Daily Routine	Dutch	Tender Care and Early Learning	French
Assessment	Dutch		
Teacher's Idea Book 1	Dutch	Child Observation Record	French
Child Observation Record	Dutch	Educating Young Children	Turkish
Program Implementation Profile	Dutch	Educating Young Children	Arabic
		Child Observation Record	Korean
Educating Young Children	Dutch	Young Children in Action	Finnish
Young Children in Action	Spanish	Child Observation Record	Finnish
		Child Observation Record	Chinese
Children as Music Makers	Spanish	Child Observation Record	Polish
Workshops for Parents and Teachers	Spanish	Child Observation Record	French
		Young Children in Action	Chinese
Good Beginnings	Spanish	Collection Titled: Supporting Young Learners	Chinese
Round the Circle—Key Experiences in Movement for Young Children	Spanish	Round the Circle—Key Experiences in Movement for Young Children	Chinese
Program Implementation Profile	Spanish	Teachers Idea Book 1	Chinese
Adult-Child Interaction	Spanish	Teachers Idea Book 2	Chinese
Outdoor Classroom	Spanish	Teachers Idea Book 3	Chinese
Young Children in Action— Study Guide	Spanish	Young Children in Action	Dutch
		Young Children in Action— Study Guide	Dutch
Child Observation Record	Spanish	Round the Circle	Dutch
Daily Routine	Spanish	Young Children in Action	Norwegian
Key Experiences in Preschool	Spanish		
Observation/Evaluation/ Planning	Spanish	**Videos**	
Parent Participation	Spanish	Adult-Child Interaction	French
Settings for Active Learning	Spanish	High/Scope Curriculum: Daily Routine	Chinese
Tender Care and Early Learning	Spanish	Setting up the Learning Environment	Chinese
Educating Young Children	Chinese		
Models of Early Childhood Education	Chinese	High/Scope Curriculum: Plan-Do-Review	Chinese
Getting Started: Materials and Equipment for Active Learning Preschools	Chinese		

High/Scope Board of Directors
July 1970–January 2002

Abrahamson, Lucille, Director
Jan 92–Jan 96, resigned
Civic Volunteer, San Francisco, CA

Austin, William H., Director
Jan 01–present
Attorney, Parker, Siemer, Austin,
Resch & Fuhr, Effingham, IL

Barr, John, Director
Jan 95–present
Vice Chair (99–present)
Attorney, Barr, Anhut & Gilbreath,
Ypsilanti, MI

Lord Bhatia (Amir), Director
May 86–Dec 97, end of term
Chairman, Forbes Trust, London,
United Kingdom

Bowman, Barbara, Director
Sep 86–Sep 93, resigned
President, Erikson Institute,
Chicago, IL

Brown, Bernice, Director
Sep 90–Dec 98, end of term
Dean, San Francisco State, San
Francisco, CA

Clark, Terry (Ph.D.), Director
Jan 94–Jan 99, resigned
President, Education Resources
Group, Princeton, NJ

Dannemiller, William*, Director
Jul 70–Dec 01, deceased Dec 01
Secretary (70–86)
Attorney, Ann Arbor, MI

**Egbert, Robert (Ph.D.),
Director**
Jan 75–Dec 94; Jan 96–Sep 01,
deceased
Charles W. Holmes Professor,
University of Nebraska Teachers
College, Lincoln, NE

**Egertson, Harriet (Ph.D.),
Director**
Jan 95–Dec 02, end of term
Secretary (01–02)
Administrator (retired), Nebraska
Deptartment of Education,
Lincoln, NE

Finberg, Barbara, Director
Jan 98–Present
Vice President, MEM Associates,
New York, NY

**Foster, Philips (Ph.D.)*,
Director**
Jul 70–Dec 95, resigned
Vice Chair (70–74)
Professor, Agricultural Economics
University of Maryland, College
Park, MD

Fruehauf, Kenneth, Director
Jan 99–Apr 00, resigned
Broker and Vice President, Merrill-
Lynch, Scottsdale, AZ

**Gleason, David (Ph.D.),
Director**
Jan 01–present
President, Bright Horizons
Foundation for Children,
Franklin, TN

Gosselink, James (Ph.D.)*, Director
Jul 70–May 86, resigned
Professor, Sea Grant, University of Louisiana, Baton Rouge, LA

Hennessee, J.W. Matt, Director
Jan 97–present
Chair (01–present)
President & CEO, Quiktrak Inc., Lake Oswego, OR

Keith, George (Ph.D.), Director
Jan 98–present
Treasurer (01–Present)
Vice Chancellor for Academic and Student Affairs, Oakland Community College, Bloomfield Hills, MI

Lund, Thomas, Director
Jan 88–Jan 91, resigned

Molder, Joseph*, Director
Jul 70–present
Chair (00–01)
Vice Chair (75–98)
Headmaster, retired, Westover School for Girls, Middlebury, CT

Moore, Donal, Director
Jan 89–Dec 97; Apr 99–present
Treasurer (93–97)
Vice President, Automotive Sales, Polytech Netting Industries, Icking, Germany

Neugebauer, Roger, Director
Apr 95–present
Publisher, *Child Care Information Exchange*, Redmond, WA

Pittman, Karen, Director
Jan 01–present
Executive Director, Forum for Youth Investment, Washington, DC

Porter, John (Ph.D.)*, Director
Jan 70–Dec 78; May 86–Dec 94, end of term
President, retired, Eastern Michigan University, Ypsilanti, MI

Sackett, Ross, Director
May 93–Dec 99, end of term
Chairman, Child's Play, Eureka Springs AR

Smith, Robin, Director
Jan 94–Feb 95, resigned
Executive Director, Student Mentor Program, New York, NY

Thomas, Marilyn, Director
Jan 95–Dec 02, end of term
President/CEO, retired, Miami Valley Child Development, Center, Dayton, OH

Tupper II, Leon, Director
Treasurer (98–00)
Apr 95–present
President/CEO, Gilreath Manufacturing, Southfield, MI

Uribe, Juan Pablo (MD), Director
Jan 00–Apr 00, resigned
Public Health Specialist, World Bank, Washington DC

Washington, Valora (Ph.D.), Director
Jan 00–Apr 00, resigned
Executive Director, Unitarian Universalist Service Committee, Cambridge, MA

Wallgren, Charles, Director
Treasurer (86–92)

Secretary (87–00)

Jan 86–Dec 00, retired

Chief Operating Officer, High/
Scope Educational Research
Foundation, Ypsilanti, MI

Weikart, David (Ph.D.)*,
Director

Jul 70–03, deceased

Chair (70–00)

President (70–00)

President Emeritus, High/Scope
Educational Research
Foundation, Ypsilanti, MI

Weikart, Phyllis*, Director
Treasurer

Jul 70–Dec 85, resigned

Director, Movement and Music
Education, High/Scope
Educational Research
Foundation, Ypsilanti, MI

Williams, Elizabeth, Director

Dec 85–Dec 86, resigned

Board Member, Williams Energy
Corp., Solvang, CA

** CHARTER MEMBER of High/Scope Board
of Directors*

David Powell Weikart died on December 9, 2003,
after a long struggle with leukemia.